D1519403

Meaning in
Mid-Life
Transitions

Meaning in Mid-Life Transitions

Edmund Sherman

State University of New York Press

Published by
State University of New York Press, Albany

For information, address State University of New York Press, State University
Plaza, Albany, N.Y., 12246

Library of Congress Cataloging-in-Publication Data

Sherman, Edmund A.
    Meaning in mid-life transitions.

    Bibliography: p.
    Includes index.
    1. Middle age—Psychological aspects—Case studies.
2. Life change events—Case studies.   I. Title.
BF724.6.S53   1987   155.6   86-5999
ISBN 0-88706-384-5
ISBN 0-88706-385-3 (pbk.)

CONTENTS

PREFACE

The idea for this book began in clinical practice where I was encountering an interesting and changing configuration of problems and persons requiring treatment. This practice was in a center for psychotherapy where individual, family, and group treatment were provided by practitioners of psychiatry, social work, and psychology. Several of the female practitioners had developed therapy groups made up entirely of women who were going through various marital, family, and individual adjustment problems. Although my practice at the center began with a fairly even mix of men and women in individual and family treatment, it became almost entirely male by the end of a year.

Men whose wives were in either individual or group treatment were coming for treatment themselves because of their wives' insistence that they seek help for their individual and marital adjustment problems. In a majority of these cases, the wives had already made up their minds that they wanted a divorce, and they wanted their husbands to get help in coping with the likely event of separation. Most of these men were either in or just entering mid-life, and were usually quite ambivalent about seeking professional help. They were particularly wary of female therapists, often feeling that their wives would not be acting up if it were not for the suspected feminist orientations of the female therapists that their wives were seeing.

What was striking me most about these situations was the apparent lack of preparedness, or even any real awareness on the part of the men, concerning the imminent breakdown of their marriages and family lives. This lack of awareness did not seem to be true for most of the women my colleagues and I were seeing whose husbands were initiating marital separation. Most of them, particularly the women in mid-life (late thirties through their fifties), had been aware for several years that something was seriously wrong in their marriages. Even in those cases where their husbands suddenly informed them that they wished to leave for another woman, there seemed to be some degree of awareness, if not anticipation, among the wives. Consequently, when separation became imminent, the women seemed less devastated by the ensuing crises than the men. Because of this, I found it necessary to develop a men's support group as an adjunct to the treatment of the increasing number of men I was seeing in individual and marital counseling.

These impressions and developments could have been due almost entirely to the happenstance of the cases and persons coming to that particular center at that particular time. In other words, they might not have anything to do with general differences between men and women in coping with such marital crises. However, my curiosity was aroused, and I wondered whether there were indeed such differences between the sexes. Further, I wondered if there were any gender differences in coping with mid-life transitions other than marital separation.

Fortunately, as a faculty member, I was able to obtain a small research grant from the State University of New York at Albany which enabled me to initiate a study of the phenomenon. It was to be a two-phase study. The first phase would consist of a statistical analysis of available nationwide survey data from the National Opinion Research Corporation (NORC) of the University of Chicago. The analysis included data for men and women in the forty to sixty year age range. The second phase of the study was designed to obtain primary data through an intensive interview survey, including some psychological testing of individuals who had experienced certain kinds of mid-life crises. The initial pretest for this second phase was undertaken in mutual support settings and groups, such as Parents Without Partners and Widowed Persons, which were apt to have some middle-aged members who were seeking peer support for coping with the crises of separation, divorce, and widowhood.

This phase of the research was intended to obtain a more detailed and individualized picture of how middle-aged persons cope with crisis events than could be obtained from the generalized findings of the statistical analysis of the NORC data. The unique, individualized experiences uncovered by the interview survey were so rich and varied in content and in their implications for understanding mid-life transitions and crises that the generalizations from the NORC data, based on statistics rather than experiences, seemed somewhat thin and simplistic in comparison. These statistical findings showed some interesting gender differences, and these are reported in Chapter One. The more I learned about the individual crisis experiences, together with what I already knew from my practice, the more I wanted to qualify many conclusions that might be drawn from the statistical findings.

Fortunately, at the time these questions arose about the statistical findings, I had the opportunity to take a semester's sabbatical from teaching. This enabled me to consult with several persons who had conducted large-scale studies in similar areas of adult development, as well as with some persons who were knowledgeable about qualitative research and case study methods, which seemed more suitable for the promising experiential data I was obtaining in my research interviews. This semester of consultation and further study convinced me that I should undertake an in-depth study of individual cases of mid-life crises from both the clinical practice and the field research interviews I was conducting. Also, my emphasis would shift from *measurement* of variables related to crisis experiences to the *meaning* of transition experiences for the individuals involved.

Thus, what started out as a search for possible differences between *groups* of men and women based on a probability sample and statistics became a search for the patterns or structures of experience and meaning for *individual* persons, regardless of gender. Indeed, I was becoming acutely aware from both my clinical and research interviews with persons undergoing mid-life transitional crises that there was in fact a "structure" to their crisis experiences. Furthermore, it became evident that the most promising way to capture and understand these "structures of experience" was through a combined cognitive and phenomenological approach, because such an approach seemed to provide the best access to the subjective side of the experience for the people involved.

So, this foray into research on the middle years convinced me that the evolving cognitive-phenomenological approach was applicable not only for clinical practice but for understanding the processes and problems of adult development and aging. Therefore, the primary focus of this book is on an understanding of mid-life transitions from the perspective of both clinical practice and qualitative human science research, rather than from quantitative behavioral science research. The essential method to be used is a structural case study approach, which will be introduced and explicated in the first two chapters. The four following chapters will consist of the case studies, and the last chapter will draw conclusions and implications for both practice and research.

I wish to thank a number of persons who were particularly helpful to me in this endeavor. First, Professor Daniel Levinson of Yale University, whose concept of the individual life structure was central to the study method of this book. I also wish to express appreciation for his personal consultation on some of the case material presented here. Others who provided helpful consultation along the way were David Chiriboga of the University of California, San Francisco, Joseph de Rivera of Clark University, and Amos Handel of the University of Haifa, Israel. My thanks to all of them for their particular contributions.

Thanks also to Stuart A. Kirk, Dean of the School of Social Welfare at the State University of New York at Albany, for his continued interest and support which were instrumental in the completion of this endeavor. I am indebted also to the University for providing the reserach grant and the sabbatical leave that enabled me to complete the bulk of the work on this project under the auspices of its Ringel Institute of Gerontology. I am especially thankful for the support services provided by the School, the Institute, and the University along the way. The secretarial staff were most helpful, and I am particularly grateful to Gail Texter for her excellent and remarkably efficient typing of this manuscript on the School's word processor.

It is to my wife, Arleen, that I owe the greatest debt for the emotional support she provided me with during the whole research and writing process. Her willingness to act as buffer between me and so many of the demands of the "outer world" were absolutely essential to the completion of this book. Her careful reading and thoughtful responses to the manuscript made her indispensible to the whole effort.

Finally, I must express my great indebtedness to the men and women who are represented in these case studies. Although their identities and circumstances have been heavily disguised to insure annonymity and confidentiality, it was their willingness to share their crisis experiences that made this book possible. If any significant new understanding comes out of this effort, it is they who provided it.

Chapter 1

INTRODUCTION

This book is intended to contribute to an understanding of the psychosocial transitions and crises of mid-life by focusing on the unique personal meaning of the transitional event or experience for the individual.

There is an implicit structure to the way in which such a transition is experienced by the individual, and this can be made explicit by the techniques and methods of the approach to be outlined and illustrated in this book. The value of fully explaining this structure enables us to understand and assess the nature and dimensions of the transition, to know whether or not it will reach crisis proportions, and to assess possible intervention strategies. Therefore, this book should be of interest to human service practitioners as well as teachers and students of human development and behavior.

This structural approach to the study and understanding of mid-life transitions can be defined as "idiographic" in its methodology. Idiographic simply means to describe things individually. Therefore, the approach here will be to describe the background, nature, and outcome of the mid-life transition or crisis of each individual studied. This focus on the individual will stress the uniqueness and variability as well as the representativeness of each mid-life transition that is depicted. This is markedly different from most studies of such developmental phenomena. Most studies utilize representative samples of individuals, drawn from the population of interest, for the purposes of making generalizations about that population based on findings from the sample. This type of methodology is called "nomothetic," and is characteristic of most current behavioral research. Kerlinger (1979) has stated that nomothetic means law-making, and that its basic purpose is to set up general laws. He notes that its emphasis, therefore, is on generalization rather than individualization, and its "results are always statistical."

Although there will be reference along the way to some of the statistical findings from nomothetic research on the developmental problems of middle adulthood, the primary emphasis throughout this book will be on the unique individual who has experienced a mid-life transition or crisis. Therefore, the basic methodology has to be idiographic.

The foremost proponent of idiographic approaches in the social and behavioral sciences has been Gordon Allport (1961). His position has been described as essentially phenomenological in nature because he consistently takes "the client's own view of himself as a unique being-in-the-world" (May, 1968). This is certainly the approach of this book. As such, it relies basically on the case study method. Runyan (1982) contends that the case study may be the most effective single method of describing the experience of a single person in order to develop "idiographic interpretations" and explanations of that experience, as well as to develop courses of action and decision-making for that particular person. It is not surprising, therefore, that the case study method has been the traditional approach of all clinical research and that much of the knowledge common to most clinicians was discovered by it (Bolgar 1965).

Most of the case studies illustrated in this book come out of clinical settings or were selected for study purposes from self-help organizations and groups dealing with certain problems and crises common to the transitions of middle adulthood. In some respects, then, the persons illustrated in the cases were self-selected by their search for some sort of help or support in dealing with their problems and crises. These individuals were willing to participate in the rather intensive interviewing and testing procedures involved in the structural approach. They had to be capable of comprehending and responding appropriately to these procedures. Therefore, they do not represent the full range of educational, occupational, or other demographic features of the general population. Such representation was neither intended or possible. However, these persons were willing to share in considerable detail and depth the complex, trying, and frequently painful personal experience of a mid-life transition or crisis. Further, their experiences tend to illustrate some of the more salient and significant themes and crises of middle adulthood, and this is the primary basis for the selection of the specific cases depicted in this book.

STRUCTURES OF MEANING

In attempting to understand and assess each transitional or crisis situation, the overall structural approach to these themes and crises of middle adulthood includes three different but related types of structure. The first type is the "individual life structure" which comes from the adult development theory of Daniel Levinson and his colleagues at Yale (Levinson, Darrow, Klein, & McKee 1978). They define it as "the basic pattern or design of a person's life at a given time" (Levinson et al. 1978, 318). The second type of structure is called the "structure of experience," which comes from structural phenomenology and psychology. It will be explained more thoroughly a bit later, but for our purposes right now, it can be described as the unique way in which a mid-life transition is subjectively experienced by the person. The third type of structure is the "cognitive structure," as that concept has been developed and applied in cognitive theory, research, and psychotherapy. Cognitive structures or schemata can be described as the ways in which the person cognitively structures, constructs or construes his or her world. A whole current life situation, or life structure, can be construed in this way, or a more immediate and circumscribed situation, event, or circumstance, can be so structured and construed. Those who work with older persons recognize that there is even a cognitive structuring and often a cognitive "restructuring" of the older person's past in a life review process (Butler 1963).

These three types of structures, particularly the latter two, will be covered in more detail in the second chapter in terms of their theoretical and empirical backgrounds. For the moment, it can be said that the three types of structure will provide the basis for an understanding and assessment of the impact, meaning, and clinical implications of crisis-laden mid-life experiences. We begin by assessing the current life structure of the individual. The next step is to determine the meaning of current or foreseeable events of potential or actual critical dimensions in that life structure. This meaning is invariably made up of multiple concerns and meanings, but these are related to one another in a patterned or structured manner. This structure of meaning can be determined and made explicit by utilizing certain phenomenological approaches in exploring it with the person who is experiencing it, and then by explicating the cognitive-structural elements of the situation through the use of certain assessment instruments which are currently available to clinicians and researchers.

Something more needs to be said about the individual life structure at this point. Levinson and his colleagues call it "the pivotal concept in our entire work . . .," and they go on to say, "by 'life structure' we mean the underlying pattern or design of a person's life at a given time" (Levinson et al. 1978, 41). The "underlying pattern" idea indicates the implicit rather than explicit nature of the individual life structure. This book attempts to make that pattern explicit in each and every case. Thus, the individual life structure provides a framework for viewing and understanding a crisis-laden event within the context of the person's current life circumstances. Yet, at the same time the life structure takes into account salient factors from the past and potential factors in the future. This structure also has both inner and outer dimensions. The inner is related to the *self* and the outer is related to the *world,* which includes the immediate social and physical environment as well as aspects of the larger societal and cultural milieu.

As Levinson and his colleagues note, part of the self is conscious, part is unconscious, but both parts must be considered in assessing the individual life structure. Further, some aspects of the self are lived out whereas other aspects are inhibited or neglected. It is important to note here that "the self is an intrinsic element of the life structure and not a separate entity" (Levinson et al. 1978, 42). For this reason, a considerable amount of attention will be given, both in concept and application, to the *self* in this book—especially to such elements of the self-system as the self-concept, the self-ideal, and self-esteem.

In assessing the individual life structure it is necessary to examine the person's participation in the external world in terms of its terrain, its cast of significant characters, and the various resources and constraints available to the person for dealing with or changing elements of that world. Clearly, the person's participation in the world involves transactions between self and world. As Levinson says, these "transactions take obvious forms, but subtle meanings and feelings play an important part in them."

These "subtle meanings and feelings" bring us directly to the importance of the structure of meaning within the structural paradigm of this book. A structural psychologist has referred to the structure of meaning as "inseparable from the 'situation experienced by the subject,' since it is the structure that organizes and gives a meaning to the whole of (the) experience . . . while at the same time it reveals a 'dynamic' of the personality . . ." (Mucchielli 1970, 124). This is a good understanding of the structure of meaning for our purposes. It comes from Roger Mucchielli of the University of Nice in France. Although he calls himself a structural psychologist, Mucchielli was very much influenced by the noted French phenomenologist, Maurice Merleau-Ponty (1942/63; 1945/62), whose ideas will be referred to again in the second chapter. At any rate, the structure of meaning is very much a phenomenological concept and is often referred to as the "structure of experience." A phenomenological psychologist put it this way: "One way to clarify experience is to seek what events *mean* to us. In asking this question, we discover that conscious experience has a certain *structure.* Indeed, we might say that the 'structuredness' of experience *is* the meaningfulness of experience. Structureless experience would be a meaningless experience" (Keen 1975, 19).

Mucchielli (1970) noted that he used certain projective tests such as the Rorschach, TAT, and sentence-completion to get at the structure of meaning, but these did not include some of the more current cognitive assessment instruments which this author and others have found particularly helpful for both clinical practice and research applications (Merluzzi, Glass, and Genest 1981).

It should be clear that the cognitive structure concept is very intimately related to the structure of meaning. It has been defined as "the system of interrelations among thoughts that allow the individual to respond appropriately to incoming sensations from the environment" (Wegner & Vallacher 1977, 4). Knowledge of the person's cognitive structure enables us to know how the person will process an event (incoming sensation) of potential crisis proportions—that is, how the event will be perceived, evaluated, and possibly acted upon. Certainly, cognitive structure in this sense overlaps with the structure of meaning. In fact, one can say that the cognitive structure mediates much of the meaning of the event.

Since the concepts of structure of experience and cognitive structure will be handled in more detail in the next chapter, it would be helpful to return to the individual life structure concept at this point. There are two predominant components to the life structure of most adults and these two are the same ones to which Freud attributed such universal significance—love and work. It is of interest to note how much this important dyad continues to provide the focus of attention for behavioral scientists everywhere. This was underscored when the sociologist Niel J. Smelser and the psychoanalyst Erik Erikson jointly organized a conference of eminent behavioral scientists and then edited a volume entitled *Themes of Work and Love in Adulthood* (1981), based on papers presented at that influential conference in Stanford, California, 1977.

As far as the individual life structure is concerned, there are numerous themes that revolve around the twin issues of work and love. In fact, we might call love and work "meta-themes" in this approach. With reference to mid-life crises, there are apt to be themes of conflict, attachment, separation, abandonment, and so on within the love dimension. This dimension includes marriage, family, friends, and other intimate and significant relationships. Examination of the work dimension in a mid-life crisis might uncover themes related to personal identity, to achievement of life goals, or more likely to despair over failure to achieve the goals, and, sometimes, a sense of meaninglessness once the goals are achieved.

One of the most frequent causes of critical transitional problems in middle adulthood is the emergence of an imbalance or dissonance between the two components of work and love. Thus, a rather common type of problem that often reaches crisis proportions is the disproportionate amount of time, effort, and *self* some middle-aged men put into their work and careers at the expense of their marriages and families. This can continue to the point where the wives are alienated and the teenage children estranged. Not infrequently, of course, this leads to separation and divorce, which introduce additional themes of stress and crisis. This problem illustrates an instance in which some aspects of the self were neglected in favor of aspects of the external world (job) within the individual life structure. It can be said that certain implicit choices had been made by the men in such cases with respect to their individual life structures. Since those structures are in jeopardy, each man will need to make some explicit decisions and act upon them.

This problem points out something about the evolution of the life structure. There is a sequence which consists of alternating stable (structure-building) periods and transitional (structure-changing) periods which shape the course of psychosocial development in adulthood. Levinson notes that the primary task of every stable period is for the individual to build a life structure by making critical choices, form a structure around them, and then pursue preferred goals and values within that structure. "The primary tasks of every transitional period are to question and reappraise the existing structure, to explore various possibilities for change in self and world, and to move toward commitment to the crucial choices that form the basis for a new life structure in the ensuing period" (Levinson et al. 1978, 49).

Thus, choices are a crucial element in the development of individual life structure. Most of the clinical work of this author with middle-aged persons experiencing severe transitional problems (i.e., crises) has revolved around this issue of choices. This work required a more conscious and purposeful assessment of the individual life structure and the stresses, fissures, and changes bearing on that structure. Then an exploration and assessment of the meaning of that structure, those changes, and the new possibilities for the person (the structure of meaning) would follow. This exploration process usually involved the use of cognitive assessment instruments for the purposes of determining the person's cognitive structuring of the situation. This approach and these procedures were very helpful in understanding and articulating the various alternatives and the kinds of choices that needed to be made. It also helped to clarify a number of the underlying assumptions and values that had been guiding the person's life decisions up to that point. By making these assumptions explicit, the crucial decision making aspect of the work was enhanced.

In principle as well as in practice, the structural approach of this book views the person in each case as a participant and a partner in the mutual endeavor of understanding all these aspects of the crisis situation. For this reason, the word "person" will be favored over the terms "client" or "patient" in the clinical cases to be described. It will also be favored over the terms "respondent" or "subject" in the field research cases. Also, since the professional doing the interviewing and testing in the case studies may be acting in either a clinical or a research capacity, the generic term "practitioner" will be used hereafter to refer to either a clinical or a research practitioner.

THE MEANINGS OF MID-LIFE, TRANSITION, AND CRISIS

Two questions have to be addressed before we go any further with this exposition on the transitions and crises of middle adulthood. One is the question of just what we mean by "mid-life, " and the second is what we mean by the related terms of "transition" and "crises." In order to answer the first question there needs to be some exploration of the various age ranges that have been identified by different authorities in the field to represent mid-life.

Daniel Levinson, whose concept of the individual life structure is so central to the approach to this book, has written: "Various discussions of 'mid-life crisis' refer to times of great difficulty in 'the middle years,' which may cover any part of the span from thirty-five to sixty-five. Crises occurring at different stages within this span have many features in common" (Levinson et al. 1978, 159). However, Levinson prefers to use the term "mid-life crisis" only for the one that occurs with the "Mid-Life Transition" (the ages of forty to forty-five) of this developmental model. Thus, he would see mid-life as beginning at about forty years of age. Furthermore, he conceives a transition as a bridge or boundary zone between two stages of greater stability in adult development.

I prefer Naomi Golan's (1981) working definition of a transition as "a period of moving from one state of certainty to another, with an interval of uncertainty and change in between." This is preferred because a transition can be identified not only by time periods (passages from one chronological stage to another in the life cycle) but also by role shifts (homemaker to breadwinner, wife to widow, etc.) and marker events (marriage, divorce, death of a spouse, retirement, etc.). Whether or not these transitions reach actual crisis proportions is very dependent upon certain factors which will be outlined shortly.

Roger L. Gould (1978), in contrast to Levinson, refers to the "mid-life decade" as thirty-five to forty-five years of age and sees the critical aspects of the mid-life transition as beginning in the late thirties. In his highly influential essay, "Death and the Mid-Life Crisis," Elliott Jaques (1965) also proposed that the mid-life crisis begins in the middle or late thirties with the recognition of one's mortality and finitude. Cath (1980) agrees that it is "the common heritage" of the decades beginning at age thirty-five that one is confronted by this very personal meaning of aging and death.

The kinds of questions and themes raised by Jaques and Cath are very similar to the mid-life experiences of the men and women represented in the case studies of this book, regardless of whether the cases come from clinical practice or field research. For this reason, the term "mid-life" will be used here to refer to the period beginning at about age thirty-five and extending to approximately age sixty. If there is one theme that runs through all the cases to be presented, it is an awareness of time left in life; of one's personal finiteness, which means limited time to experience and achieve what one thinks should be personally experienced and achieved.

Now that it has been clarified what is meant by mid-life and transition, what is meant by a "crisis?" In its simplest terms, it has been defined as "an upset in a steady state" (Parad, 1965). This definition assumes that people ordinarily strive to maintain a constant series of adaptive maneuvers and characteristic problem-solving activities through which basic needs for survival, security, self-esteem, love, and relatedness are met. In mid-life situations, events can occur which lead to sudden discontinuities and consequent transitions, such as an unexpected death of a loved one, a serious illness or disability in one's self or loved ones, and so on. There are also transitions marked by the accumulation of progressive physical, social, and psychological changes which lead to a point of discontinuity and which result in a state of major disequilibrium in the individual life structure. In either case what we are concerned with are *transitional crises;* those that mark a shift from one life structure to another in mid-life, terminating the existing one and creating the possibility for a new one (Levinson et al. 1978).

Ordinarily, the individual might possess adequate coping capacities and mechanisms for re-establishing the previous equilibrium. However, in a crisis, by definition, the habitual problem-solving activities are not adequate and do not rapidly lead to the previously achieved balance state. The stressor event or transitional change requires a solution which is new in relation to the individual's life experience.

The person's perception of the event or state is central to the determination of whether the situation will become a crisis. "To transform a stressor event into a crisis requires an intervening variable that has been variously termed, 'meaning of the event' or 'definition of the event,'" according to Reuben Hill (1965, 36). He provides the following formula for determination of a crisis: A (the event)→*interacting* with B (the person's or family's crisis-meeting resources)→*interacting* with C (the person's definition of the event)→*produces* X (the crisis). Thus, the key lies in the *meaning* dimension of this paradigm. The event may or may not eventuate in a crisis depending on what kind of definition (meaning) the person gives to the event. Here, again, the importance of the structure of meaning element in the structural approach becomes very evident.

The problem created by a stressor event can be perceived by the person as a threat, a loss, or a challenge. The threat may be to fundamental instinctual needs or to the person's basic sense of integrity. The loss may be actual or may be experienced as a state of acute deprivation. For either of these states there is a characteristic way the person tends to respond emotionally. A threat to need and integrity is met with anxiety. Loss or deprivation is met with depression. Indeed, the two emotional states of anxiety and depression are ubiquitous and are the ones that practitioners most often encounter in persons coming to them for help in dealing with life crises.

There is another way in which the problem can be perceived, and that is as a challenge. If it is perceived in this way, it is more likely to be met with a mobilization of energy and purposive problem-solving activities (Rapoport 1965). Thus, not only is the "meaning" or perceptual dimension the key to whether the stressor event will produce a crisis, but it also plays a major role in determining both the nature and extent of coping behaviors. Characteristic modes for organizing perceptual and intellectual activities have been referred to as cognitive styles, and Witkin's (1981) formulation of field-dependent and field-independent cognitive styles has been one of the most influential ones in current cognitive theory. His cognitive field theory will be discussed somewhat more in the next chapter as one of the phenomenological field theories that underlies the structural approach of this book. For the moment, suffice it to say that his identified cognitive styles correspond to the characteristic adaptive and defense mechanisms of persons under stress.

> For example, under stressful situations, a person whose cognitive style is identified as "field-dependent" is very dependent upon external objects in the environment for orientation to reality. This type of individual tends to use such coping mechanisms as repression and denial. In contrast, the "field-independent" person will tend to prefer intellectualization as a defense mode (Aguilera & Messick 1982, 67).

Nancy Haan (1969) identified intellectuality at the higher end of her continuum of adaptive capacities of the ego. Her continuum was adapted and applied by Vaillant (1977) in his study of middle-aged men. He found intellectualization and other such "neurotic defenses" to be more adaptive than the "immature" mechanisms like projection, or "psychotic" mechanisms like denial, for the middle-aged men depicted in his book, *Adaptation to Life*. It is very likely that characteristic defenses are part and parcel of one's being-in-the-world, the way one perceives and acts upon events in the external world. Thus, a person who characteristically uses intellectualization, or higher mechanisms such as humor and anticipation (per Vaillant's hierarchy) is more apt to perceive problems created by stressor events as challenges, *because* her/his characteristic defenses are generally more adaptive. These would be valuable resources in Hill's paradigm (above). On the other hand, a person who is more stress-prone or "stress-preoccupied" (Lowenthal, Thurner, Chiriboga & associates 1975), is apt to be a person who not only tends to see stressor events as threats, but also characteristically has a less adaptive defensive style and uses mechanisms like denial and projection. Thus, perception or meaning of a stressor event and adaptive style are intimately and reciprocally related to one another.

To the extent an event is perceived realistically, problem- solving can be appropriately oriented toward tension reduction and problem solution. Mechanisms like humor and anticipation provide a certain distance and perspective on the problem, a perspective which will be more realistic than one distorted by projection and denial. This speaks to the importance of the mediating cognitive process of "appraisal" which is so central to Richard Lazarus' (1966 and 1980) "cognitive- phenomenological" approach to the study of coping. The appraisal process will determine the various coping methods used by individuals and will, of course, be influential in forming the person's definition of the situation. Thus, whether the situation becomes a full-blown debilitating crisis is very much dependent upon the subjective meaning of the situation in terms of its dimensions and the person's perceived capacity to deal with it. This is clearly within the realm of the structure of meaning, as noted earlier in this chapter.

What we are talking about here, of course, are mid-life transitions and problems of rather major proportions. There has been some question in adult development literature as to whether women or men are better able to cope with these problems. It will be recalled from the Preface that my original interest in this area came about as a result of clinical experience, where it appeared that middle aged women seemed better able to cope at least with the problems of conflict and separation in marriage. It should be helpful to pursue this issue in more detail now.

GENDER AND MID-LIFE PROBLEMS

In attempting to understand why women seemed to cope better than men in dealing with certain mid-life problems, I began by empirically studying whether women were generally more satisifed and adjusted to middle-age in general. Then, it was necessary to see what factors were most important for life satisfaction in women as compared to men in the hope that this might shed some light on what appeared to be better adaptability among women in the admittedly small and biased sample I had seen in clinical practice in a center for psychotherapy.

Some of the results of this study have been presented elsewhere (Sherman 1982), but it involved analyzing the life satisfaction of a national sample of middle-aged (forty to sixty) men and women based on a measure of self-reported satisfaction in life areas of marriage, family, friendships, finances, health, and leisure. The kinds of crisis-provoking events included in the study were death of spouse, illness, divorce, separation, and job loss, including retirement and layoffs. The impact of these events were measured by a modified Holmes and Rahe (1967) social readjustment scale, with death of spouse having the highest stress rating (one hundred points) and retirement the lowest (forty-five points), from the stressor events most relevant to mid-life which were recorded in the NORC data file.

The analysis showed that there were no significant differences between the sexes in terms of their social readjustment ratings, which meant that there was no greater general incidence or degree of stressful mid-life events for men than women. Also, there was no significant difference between the sexes with respect to life satisfaction, so that it appeared that they were similar in the degree of satisfaction with their current lives. However, when the stress measures (social readjustment ratings) were entered into the analysis, the men showed a significantly lower life satisfaction than the women. This finding was consistent with the general idea that women seemed to retain better morale in the face of stressful events in mid-life.

The findings concerning the effect of marital status on life satisfaction were particularly noteworthy. They indicated that marriage was a more positive source of support in mediating stress for men than it was for women. Indeed, it looked as though marriage might be a major source of stress rather than support for women, because being married had a significant negative relationship to life satisfaction for women. In fact, the life satisfaction scores of married women were somewhat (though not significantly) lower than women who were widowed, divorced, or separated. Just the reverse was true for married men, who showed a significantly higher level of life satisfaction than men who were widowed, divorced, or separated. These findings appeared to be consistent with the contention made by sociologist Jessie Bernard (1972) a decade earlier that middle-aged women as a group were quite dissatisfied with their marriages.

Early on in the second phase of the research designed to study the individual strategies and attitudes in coping with mid-life crises, it became apparent that women more readily used outside sources of support in coping than did men. This might serve to explain in part why the men in the NORC sample did not seem to deal as well in general with stressful events.

The women in this initial group did indeed seem to seek support from family, friends, and professionals more readily and more frequently than did the men. The women showed a wider range of sources of help for dealing with the stressful events, with most women identifying at least three sources, whereas the men identified between one and two sources. The sources included friends, family, professional (clinics, social agencies, and private practitioners), spouse, peer support groups, clergy, self-help books, and so on.

It is interesting to note that among this early group of forty-six persons who were interviewed and tested, the highest ranked source in terms of helpfulness were identified by women in the following numbers: friends (8), family (6), professional (5), spouse (1), support group (2), other (1); whereas the men identified the following: friends (4), family (0), professional (3), spouse (6), support group (0), other (0). The most remarkable figure here is that the highest ranked source of help most frequently identified by men was the spouse. Although the numbers are very small, what makes this remarkable was that this initial group came entirely from Parents Without Partners groups in which the major problem or crisis the respondents identified was the divorce or separation from the spouse. This means that a number of men actually relied on their estranged wives to help them cope with the stress occasioned by the divorce or separation. Indeed, these men said they did this because they had no one else to turn to with whom they felt close enough to confide in and seek emotional support from. The one woman who identified her spouse as the most helpful source did so because of a serious behavioral problem of one of their teenage children who was living with her.

During marriage men generally tend to rely on their wives to coordinate and maintain relationships with family and mutual friends, so that when separation and divorce occur the wives are more apt to have a ready-made support network than are the husbands. Further, the men more commonly come to rely on their spouses as their sole confidantes during marriage than do women (Fiske 1979). This would help to explain some of these early findings.

Another noteworthy early finding was the fact that they had to rely almost entirely upon themselves to deal with the crisis, whereas none of the women said this. Quite a few said they relied mostly on themselves, but they also claimed to get important help from significant others. Of course, the fact that the men said they "went it alone" more than the women is consistent with the idea that they probably had fewer confidants.

This might seem to paint a very bleak picture for the men as a group. However, this would be somewhat deceiving. A few of the men interviewed in the beginning of the second phase of the study seemed to be doing quite well despite the fact that their wives initiated the separation, and that they did not continue to use their wives or other women as confidants. They found themselves apartments, cooked their own meals, and learned to fend for themselves quite adequately. Although they were going through considerable emotional turmoil as a result of their separations from wives and children, they seemed to be able to cope with the emotional as well as the practical, instrumental aspects of the separation crisis on their own.

This seemed to run counter to some widely held beliefs about the way men and women cope in the face of stress and crisis. The two major ways of coping that have been identified are *expressive* and *instrumental*. The expressive type has to do with emotions, including anxiety, feelings of tension, anger, fear, hostility, sadness, and so on. The issue for this type of coping is how well the person expresses, handles, and generally manages these emotions, which can sometimes be overwhelming and prevent any healthy problem-solving in the face of the crisis. The instrumental type of coping has to do with the practical, concrete steps in terms of planning actions for healthy problem-solving, such as making necessary changes in financial, occupational, locational, and other living arrangements.

It has been generally assumed that men are better at instrumental coping, because in the conventional roles of husband and father, they have been the breadwinners and the financial managers of their families. It has also been assumed that women are better at expressive coping. According to the older socialization norms of our society, girls and women are supposed to be more expressive of their feelings and emotions, whereas just the opposite is supposed to be true of boys and men. Furthermore, women have had the traditional roles of wife and mother in which they have been the nurturers and the managers of the emotional and affiliative needs of their families. Certainly, the preliminary impressions from the second phase of my study indicated that the women were much more effective at maintaining and using helping networks of family and friends to meet their affiliative and emotional needs in the time of crisis.

This does not necessarily mean that women are better at coping with transitional crises, for it often takes more than the support of others to make it through a crisis. As Fiske (1980) noted, having the resource of close interpersonal relationships did not protect the middle-aged women from a "proliferation of symptoms" related to the post-parental stage. To this should be added the observation that exclusive reliance upon either expressive or instrumental coping is not good for adaptation. Too much uncontrolled emotion and assumption of emotional dependence on others does not lead to effective, autonomous, problem-solving activities. Conversely, failure to adequately ventilate and handle the pent up emotions and cumulative stress and to deny expression of the emotions while engaging in instrumental problem-solving has been shown to lead to disproportionate instances of later emotional breakdown—notably in the form of depression (Caplan 1964; Lindemann 1944). The use of both expressive and instrumental coping concurrently has been found to be the most effective way of dealing with crises, particularly those involving loss of significant others (Rapoport 1965).

Probably the most comprehensive ongoing study of men and women during the transitions and crises of adult life was that begun by Marjorie Fiske Lowenthal and her colleagues at the University of California, San Francisco (Lowenthal et al. 1975). That study, which included samples of high school seniors, young marrieds, young middle age (late thirties and early forties), and older middle age (up to age 58), were followed longitudinally into adulthood and old age respectively. More than any other study, theirs shed some light on the diverse statistical and direct interview impressions I was finding in my own study, so it should be helpful to summarize here some of the relevant points from the San Francisco study.

Those investigators came to the conclusion that women and men were indeed different in most ways of living and coping. The felt that women were much more like each other at all stages of life than like men. However, in their middle years, women tended to be more "stress preoccupied" as a group than any other age cohort in the study, whether male or female, and whether young or old. This was particularly true of the nonworking married women who were less satisfied with their family lives and their lives in general than the working married women and the men in the middle-aged group. At the same time, divorce and widowhood were more traumatic for the men than the women in this group. The investigators thought this was due in large part to the fact that men were less likely to have confidants other than their spouses, and this fact probably helped to explain the more hasty remarriages among the men.

Five years after the publication of the above study, Marjorie Fiske (Lowenthal) made the following summary statement: "In the current study of transitions in adult life, from youth to old age, on most measures the differences between men and women within a given stage are greater than those between the young and the old of each gender" (Fiske 1980, 343). She also noted that Richard Lazarus (1966, 1980) was pursuing a "highly innovative" and "intensive study of middle and later middle-aged men and women who are being followed up frequently and regularly" (Fiske 1980, 344). She felt that Lazarus' focus on day-to-day stress would give a much clearer picture than had been obtained on stress and coping among the middle-aged up to that time. However, when Lazarus and his coresearcher, Susan Folkman, reported their findings from a middle-aged community sample (Folkman & Lazarus 1980), my prior conceptions of the relationship between gender and coping had to be altered somewhat. They identified two functions of coping, problem-focused and emotion-focused, which are similar to instrumental and expressive coping, respectively. They noted that contrary to cultural stereotypes, there were no gender differences in emotion-focused coping, but men used more problem-focused coping in the context of work. However, the authors thought that this finding probably reflected "gender differences in jobs rather than a general disposition" on the part of males to use more problem-focused coping than females (Folkman & Lazarus 1980, 235). They felt that this was due to the fact that more women than men hold lower-level jobs in which there are fewer opportunities to engage in problem-solving processes. Overall, they felt that "the results offer relatively little confirmation for the gender differences that conventional wisdom leads us to expect" (Folkman & Lazarus 1980, 233).

This seemed to be somewhat at odds with the observations by Fiske. However, I had the good fortune to be able to confer with some of the people involved in the foregoing studies. These people included some of the major coinvestigators in the transitions study begun by Marjorie Fiske (then retired), as well as some people associated with the Lazarus and Folkman study.* They indicated that the whole broad area of stress, crisis, and coping was very much in flux. There are very many complex, interrelated factors and variables that require considerably more systematic and controlled study. Although the much more intense and detailed cognitive-phenomenological analysis of psychological stress by Lazarus and his colleagues is giving us considerably more valuable information about how people cope with the daily hassles or mundane varieties of stress, it was not designed to demonstrate what types of coping are most successful for some of the more acute kinds of problems and crises that can occur in mid-life.

Further, there was some evidence from the transitions study that it is not necessarily functional for certain persons to self-consciously attempt to cope with their crises. This observation raised some obvious questions about certain aspects of formal or professional crisis intervention. Also, the study found that interpersonal supports are not necessarily positive coping resources for some older persons. Sometimes the availability of genuine social support might well be conducive to such outcomes as admission to the psychiatric wards of a hospital. As Fiske has noted, "In fact, lack of such support, or a degree of social invisibility, may provide a certain amount of protection against hospitalization once mental or emotional difficulties develop" (Fiske 1980, 351).

This is probably due more to the nature of the person than to the availability of the social support. That is, some persons immediately look to other people for support when they experience any undue stress in their lives. If we can change the words of a popular song, "people who need people (desperately) are *not* the luckiest people in the world." Even if a support network is available for such a person, the aura of desperate neediness could well drive possible supporters away. Such persons very much fit the description of the "succorance seeking" pattern of aging found in the famous Kansas City study of aging (Neugarten, Havinghurst & Tobin 1961). Needless to say, this was not the most successful or adaptive pattern of aging found in the study.

It is possible that although women have been shown empirically to have more social supports than men, it might be that a significant number of

*Notably David Chiriboga and Majda Thurner, co-authors with Marjorie Fiske of *The Four Stages: A Comparative Study of Women and Men Facing Transitions* (1975).

women rely unduly (like the succorance seekers) on others for coping. If so, this might explain why the transitions study did not find middle-aged women, as a group, to cope better than men in the same age group.

Coping aside, there is considerable evidence that men and women show different patterns of personality development in their middle years, and these differences can have some bearing on the problems of concern here. For example, David Gutmann's (1969) cross-cultural studies have indicated that as the middle years wear on, men tend to become more affiliative and interested in love than power, more diffusely sensual and less aggressive, more present than future oriented. Although in the earlier years of marriage husbands tend to be dominant, as they move from their middle into their later years they tend to become more dependent. During these same years women are becoming more independent as well as more aggressive and domineering.

These changes appear to be consistent with Jung's (1971) contention that there is an integration of two basic psychological functions, "feeling" and "thinking" in the process of individuation in the later stages of life for both men and women. In this process men become more open to the feminine side (the *anima*) of their personalities while the women become more open to the masculine side (the *animus*) of their personalities. Indeed, Costa and McCrae (1976) found in an empirical study of structural change in the age groups of men from twenty-five to eighty-two that there was a significant change in degree of openness to affective as well as cognitive experiences in middle age. These researchers felt that these findings tended to support Jung's contention. Ryff and Baltes (1976) have also found evidence for this sex role reversal and greater similarity between middle-aged men and women in personality traits. The middle-aged women showed more masculine traits such as ambition, competence, and courage compared to their younger counterparts.

These findings of greater ambition, aggression, and independence among middle-aged women explain why the NORC sample findings showed that unattached women (single, divorced widowed, and separated) fared much better in terms of life satisfaction than the unattached middle-aged men. Furthermore, the increased need for affiliation and nurturance among middle-aged men would tend to work against these unattached men, who were missing their primary and often sole sources of affiliation and nurturance (their former wives).

PROBLEMS AND THEMES OF THE MIDDLE YEARS

There seems to be a remarkable consensus of opinion among researchers and adult development theorists that entrance into middle age is frequently stormy and stressful (Chiriboga 1981). The transition into mid-life and the normative kinds of transitional events that often occur between the years of thirty-five to sixty can be dramatic, and they have received a great deal of empirical and theoretical attention. These tend to include expectable events such as the empty nest, death or serious illness of aging parents, menopause, the inevitable physical changes and common medical problems of middle age, and so on. However, these are apt to be much less devastating than the nonnormative or unanticipated events such as death of child, loss of a spouse, forced unemployment before retirement, divorce, and so on. The normative and expectable events can of course be prepared for, and that is probably why they are usually less devastating.

Even though the non-normative events may become more salient in the middle and later years, they have received far less attention than the normative ones, and relatively little is known about them beyond their very disruptive qualities (Chiriboga 1981). Levinson's stage model of adult development is primarily concerned with normative or expectable changes. The disruptive effects of even normative transitional events are well represented in his study of the process of change involved in the shift from one life structure to another in the stages of development. However, there is not much systematic attention given in his model to the effects of unexpectable events.

The social psychiatrist C. Murray Parkes (1971) utilized the concept of an "assumptive world" in his study of adult transitions. The assumptive world is very similar to Levinson's life structure concept in that it is developed by each person out of his or her unique set of experiences. Just as in the case of the life structure, whenever a major change occurs in the person's life situation he or she needs to revamp his or her plans for living within the world. The person also needs to *restructure his or her ways of looking at the world*. This latter point fits very well with the approach of this book and provides an important perspective on the mid-life transitions and crises depicted in the later chapters. The need to restructure ways of looking at the world is certainly implicit in Levinson's approach to transitions and crises, but Parkes clearly explains this concept in a way that enables us to comprehend somewhat better the impact of unexpectable mid-life events.

He uses the term "psychosocial transitions" to describe major changes in a person's life space which take place over a relatively short period of time, but which affect large areas of the person's assumptive world and are also lasting in their effects. The internal assumptive world is the person's total set of assumptions and interpretations which are built upon the basis of the person's past experiences in dealing with the outside world and on his or her expectations about the future. If the changes and transitional events encountered in mid-life fulfill the person's expectations and do not happen suddenly, the person is able to prepare gradually for the necessary restructuring and to cope effectively with the changes.

However, if the events and the changes are sudden and unexpected, as well as major in their dimensions (psychosocial transitions), they will call for a major restructuring and the abandonment of one set of assumptions for a fresh set which will enable the person to cope with the newly altered life space. Obviously, these situations are much more likely to become crises, because the person is less prepared to learn and implement new, appropriate coping strategies. Furthermore, the *meaning* of the event is apt to be more devastating in its overtones because the person has not been able to adequately restructure his or her ways of looking at the sharply altered world.

Not only does Parkes's formulation enable us to better understand the impact of unexpectable events, but it highlights the relationships of the meaning of events (expected and unexpected) to the assumptive world of the individual. It might be argued that the meaning of each event is going to be so unique to the very particular assumptive world of each individual that it will be impossible to identify any general, salient issues and meanings in mid-life transitions. However, it is possible to identify common themes which tend to permeate the unique experiences and meanings of mid-life events and crises for the people encountering them. Thus, we can speak about common pervasive themes such as loss and separation.

ALTERNATIVE PERSPECTIVES ON MID-LIFE PERSONALITY DEVELOPMENT

It has already been noted that Levinson's theory of adult development is primarily concerned with normative changes and that he does not give much attention to unexpectable changes. Furthermore, he is quite insistent that the chronological stages he has outlined do indeed evolve "through a relatively orderly sequence during the adult years" (Levinson et al. 1978, 49). Orville Brim was quite critical of this aspect of Levinson's theory. In writing about the "male mid-life crisis" he noted that "there is as yet no evidence for developmental periods or 'stages' in the mid-life period, in which one event must come after another, or one personality change brings another in its wake" (Brim 1976, 8).

Stage theories of adult development in general have been criticized by a number of investigators in gerontological and life span research. By delineating progressions of change that follow orderly and sequential patterns, stage theories have been seen as too rigid, restrictive, unidirectional and irreversible. They seem to belie much empirical evidence of individual differences, social change, cohort effects, and personal idiosyncrasies (Baltes 1979). This evidence has led some psychologists to view human development as a continuous operation of various developmental processes rather than one involving discrete stages. Klaus Riegel (1976) has proposed that human development is a dialectical process marked by contradictory ideas or actions caused by constant changes occurring in the person and in the person's environment. Additionally, these contradictions are not seen by Riegel as deficiencies but as invitations to a new level of integration, even though they may seem disruptive and discontinuous in any one life.

Thus, some psychologists have taken an explicitly non-lifespan perspective, if only for heuristic purposes: "With regard to the description of psychological aging, the author's belief is that a nonlife-span discontinuous posture seems useful at the present time . . ." (Baltes 1973, 463). Then other investigators have taken a somewhat different perspective in criticizing stage theories of development. Costa and McCrae (1980), for example, have argued that there is no essential change in the later half of life. Although it was noted earlier that these same two investigators found an increased openness to affective experience among middle-aged men, they do not see any significant changes *after* middle age. They claim, in fact, that enduring personality dispositions (notably neuroticism and extraversion) antedate and predict measures of personal adjustment in later years, especially in old age (Costa and McCrae 1981). This is somewhat different than the perspectives of Riegel and Baltes, which appear to emphasize the continuous potential for change throughout the life cycle. However, both perspectives are critical of Levinson's type of stage theory for different reasons. I tend to prefer the dialectical perspective of Riegel because it can better deal with the discontinuous and often unpredictable events involved in mid-life transitions.

Another criticism of Levinson's model is that it does not fit the experience of women. Since his model was developed from the study of men it tends to reflect the norms and role patterns of the careers and family lives of men. Gilligan (1982) has contended that women's development is more intricately tied to human relationships with more emphasis on caring, nurturance, and attachments across the life cycle. Therefore, women would experience generativity, for example, earlier than men and sustain it further into the life cycle.

Lillian Rubin (1983) not only agrees with Gilligan's contention about the greater relevance of attachments, intimacy, and relationships in the adult development of women, but claims there are fundamental differences in the development of men and women that begin early in childhood and continue throughout the life span. Rubin's perspective is important for our purposes here because she deals with the critical themes and problems represented in many of the cases in this book, including attachment, separation, individuation, and reattachment. Her perspective also helps to explain why the women in my interview survey had and used a support network of friends and relatives in a way the men did not.

Rubin draws upon object relations theory, particularly the separation-individuation issues raised by Margaret Mahler (1979) on the basis of her research on mother-child relationships in early childhood. According to this theory, there is a separation struggle for both boys and girls in order to set up "ego boundaries"—the personal psychological boundaries of the self that sets a person off from others and the rest of the world. This struggle begins in the primary relationship with the mother, who has to provide the basic emotional security and sustenance to enable the young child to separate and venture out in the world so as to individuate (become a more distinct self and "object"). At the same time she also has to be available to reassure and replenish the child emotionally after each such venture. Not only is the mother the main care-giver and source of attachment, but also the primary source of identification for both boys and girls. However, in order to achieve *gender identity* boys have to give up their primary identifications with their mothers, and this is a fundamentally wrenching experience that affects the object relations of boys and men for the rest of their lives. Rubin puts it as follows: "Now, in order to identify with his maleness, he must renounce this connection with the first person outside of self to be internalized into his inner psychic world—the one who has been so deeply embedded in his psychic life as to seem a part of himself—and seek instead a deeper attachment and identification with father" (Rubin, 1983, pp. 55-56). However, father has been a shadowy and secondary character in the boy's internal life up to that point, which makes such an attachment difficult.

In order to repress his identification with his mother, the boy must build up a set of defenses that allows him to develop ego boundaries that are firm and fixed, ". . . barriers that rigidly separate self from other, that circumscribe not only his relationships with others but his connection to his inner emotional life as well." This is in marked contrast to the developmental scenario for girls:

> The context within which separation takes place and identity is forged means that a girl never has to separate herself as completely and irrevocably as a boy must. Her sense of herself, therefore, is never as separate as his; she experiences herself always as more continuous with another; and the maintenance of close personal connections will continue to be one of life's essential themes for her (Rubin 1983, 58-59).

Although this is a greatly abbreviated and truncated rendering of Rubin's formulation, it can be seen how it might help explain the differences I found between men and women in their willingness and capacity to use the support of others in dealing with their mid-life marital separation. In this study, there will be occasion to refer to Rubin's formulation at various points.

Whether or not the gender differences identified by Gilligan, Rubin, and others sustain themselves with the same magnitude and intensity in all phases of the life cycle is still open to question. Ryff and Dunn (1983) found that men's personality development scores are better predicted by their life event ratings than women's, which would tend to support Gilligan's (1982) contention that women's development is less tied to particular life events or status transitions and more to human relationships. More recently, however, Ryff (1985) has raised question as to whether there really are such great experiential differences between men and women throughout the life cycle. Her recent research on the subjective experience of aging for both men and women led her to the following conclusions:

> Finally, the question of sex differences in adult personality processes also produced mixed findings. Initial studies found that men and women differed in terms of their perceived value changes and on certain personality dimensions. However, as we moved closer to developmental scales, that is, those constructed on the basis of developmental theory, sex differences dropped out of the findings. The patterns described in the final study did not differ by sex. Such outcomes suggest that certain aspects of Eriksonian theory may characterize the subjective experiences of both men and women. As with the stage theory issue, there is need to move beyond either/or posturing to more precise questions of which parts of what theories are or are not appropriate for men and for women. We would argue that equally important questions pertain to the significance of such changes for men and women (Ryff 1985, 106).

So, we are left with many remaining questions, not only about gender differences but also about stage theories. Ryff (1982) has called for phenomenological studies of the experience of aging, which she feels would add more dimension to and understanding of the mixed findings we are getting from much of the quantitative empirical work in these areas.

Before leaving the developmental literature, there is one other theorist who has some pertinent things to say about these subject areas. Robert Kegan, whose book, *The Evolving Self* (1982), manages to incorporate and accommodate a number of the developmental issues raised here so far. He incorporates object relations theory, which is essentially psychoanalytic in its origins, and effectively combines it with a neo-Piagetian cognitive perspective. He calls it the "constructive-developmental" approach in that the cognitive aspect of development has to do with the construction of meaning, or "meaning-making" throughout the life cycle. Rather than taking the essentially "male" position that individuation and autonomy represent the highest form of adult development, or the "female" position that relationship and caring represent it, he claims that *both* positions represent basic processes (named "differentiation" and "integration," respectively) in human development. As he says, "subject-object" relations emerge out of a lifelong process of development: a succession of qualitatively more extensive objects with which to be in relation created each time; a natural history of qualitatively better guarantees to the world of its distinctness; successive triumphs of "relationship to" rather than "embeddedness in."

This distinction between relationship and embeddedness is a crucial one and will be called upon in relation to some of the case material to be presented and to some of the conclusions to be drawn from those cases. It is also important to note that this lifelong process is a *dialectical* one in which contradictions in thought and feelings (personal constructions) brought on by inside and outside changes is basic to the growth and development cycle. Although dialectical, it evolves in stages, called "truces," of a hierarchical and circular (helix) nature, beginning with the "incorporative" (infant) stage through to the sixth and highest "interindividual" stage. Thus, Kegan's model contains elements of stage theory but is still dialectical. It is perhaps best summed up by Kegan himself:

> I suggest that human development involves a succession of renegotiated balances, or "biologics" which come to organize the experience of the individual in qualitatively different ways. In this sense, evolutionary activity is intrinsically cognitive, but it is no less affective; we *are* this activity and we experience it. Affect is essentially phenomenological, the felt experience of a motion (hence, "e-motion"). In identifying evolutionary activity as the fundamental ground of personality I am suggesting that the source of our emotions is the phenomenological experience of evolving – or defending, surrendering, and reconstructing a center (Kegan 1982, 81-82).

It can be seen that Kegan takes not only a dialectical and cognitive stance in his developmental scheme but also a phenomenological one. This takes account of one area of Ryff's concern, and it is most certainly a central area of concern for this book. Therefore, there will also be occasion to draw upon Kegan's scheme as the book progresses.

TRANSITIONAL THEMES AND CRISES

It was noted earlier that there are certain issues and themes which seem to run through many of the transitional events and crises of mid-life. The rather pervasive themes of loss and separation were mentioned in this regard. Because of the ubiquitous nature of these themes, each crisis situation to be illustrated in this book represents a salient theme or problem for many persons in their middle years. Some of these themes have become well known in the developmental literature, for example, Erikson's conceptualization of the polarity "generativity vs. stagnation" as the central theme or task in middle adulthood. The use of such thematic polarities has also been adopted by Levinson (1978), but with greater specificity for the middle years. Thus, he speaks of four primary tasks in the mid-life individuation process, each of which involves the reintegration of a fundamental polarity in the character of living. The four thematic polarities are: Young/Old, Destruction/Creation, Masculine/Feminine, and Attachment/Separateness. Some of these polarities have particular relevance for the case material to be presented later concerning crises of attachment and separation, while Erikson's polarity has specific relevance for the case material in Chapter Four concerning generativity, stagnation, and crises of identity in mid-life.

Obviously, some authors have more to say than others about certain themes and problems of the middle years. Therefore, the work of theorists and researchers who have been particularly concerned about the issues and themes of each chapter will be drawn upon when introducing the case material to be presented in those chapters. The selection of problems and themes for a book such as this is, of course, arbitrary to some extent. Because of this, the selection has not been guided entirely by the developmental literature.

The realities of clinical practice suggested some problems and themes that have not been given much systematic attention by theoreticians and researchers. For example, very little attention has been given to the transitional problems of people who are attempting to establish new relationships after separation, divorce, or death of a spouse in their middle years. Yet, this is a pervasive problem in the lives of many middle-aged persons. Therefore, the theme and problems of reattachment will be considered in the same chapter with the related theme and problems of loss, which have received much more theoretical and empirical attention.

The cases here have been selected in large part to serve the subject focus of this book, which is on understanding the nature, course, and outcome of mid-life transitions.** The emphasis will be on the transitional or crisis experience, with or without psychotherapy. Therefore, the cases were not selected primarily to illustrate practice principles and procedures in mid-life crises. However, the first two cases to be presented in the book (in Chapter Three) will go into considerably more detail about treatment methods and techniques, particularly cognitive approaches. This is because those two cases represent the two most prevalent emotional problems associated with transitional crises: anxiety and depression. Thus, although the primary emphasis is still on understanding in those two cases, they should serve to illustrate how cognitive approaches might be applied in mid-life crises. The remaining

---

**It should be emphasized here that all the names and other possible identifying information about the persons represented in the cases have been changed and heavily disguised so as to insure both anonymity and confidentiality.

cases, some of which were not treatment cases, will be presented essentially for the purpose of understanding the transitional or crisis experience. However, in the last chapter of the book there will be a section devoted to the clinical implications of this structural approach for intervention in mid-life crises.

Chapter 2

THE STRUCTURAL APPROACH: THEORY AND METHODS

The purpose of this chapter is to describe the theoretical background and the basic methods of approach that will be applied to the mid-life transitions and crises that are analyzed and illustrated in the case materials of this book. The theoretical and empirical background of the approach represents an amalgam of perceptual, cognitive, and phenomenological concepts and methods for determining structures of meaning in mid-life transitions. When applied to cases, the approach incorporates the three types of structures noted in Chapter One: the individual life structure, the cognitive structure, and the structure of experience. In this chapter, the methods and instruments for incorporating this in research and clinical practice will be explicated, along with the theoretical and empirical background material presented in this chapter.

THE STRUCTURAL APPROACH AND STRUCTURALISM

The uses, abuses and definitions of the term "structural" in the social and behavioral sciences have been so extensive and varied that they almost defy classification. The term has been applied to such disparate fields as anthropology, economics, linguistics, psychology, and others. Actually, no one discipline or school of thought can lay sole claim to the term, for as Piaget (1970) has said, "structuralism is a method, not a doctrine."

Gardner (1972) has identified three principal elements or aspects in the structural approach: the strategic aspect, the formal aspect, and the organismic aspect. The strategic aspect involves searching for the relationship between elements rather than the elements *per se* within the organism or system under study. Procedurally, this means that one looks first at the whole system rather than focusing on its parts in attempting to understand the dynamics of the system. The organismic aspect of structuralism holds that structures can be seen as wholes with a dynamic as well as static aspect to them, and no part of the structure can be altered without affecting the entire structure. Also, while each whole contains parts, it is part of a larger whole. In short, the organismic aspect of structuralism stresses the perception of *relations* and configurations rather than absolute properties. Then, in line with the formal aspect of structuralism, the aim is to formalize all relationships of the identified elements into some type of logical model or system.

The approach of this book incorporates all three of the above aspects, and it includes another notion that has been associated with structuralism. Broughton (1981) has noted that structure as a concept has always implied the notion of *interiority*. That is, structure is not something superficial but rather something underlying immediate appearances. Thus, we can speak of various levels of interiority, such as the "surface structures" and "deep structures" identified by Chomsky (1968) in his conceptions of language and mind.

Claude Levi-Strauss (1963) represents a structural approach to anthropology which is aimed at analysis of deep structures. These structures are not only not obvious in terms of surface appearances, but they are not at all readily accessible to human consciousness. The structural approach to be presented is definitely not aimed at the type of deep structure identified by Levi-Strauss. It is much closer to the phenomenological structuralism of Maurice Merleau-Ponty (1942/1963) and his definition of structure as "a whole significant for a consciousness which knows it." Indeed, the approach to be outlined here assumes that even if the structure (i.e., the whole) of an experience or event is not immediately apparent or accessible to a person's consciousness it most certainly can become so. A number of methods to be described later in this chapter are designed to make explicit or conscious that which is implicit in the experience.

In order to demystify the concept of structure even more, we can readily accept the notion of a structure as ". . . an abstract construct, not something different from the ongoing interactive processes but rather a temporary accomodative representation of it at any one time . . ." (Buckley 1967). This conception of structuralism has been utilized in general systems theory (von Bertalanffy 1951/1968), and in Kurt Lewin's (1935) field theory. It has even been used in ego psychology, in which the ego has been described as "process and structure" (Loevinger 1976). The versatility of this notion of structure should provide for a certain universality of discourse and understanding by readers with different theoretical orientations toward personality and psycho-social development.

PERCEPTUAL THEORIES AND METHODS

Perhaps the best starting point for presenting the background of this approach lies in the perceptual theories of personality, which have very clear connections with the phenomenological and cognitive concepts and methods which follow. In fact, some of these personality theorists have identified their theories as essentially phenomenological (Combs 1949; Combs, Richards, and Richards 1976; Combs and Snygg 1959; Frenkel-Brunswick 1951; Snygg 1941). If one conceives of perception as Schachtel (1959) did—as an aspect of total personality which includes the sensory, experiential, emotional, and intellectual—then one can see how closely related it is to phenomenology's concern with "lived experience." Merleau-Ponty, (1964) perhaps more emphatically than any other phenomenologist, has asserted the primacy of perception, and the notion that the perceived life-world is the primary reality for human beings.

The perceptual approach to personality has been a major force in American psychology for over four decades. The central idea in this view of personality is that persons view and interpret the world selectively and differently from one another. This perceptual or phenomenal world has been variously called the "assumptive world," (Frank 1974, and Parkes 1971), the person's "reality world" (Cantril 1957), and the "personal construction" of the world (Kelly 1955). Whatever it is called, it is obviously a concept that is kindred to phenomenology's concept of being-in-the-world, which will be explained shortly.

There are several key ideas, findings, and related methodological approaches in perceptual psychology which have very clear implications for the study of adult transitions and crises. One prominent American psychologist, George S. Klein (1970), proposed a concept based on his experimental work in human perception. It is called a "perceptual attitude," which Klein describes as a "personal outlook on the world." This is a rather broad description, but what it means is that perceptual attitudes represent "personal styles" in the use of the adaptive properties of perception, and in particular, their use in reality appraisal. A perceptual attitude "acts very much as a 'selective value' of what is or is not to be ignored" (Klein 1970, 136).

Klein identified and pursued research on several types of perceptual attitudes, some of which have particular meaning for the change inherent in adult transitions. One of these he described as an attitude that requires that reality remain stable and unchanging, especially in its outward appearances.

"In order for such a person to be comfortable, things must appear as they are *known* to be . . ." (Klein 1970, 148). This was tentatively identified by Klein as an "intolerance for the unstable or the equivocal." This is closely related to a perceptual pattern which was originally identified by Frenkel-Brunswick (1949) and called an "intolerance of ambiguity." It is a process of increased rigidification of perception which shuts out uncertainties by a narrowing of the person's cognitive structure or "map" into rigidly defined tracks. This imposes a specious clarity and simplicity as a defense against underlying conflict and confusion. Thus, persons with less severe underlying confusions should be able to face ambiguities more openly, in a pattern with a broader integration of reality, which allows more flexible adaptation to changing circumstances and life events.

It should be evident that this dimension of tolerance/intolerance could play a major role in the stressful context of changes and choices involved in adult transitions and crises. Such transitions are of necessity ambiguous, complex processes fraught with unclear, anxiety provoking impressions and meanings. Indeed, there is empirical evidence from longitudinal studies to show that a tolerance for ambiguity is functional for weathering the crises of middle and later adulthood (Fiske 1980).

Those persons who are intolerant of ambiguity will bring rigid patterns of perception when trying to reduce the initial anxiety brought on by the complexity of the situation. Much of reality, and therefore many options and choices, will be excluded in the decision making that is crucial for coping with mid-life crises. On the other hand, the person with a tolerance for ambiguity will be able to bear the initial anxiety and remain open to perceive more of reality and, consequently, to recognize more of the options and opportunities available.

One of the most widely used instruments in assessing this dimension is Budner's (1962) Intolerance of Ambiguity Scale, which has operationalized and developed with Frenkel-Brunswick's concept in mind. Intolerance was defined by Budner as "the tendency to perceive ambiguous situations as sources of threat." He constructed a questionnaire consisting of sixteen statements requiring responses on a seven-point Likert-type scale going from "strongly agree" to "strongly disagree." Four of these statements form a subscale of responses which Budner calls "phenomenological denial." The statements are:

1. "There is really no such thing as a problem that can't be solved."
2. "An expert who doesn't come up with a definite answer probably doesn't know too much."
3. "People who insist upon a yes or no answer just don't know how complicated things really are."

4. "Many of our most important decisions are based upon insufficient information."

What these statements are attempting to get at, of course, are responses that indicate a denial of the complexity inherent in so much of the human condition and in life situations. Obviously, such responses can be very revealing and useful for the purposes of assessing how individuals might respond to critical life events and decision points, as will be illustrated in some of the case materials.

Another perceptual attitude which has important implications for the study of mid-life transitions is one that is often referred to as locus of control. Essentially, this is the person's perceived control over events, and as such, it may have a profound effect on the way in which the person will respond to the events and stresses of mid-life. The internal/external locus of control framework developed by Rotter (1966) has been by far the most frequently used of its sort in the study of aging, and it has been especially useful because it assesses the extent to which the person feels in control of events—that is, the extent the person feels able to obtain rewards or satisfactions from the environment based on his or her own behavior. In short, it indicates how self-determining one feels, or conversely, how much one feels determined by others or outside forces. Clearly, persons with an external locus of control (i.e., those who see events as largely outside their control) are likely to have more difficulty in coping with transitional changes and stresses than those with an internal locus, who will tend to show greater initiative and adaptiveness with respect to such changes (Kuypers 1972).

The assessment of a person's locus of control is relatively easily done by use of the Rotter (1966) Scale, a self-report instrument which measures this perceptual attitude by responses to pairs of alternative statements such as the following:

1. a. Becoming a success is a matter of hard work, luck has little or nothing to do with it.
   b. Getting a good job depends on being in the right place at the right time.
2. a. Many times I feel that I have little influence over the things that happen to me.
   b. It is impossible for me to believe that chance or luck plays an important role in my life.
3. a. What happens to me is my own doing.
   b. Sometimes I feel that I don't have enough control over the direction my life is taking.

Respondents have to circle either the "a" or "b" in the above statements, whichever comes closest to their opinions. There are twenty-nine pairs of statements, and administration of the test is not difficult or time-consuming for either clinical or research purposes. Such an instrument can be a very useful complement to an estimate of the person's intolerance of ambiguity when assessing the meaning of a transitional event in the life of a middle-aged person. For example, it is quite conceivable that a person could have an external locus of control together with a rather high tolerance of ambiguity. This might mean that the person would experience a low degree of threat or anxiety in the face of the ambiguity created by transitional events and change. There might instead be a fatalistic acceptance or passivity in the form of the adage, "Whatever will be, will be." On the other hand, a person with an external locus of control and a high intolerance of ambiguity might experience extreme anxiety and feelings of helplessness in the face of the changes, thereby experiencing a truly traumatic transitional crisis.

Charlotte Buhler (1962), who collaborated with Else Frankel-Brunswick at the Psychological Institute of the University of Vienna and who outlined an influential life-span developmental paradigm of her own (Buhler 1968), identified the central importance of values and beliefs when facing the ambiguities and problems encountered in negotiating the transitions of the life cycle. Values, of course, can range from fairly superficial preferences in mundane matters to deeply held beliefs about human conduct and existence. Psychologists like Buhler, who emphasize a perceptual view of personality, see values as permeating and explaining a wide range of behavior. Therefore, Combs and his colleagues (1976) and especially Gordon Allport (1955), with his focus on value schemata, would view the exploration of values as essential in any effort to understand human experience and behavior. In short, the personal meaning of transitional events in mid-life will be greatly affected by the existing value schemata of the person experiencing those events.

There is good empirical evidence to show that intentional articulation of one's behavior in terms that are congruent with one's goals or values translates into highly adaptive adult development (Lowenthal 1980). Lack of congruence between a person's global goals (values) and concrete goals in behavior can be particularly problematic in certain adult transitions. For example, when the middle-aged person can no longer effectively act upon or hope to realize the high aspirations for achievement and advancement (global goals or values) which have been so much a part of the person for most of his or her life.

In such instances the achievement values have become an intrinsic part of the person's self-concept and identity. It is important to add that it is the values which impinge most heavily on the self-system that will be the values that have the greatest effect on the person's thinking, emotions, and behavior. Such values tend to have evaluative descriptive meaning represented in terms such as "good," "ambitious," "honest," "valuable," "hard-working," and so on.

These have been referred to as "self-values," and they have been shown empirically to have a significant relationship to negative self-assessments in particular (Rosenberg 1979). Thus, the middle-aged person who no longer has the stamina, capacity, or opportunity to achieve the status or position identified with the evaluative concept of self as "successful" will experience sharply lowered self-esteem, possible demoralization, and even the type of depression often identified with the "mid-life syndrome."

When we look at many of these self-values it becomes apparent that they are instrumental rather than terminal values; that is, they are beliefs about desirable modes of conduct rather than beliefs about desirable end states of existence. The importance of this distinction for the purposes of intervention has been shown experimentally by Rokeach (1973), who found that it is easier to change instrumental values and that constructive value change could be brought about by showing the person the inconsistencies or incongruence between his or her identified instrumental values and the identified end-state or terminal values of the person. The use of Rockeach's instruments and procedures will be illustrated in certain case materials later in the book. Value items from Yalom's (1980) existential approach to therapy will also be illustrated.

It can be seen from this discussion of self-values that the concept of self and its delineation is essential for an understanding of structures of meaning in adult transitions. As we have seen, it is a central concept in Levinson's adult development theory, and it will be indispensible for applying the individual life structure construct to the subject matter and case materials of this book.

The concept of self as the implicit sense of who one is can be viewed essentially as a cognitive perception of self. Although implicit, one can usually make it explicit by the use of adjectives describing personal traits, features, and behaviors. This very process of description speaks to the cognitive nature of the self-concept; that is, what the person thinks he or she is like.

This idea follows Carl Roger's (1965) earlier view of the self. In his scheme, the self-concept is cognitive in nature, but self-esteem, another element in his conception of the self-system, is seen as largely affective or emotional in nature. Self-esteem is how one *feels* about oneself in terms of the congruence or discrepancy between one's self-concept and one's *ideal* self. This ideal self or self-ideal consists of an amalgam of standards for conduct, belief, achievement, and so on, based upon the internalization of examples and precepts provided by significant others and the larger social and cultural milieu of the individual. When the person experiences a discrepancy between what he or she *thinks* he/she is like and what he or she *wants* to or *should* be like in behavior or response to an actual event, then there is usually a negative *feeling* (lowered self-esteem) in the form of shame, guilt, self-denigration, and the like. Thus, we can see how demoralization comes about for the person who does not achieve her or his highly valued goals by middle-age.

Butler and Haigh (1954) used a Q-sort technique to measure self-esteem in some earlier clinical and experimental work based on Roger's conception of the self-system. The assessment techniques to be illustrated in the case materials here will draw upon methods developed in certain cognitive approaches to clinical assessment, but they will be assessing the same phenomena as the earlier Q-sort method, which is the discrepancy between measures of self-concept and measures of ideal self. The value of this approach is that the crucial elements of the self-system can be assessed and depicted within the larger context of a cognitive structure, which is more in line with the holistic structural approach being pursued here. This will be pursued and operationalized further in the next section of this chapter, which covers cognitive theory and methods.

For the moment it is important to note that this three-part conception of the structure of the self-system, including self-concept, ideal self, and self-esteem, is not a static one. A static concept of the self-system would be contrary to the purposes of this study. What is needed is a dynamic person-in-situation perspective that will provide an understanding of the meaning of critical events within the context of a changing life space and life structure of the middle-aged individual. The person's sense of self is simply not identical in all situations or environmental fields. Therefore, this structural conception of the self-system has to be situated within the larger and more fluid framework of a phenomenal field.

To some extent, Robert Jay Lifton (1976) has done this with this conception of the self in terms of its "ordering of experience . . . along the various dimensions that must be dealt with at any given moment—temporal, spatial, and emotional." His interrelated concepts of *centering* and *grounding* lend a more fluid field perspective to what he called the "life of the self." Levinson (1978) cited Lifton's perspective in his own self-and-world conceptualization of the individual life structure. This perspective is also compatible with phenomenological conceptions of the self, as will be seen.

In attempting to put such a dynamic conception of self within a field, it is only natural to turn to Kurt Lewin's (1935) field theory. It is certainly the best known and most comprehensive field conception in the behavioral sciences, and it is also one of the foremost perceptual theories of personality. More importantly, his theory makes a direct connection with many of the key concepts and methods from cognitive theory and phenomenology that go into this structural approach. It has been said that:

> Lewin's grounding in the philosophy of science made it possible for him to recognize the fundamental role of phenomenology, or immediate perception, in all of science. This enabled him . . . to recognize clearly that the beginning of scientific inquiry and the ultimate test of its outcome was *somebody's experience,*

and that this called for a dynamic quite independent of the physical one (Marrow 1969, 37).

This perspective led Lewin to develop a topology or nonquantitive geometry which he felt could handle problems of structure and location in a psychological field, and which "could make possible a representation of the structural relations within the person's own psyche as in his psychological environment" (Marrow 1969, 36). It is this total psychological field or life space as perceived or experienced by the person which is particularly pertinent here.

Lewin's work was highly influential in social psychology, and nowhere more than in the contribution of Fritz Heider, whose book, *The Psychology of Interpersonal Relations* (1958), has been so influential in the development of a number of subfields in contemporary social psychology. The source of Heider's ideas and knowledge about interpersonal relations was a commonsense or naive psychology which was expressed in the everyday language and experience of the ordinary person. He said that "the ordinary person has a great and profound understanding of himself and of other people which, though unformulated or only vaguely conceived enables him to interact with others in more or less adaptive ways" (Heider 1958, 2). This is very much like Michael Polyani's (1966) conception of "tacit" vs. "explicit" knowledge, and it is highly compatible with phenomenology's conception of human knowledge and epistemology. Compare Heider's "naive psychology" to Sartre's (1966) idea that a phenomenologically-based "existential psychoanalysis" should enable a person "to know what he already *understands*."

Early on in his work, Lewin believed that everyday terms such as "moods," "goals," and "willpower" could be represented by geometric space concepts. In one sense this actually came about later in the form of spatial representations of cognitive structures, which will be described and then illustrated throughout the case material. In another sense, Heider made fruitful use of the intentional value of ordinary language as denoted in terms like "ought" and "can" to represent perceived value, will, capability, and so on. All of this consistently emphasizes the importance of ordinary language in the thinking of phenomenologists from Heiddeger (1927/1962) to Berger and Luckmann (1966), as will be seen.

Heider's (1959) other work on perception, event structure, and the psychological environment was also highly suggestive and helpful in this structural approach to mid-life crises. This is especially true for his work on the combined interpersonal and intrapersonal perspectives on the structure of human events. Joseph de Rivera (1977) extended Heider's earlier observations on such event structures into the realm of emotions. He developed a "structural theory" of emotions which clearly depicts how emotions are experienced within the combined intrapersonal, interpersonal, and environmental forces of the event field. Aylwin (1985) has more recently explicated and empirically demonstrated some of the structural relations between thinking and emotions. Most certainly, transitional events are laden with emotions, and they can be transformed into actual crises depending upon their intensity and structure. Therefore, the cognitive correlates of the emotion involved in a transitional event can be of critical importance for understanding and possibly intervening in the situation. Some illustrations of the structural analysis of emotions related to transitional events will be provided in the case material to follow.

COGNITIVE THEORY AND METHODS

It has already been noted that there are very clear connections between perceptual theories of personality and the cognitive and phenomenological concepts and methods which follow. Perhaps more than any of the perceptual theories, field theory has a direct connection to much of current cognitive theory. In fact, Heider (1959) referred to the advent of "cognitive field theory" and identified his work and Lewin's earlier work as within that emerging theoretical stream.

Cognitive Styles—Field Dependence and Independence

The experimental work of Herman Witkin (1962) certainly demonstrates how human perception operates within a field and how cognition is affected by that fact. He identified two basic and polar perceptual modes called "field dependence" and "field independence." Most people show a tendency toward one or the other of these two basic modes, and when this tendency is strong it shows up in pervasive and characteristic ways of thinking and of construing reality among individuals. In fact, these two modes of perception are referred to as "cognitive styles" (Witkin and Goodenough 1981). Witkin and his colleagues have found that field independent people are able to keep foreground apart from environmental context on a number of perceptual tasks in certain experiments, while field dependent people have considerable difficulty in keeping foreground apart from context. These perceptual modes have been shown to be associated with a number of important areas of personality functioning. Field independent people tend to show a clear awareness of their own attitudes, needs, and feelings. Field dependent people tend to rely heavily on external sources for their attitudes, judgments, and even evaluations of themselves. This has obvious implications for the locus of control and self-system concepts that were just covered, although there is not necessarily a direct correspondence between these cognitive styles and locus of control. For example, it is possible for a person to have a high internal locus of control but a clearly field dependent cognitive style, and it is possible to be field independent and have an external locus of control. However, the way these two factors combine has a very distinct effect on the way people think, feel, and behave, as will be seen in a number of the case illustrations.

There are various forms of this perceptual test, but the one that was administered to the people in the case illustrations was the Embedded Figures Test (EFT), which was developed by Witkin and his colleagues (Witkin, Oltman, Raskin & Karp 1971). The EFT is administered by presenting the person with a set of cards containing complex geometric-like designs in which certain simple figures are embedded. Field dependent persons either cannot perceive or have great difficulty perceiving the simple embedded figure, but the field independent person immediately or very quickly is able to perceive the simple figure. Although the EFT has been shown to be related to personality types, particularly in cases of psychopathology (Witkin 1965), it should not be the sole method of assessment in any one case but should be used in conjunction with other instruments and with experienced clinical insight.

The utility of this method to gain an understanding of the subjective meaning of a transitional event for a person should become evident in some of the case illustrations. For the moment, it is worth noting that Witkin's work on field dependence and independence clearly illustrates how most modern cognitive theorists are field theorists. They are field theorists because they see cognitive development emerging and growing out of the interaction of persons in their physical and social environments. Piaget's (1954) and Bruner's (1966) work on cognitive development most certainly incorporate this basic sort of field perspective.

Cognitive Structure

The direct connection between Lewin's field paradigm and the notion of geometric space representations of cognitive structures was noted by Heider when he made the following observation:

> This new notion is, of course, implicit in the Gestalt-psychological concepts of cognitive structure. But one might say that its most consistent elaboration is found in Lewin's construct of life space. The parts of the life space are identified by their referents, they are usually characterized by the words we use to describe the objective environment. And not only the parts, but the relations between the parts, have this representational function. For instance, the fact that two regions of the life space are adjacent refers to, or symbolically represents, the fact that the referents of these regions stand in some neighboringness relation (Heider 1959, 117-18).

This excerpt pulls together several key ideas covered up to this point, and it will soon be seen how they can be operationalized by written responses to self-report instruments. These responses can then be rendered into figures or "maps" of cognitive fields or structures representing something very much like the "significant" (Lewinian) life space of an individual. "Significant" in this sense means that the representation includes referents for persons, objects, and relations that have particular meaning for the person in his or her life space. It should also be noted that the "neighboringness relation" in the above excerpt is termed the "relation of intentionality" by Heider (1959, 118). Thus, the critical concept of intentionality from phenomenology is very specifically identified as an inherent property of the field, as conceived by field psychological theorists such as Lewin, Heider, and de Rivera.

Two contemporary social psychologists who were influenced by Heider's work refer to the theories of such psychologists as "phenomenological theories," because they make use of the notion of the *phenomenal field*— "the constellation of thoughts, perceptions, and feelings" that are real for the person (Wegner and Vallacher 1977). They go on to say that "the organization of the phenomenal field, frequently called the individual's *cognitive structure,* is the system of interrelations among thoughts that allows the individual to respond appropriately to incoming sensations from the environment." These thoughts are frequently in the nature of attitudes or judgments about self, significant others, aspects of the individual's environment, and about life in general. Further, through the mathematical technique of factor analysis, different researchers have found that these judgments tend to fall into three general dimensions: *evaluation* (good-bad), *potency* (strong-weak), and *activity* (active-passive).

These three dimensions were found in repeated factor analyses of results of attitude research done with the Semantic- Differential Test (Osgood, Suci & Tannenbaum 1957). The test has particular relevance for our purposes here because it was designed to determine the *meaning* of certain concepts for the person, through measurement by scaling techniques. These concepts could cover anything from a political party or label to abstract ideas, as well as actual objects and persons, including self, ideal self, or significant others. Although it has been widely used to test people's attitudes about political and other social issues, it has also been used as an assessment instrument in psychotherapy. The test is simple to construct and administer for any purpose, but essentially it involves having the person respond to selected concepts (e.g., "me," "mother," "love," "divorce," "death") by putting a checkmark at the appropriate place on a seven-point, bi-polar scale with adjectives at each end to represent the polar opposites for describing the concept on that particular dimension of meaning. A brief, partial example is given below in which the person has to respond to the concept "My Father" on three bi-polar scales representing particular dimensions of descriptive meaning:

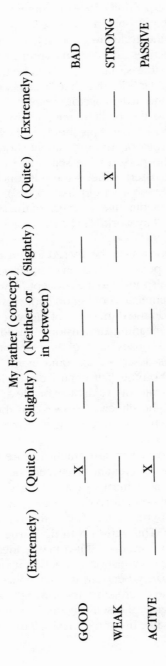

Semantic-Differential Test Sample

The semantic-differential description of the father by the person who responded to the above portion of the instrument would be that he is or was "quite good," "extremely strong," and "quite active." It can be seen that these three scales represent the evaluative, potency, and activity factors noted earlier. Any number of adjectives can be used to represent these three factors. For example, "valuable/worthless," fair/unfair" can be used to represent the evaluative factor while bi-polar adjectives like "tough/soft" and "fast/slow" can be used for the potency and activity factors respectively.

It is entirely up to the practitioner and the respondent in a mutual endeavor to determine what concepts should be included in the respondent's semantic-differential protocol. The instrument should obviously include the significant others in the person's life space and two elements of the self-system which were discussed earlier—the self-concept ("me") and ideal self ("ideal me" or "the person I would like to be"). Also, since this study is concerned with the individual life structure of the person, concepts like "my marriage," "my family," "my work," "my career," and so on should be included.

The person's responses can be scored for measurement purposes, and the scoring goes in the positive direction of the factor to be measured. Thus, in the above example, responses to the concept, "My Father" would be scored six on the evaluative dimension of "good/bad," seven on the dimension of "weak/strong," and six on the dimension of "active/passive." Since more than one bi-polar scale or meaning dimension is used for each concept, it is necessary to sum the responses on all of the relevant dimension scales. Thus, if the person's father is described as "quite good" (score of six), "slightly unfair" (score of three) on the "fair/unfair" dimension, and "quite valuable" (score of six) on the scale of "valuable/worthless," the total score on the evaluative factor would be fifteen $(6+3+6)$. In the case examples of this book, four scales for each of the three factors were included in the semantic-differential instrument used.

A particularly important measurement feature of this instrument is its capacity to measure the discrepancy between the self-concept ("me") and ideal self ("ideal me") as a means of assessing the person's level of self-esteem. The operational definition of self-esteem in this quantitative sense is the actual numerical discrepancy between the reported self-concept score and the ideal self score. This agrees with the earlier description of the self-system and the structural triad of self-concept, ideal self, and self-esteem. There is an inverse structural relationship between the degree or level of self-esteem and the discrepancy between the self-concept and ideal self in the sense that the greater the discrepancy the lower the self-esteem, and the less the discrepancy the higher the self-esteem. In other words, the more the person feels he or she is like his or her ideal self the higher is the self-esteem.

Another important feature of the instrument is that it can be used to portray in spatial and graphic form the relationships between the different concepts measured by the test in what is called by Osgood (1957) a person's "semantic space." This is done by plotting each concept in accordance with its cumulative factor scores on a grid (usually graph paper) to represent semantic space. Since there are three factors to be represented, it would be ideal to have a three-dimensional model (such as those used to portray chemical compounds) with balls to represent the concepts, and with rods connecting the different balls. However, this author prefers to portray the two most powerful factors (according to factor loadings) of the three: the evaluative and the potency factors. An example of this can be seen in the case of Doris Pierson as portrayed by Figure 3-1 in Chapter Three. Of particular note in that case is the large discrepancy between Doris Pierson's self-concept and ideal self, which is indicative of her very low self-esteem. The sum of her scores on the four evaluative scales for "ideal me" was twenty-five and the sum on the four scales for "me" was ten, for a self-esteem score of fifteen (25 − 10 for a discrepancy of 15). This author has found in his own empirical studies that this measure of self-esteem correlates very highly with other self-esteem measures, notably Rosenberg's (1979), with coefficients ranging from .86 to .93. Even without the arithmetic manipulations, it is evident from looking at the spatial model of Doris Pierson's semantic differential test results just how she feels about herself. This is also true for the descriptive meanings of important concepts like "My Family," "My Marriage," "My Life," and so on.

The remarkable versatility of the semantic-differential method for both clinical and research purposes has been noted in the behavioral science literature and is evident in the above example (Kerlinger 1973). The feature of providing a spatial representation of the significant persons, objects, and ideas in a person's life provides a great deal of insight into the structure of relationships and structure of meaning in the person's "lived experience." In addition, Osgood's semantic space model comes very close to Kurt Lewin's (1951) concept of psychological "life space." It is clearly a good instrument for the idiographic study of individuals and issues of meaning in their life space.

Another instrument which is a very effective tool in idiographic studies of persons is the Repertory Grid Test (Bannister & Fransella 1971). This is often called the Reptest for short, and it was devised by George Kelly (1955), an American psychologist, who developed it within the framework of his Personal Construct Theory of Personality. He developed this conception of personality from a theory of cognition based upon the fundamental postulate that "a person's processes are psychologically channelized by the ways in which he anticipates events" (Kelly 1955). Thus, the emphasis is on anticipation rather than reaction, and on the creative capacity of the person to represent the environment rather than to merely respond to it. The central point in Kelly's conception is "constructive alternativism," by which the person may create alternative constructions of his or her life situation. In other words, the person's life situation is not predetermined or inexorable unless he or she chooses to construe it that way.

This theory is obviously highly compatible with the basic structural approach of this book, because it assumes that human beings are actively engaged in making sense of the world as they have personally experienced it. Kelly's approach to understanding persons is to learn how they go about the task of making sense of their worlds. Each person develops a personal construct system which is a set of representations or models of the world he or she has acquired through experience, and this system is also accessible to change through new and different experiences. Kelly's model amounts to a system of interrelated constructs in which each individual construct serves to discriminate between elements of the same general class or range. An element in this system is anything that can be contrasted or compared, such as one person to another, one object to another, or one idea or concept to another. The Reptest is designed so that the person compares a list of elements, most commonly significant people in his or her life space (usually including self and ideal self), on a list of constructs which the person has chosen in order to discriminate between the elements.

The most widely used version of the Reptest is in a grid form in which the elements are usually listed vertically and the constructs horizontally. The reader can see examples of this in Figures 5-2 and 5-3 in Chapter Five. This form has been widely used by researchers and therapists who do not necessarily follow or use personal construct treatment theory and methods (Guidano & Liotti 1983; Neimeyer & Neimeyer 1981; Ryle 1975). It obviously has a number of similarities to the semantic-differential technique, and it is used in place of or together with the semantic-differential in some of the case studies to follow.

Most of the element lists in the grid are made up of significant people named by the person, although the practitioner can include elements that may be of clinical significance (e.g., self, ideal self, parents of the person). The construct list, however, should be entirely determined by the person, if at all possible. This is done by having the person describe in her or his own words how one person in the element list is like one other person but different from a third. The selection of constructs is always done in terms of these triads. For example, the person might be asked how he or she resembles either parent and how this differs from the remaining one. The person might describe him or herself as resembling the father in terms of the construct "easy-going," and that by contrast the mother is "tense." The construct is usually an adjective or descriptive phrase (e.g., "down-to-earth") as is the contrast, which always has to be specifically elicited. The contrast has a unique place within the person's construct system, so the contrast should not be assumed to be the dictionary opposite or antonym of the construct. Thus, a person might select "fun loving" as the contrast for the construct, "serious," instead of choosing "nonserious," as the contrast.

When the whole grid has been constructed in terms of elements, constructs, and contrasts, the practitioner and person can determine how the significant people in the person's life space are alike or different from one another. In fact, the grid can be used as a matching-scores matrix that is akin to a correlation matrix of positive (+ , like) and negative (− , unlike) scores which provide rough measures of association (Bannister & Mair 1968, 56). Or, the practitioner can take the list of constructs and develop the full list of elements (usually names of persons) on a separate sheet for each construct, with a rating scale of one to five or one to seven for each elements in terms of how much each is like or unlike the construct which is named at the top of the sheet (Ryle 1975, 28). Thus, a scale could go from one, "not at all like," to seven, "exactly like."

If this scoring system is used, Slater's (1965) Principal Component Analysis for grids will provide a mathematical (factor) analysis which extracts successive components—the first accounting for the most variation, the second accounting for the most residual and so on. These first and second components can then be put into a two-component graph which offers a geographical version of conceptual space. The meaning of each region is indicated by the constructs, and the location of each element in relation to these constructs and to the other elements is represented. It provides a spatial model very similar to the semantic-differential model. However, the vertical and horizontal axes of the Reptest graph are derived from a factor analysis of the elements and constructs, in contrast to the predetermined axes (notably, evaluative and potency axes) in the semantic-differential model. Such complex measurement procedures require a computer, so this author prefers to use a simpler but more convenient method of extracting the main construct dimensions directly from the repertory grid. This procedure can be done by the practitioner without a computer by what is called the "anchor method," by anchoring the factors into the specific constructs used as axes. The steps for this procedure have been described in Bannister (1965) and in Bannister and Mair (1968) and will not be repeated here. However, examples of this type of analysis in graphic form are provided in Figure 3-2 in Chapter Three and Figure 5-5 in Chapter Five.

The elements and constructs of the Reptest are directly selected by the person, whereas the evaluative and potency dimensions, as well as the bipolar scale adjectives of the semantic-differential are primarily selected by the practitioner in a predetermined form. Because of this, the Reptest is apt to be more revealing of the person's own description and experience of the key elements than the semantic-differential test. This does not necessarily mean it is the preferred test in each and every case situation. For one thing, it is more demanding of the person's time, effort, and cognitive capacity, which have to be taken into account in every case.

It can be seen that both the Reptest and the semantic- differential can be used to determine and to portray the cognitive structures of persons in general, and of mid-life transitions in particular. They are indeed "maps of the mind," to use Hampden-Turner's (1981) term. It is also interesting to note that although the two instruments are constructed in different ways, when the results are factor analyzed in repeated studies, essentially the same two factors tend to account for most of the variance: the "evaluative" and "potency" factors in the semantic-differential (Osgood et al. 1957) and the "good-bad" and "powerful-weak" factors in the Reptest (Bannister & Mair 1968). Further-more, it should be mentioned that the evaluative dimension or structure has particular importance and implication for much of the clinical work in which these two types of instruments have been applied for assessment purposes. Even when applied to political and religious beliefs, as has been done most frequently with the semantic-differential, its import has been evident. Hampden-Turner (1981) has referred to it as the "lethal structure," because it contains much of the basis for hatred between people—differences in core values and conceptions of good and evil. This will become quite apparent in several of the case illustrations, particularly with respect to object-relations and attachment-conflict issues.

Theories of Cognitive Therapy

Kelly's Personal Construct Theory is not only a theory of personality but also a treatment theory. The therapy is guided by the central tenet of the theory, which is that people can undertake alternative constructions of problems with which they are struggling and thereby gain more cognitive control over their lives. Techniques such as fixed-role therapy and other enactment procedures are based on this central thrust. However, the basic theory seems much more suggestive for the study and understanding of human behavior than it does for specific treatment techniques.

The reverse is true of most of the theories of cognitive therapy; they are in fact rather thin in regard to the underlying personality theory and much more suggestive with respect to specific treatment techniques. The core idea in the cognitive approach to psychotherapy is that negative human emotions are more a result of what people think, believe, or tell themselves about situations or events than the actual events themselves. Albert Ellis (1962) built this core idea into a cognitive "ABC" theory of emotion which underlies his Rational-Emotive Therapy (RET). In his scheme, A is the *activating event* or situation, B is the *belief* or thoughts about the event, and C is the emotional *consequence* of the belief or thoughts. Thus, the A → B → C sequence shows B to be the intervening factor or variable in the whole experiential process. If B is an irrational belief (B) it can lead to irrational and dysfunctional emotional consequences (C). The reader may recall the A-B-C-X sequence in the discussion of crisis intervention in Chapter One. The C in that sequence had to do with the meaning of the event, whereas B represented coping resources. In Ellis's ABC model B is the meaning element. If the person views an activating event (A) as catastrophic, and he or she holds this irrational belief (B) in the face of contrary evidence and views of others in the same predicament, he or she will feel devastated and demoralized (irrational consequence—C) by the event. Thus, it is the belief or idea that leads to the negative emotional consequences.

In fact, Ellis often refers to "catastrophic thinking" as a major form of irrational thinking leading to emotional problems. He says that irrational beliefs generally contain a "must," an "ought," or a "should"; an absolutistic demand that the person must obtain what he or she wants. If the person does not obtain it, the results would be viewed as awful, terrible, and intolerable. In this way, the person has set himself or herself up for some very negative emotional (C) consequences. In short, what any person might reasonably want, such as acceptance, love, and respect, is irrationally transformed into an absolute need or demand, and if it is not met this would be experienced as awful, traumatic, and utterly demoralizing.

The central focus of the cognitive approach involves teaching the person how to explore the implicit thoughts, beliefs, or "self-talk" that are associated with the explicit emotions of a dysfunctional and disproportionate nature. This is called cognitive review. The person identifies the unsubstantiated and irrational elements in the implicit thoughts, and with the guidance of the practitioner, learns how to dispute them and replace them with rational beliefs (B). This disputation (D) element is thus the core activity of the treatment process, which should lead to a new evaluation (E) of the problem situation that began with the activating event (A). Thus, there is an A-B-C-D-E sequence involved in the total RET process (Ellis 1962, 1974).

Aaron Beck (1976) uses essentially the same approach as the RET process, and as will be seen in Chapter Three, he has the person monitor the process by identifying "automatic thoughts" (self-talk) and associated emotions in a highly structured cognitive review process. Beck claims that the cognitive model differs from the classical behavioral or conditioning model, which posits the following sequence in explaining emotion (and behavior): stimulus → emotion (or behavior). The cognitive model posits this sequence: stimulus → conscious meaning → emotion (or behavior). Thus, it is the *conscious* meaning of the event or stimulus that leads to the problematic emotion of the person. In practice, Beck tends to focus on meanings that are easily accessible to consciousness in the form of "automatic dysfunctional thoughts" or self-talk, as the person monitors his or her thoughts in conjunction with the experience of negative emotions. The relative ease with which this self-talk can be monitored and then changed by new self-talk or self-instruction based on cognitive review and rational disputation have led a number of former behaviorally-oriented clinicians to add this cognitive ("B" or conscious meaning) element to their treatment repertoires and to call it a "mediating variable" between stimulus and emotional or behavioral response (Mahoney 1974; Meichenbaum 1977). This has led to a profusion of new "cognitive-behavioral" techniques in psychotherapy, some of which are illustrated in the Chapter Three cases.

Regardless of the potential or real treatment value of this "mediating" concept in short-term therapy, it is lacking in its capacity to help us understand and even to treat many of the more intransigent emotional and behavioral problems. This particular observation led Guidano and Liotti (1983), on the basis of their experience and study of hundreds of cases in the Psychiatric Clinic of the University of Rome, to develop a structural theory of cognitive processes and emotional disorders. They feel that the review and modifications of self-talk in the above cognitive and cognitive-behavioral treatment approaches get at only partial and apparent distortions of thought on a fairly superficial level. They also feel that these rather discrete and isolated cognitive phenomena are only part of a more complex, interrelated system or structure of cognitions.

They refer to "surface structures" and "deep structures" of cognition. The surface structures are the most accessible to the self-talk type of monitoring and cognitive review. The deeper structures inhere in basic conceptions of the self that go far back into the development of the individual, beginning in early childhood with preverbal experiences, involving formative interactions with significant attachment figures, primarily the mother or a surrogate. Guidano and Liotti rely heavily on Bowlby's (1969) attachment theory, which posits that individual differences in early attachment experiences will lead to different "patterns" of attachment behavior later. They even go so far as to say that attachment "might be defined as a cognitive structure that is constructed during the course of development." They add, "it is highly probable that if distorted self-conceptions regarding fundamental aspects of identity (lovableness, personal value, etc.) have been formed, these not only will determine a particular attitude toward reality, but also will notably influence the cognitive and emotional processes in course" (Guidano & Liotti 1983). This is clearly consistent with Kegan's (1982) theory noted earlier.

It is the basic conceptions of the self resulting from developmental experiences which are at the core of the deep cognitive structures. Guidano and Liotti are in agreement with Victor Raimy (1975) in his view that the most important focus for cognitive therapy in order to bring about more lasting change is with basic misconceptions about the self. However, they provide a much richer theoretical background and suggest a more sophisticated assessment and treatment approach than Raimy, who seems to rely on essentially the same general cognitive review approaches as Ellis and Beck.

Guidano and Liotti believe that it is necessary to do a developmental analysis based upon the person's recollection of early life experiences, especially those in infancy, preschool years, childhood, and adolescence, for "the way in which people recollect their experiences and the meaning they attribute to them constitute a gold mine for the cognitive therapist." They use this historical information to match their "reconstruction of the patient's faulty causal theories, basic assumptions, or irrational beliefs with his or her ongoing inner representation." As the person reports his or her own inner representations, the practitioner needs to be aware of the kind of attitude maintained toward self and reality. Careful attention has to be paid to the way in which the person uses certain important words: to be, must, can, to need, and to be worth. The way in which these verbal forms follow the pronoun "I" provides clues to the person's self-identity and self-esteem. Also, the way in which the person uses these verbal forms after other pronouns like "he," "she," "they," and "you," can provide leads to his or her attitude towards others and reality.

As noted earlier in the work of Lewin and Heider, Guidano and Liotti are sensitive to the importance of everyday language for providing clues to the person's current experiential state of existence or being-in-the-world. They suggest some very promising treatment techniques that consist of the semantic correction of the use of the pronoun "I" and verbs such as "to be," "to be worth," and "to deserve," as well as the use of "must,""ought," and so on.

They call their theory a "structural approach" to understanding and dealing with the cognitive processes involved in emotional disorders, and their theory is certainly closer to the structural approach of this book than are most of the other cognitive and cognitive-behavioral approaches. This is true for a number of reasons. First, Guidano and Liotti insist upon information about the family and developmental background of the person in order to better understand the cognitive structures and meanings operative in the person's current life situation. Most of the other cognitive-behavioral approaches focus on the role of current and easily accessible cognition in the emotional problems of the person. Because of this, they are less apt to get at the deeper, less accessible cognitive structures for more pervasive and durable change in emotional and behavioral functioning. Each of the case studies here do include background information that provides leads to understanding the person's current cognitive and emotional functioning.

Secondly, although they use certain cognitive assessment instruments, such as the Reptest, Guidano and Liotti pay particular attention to certain verbal and nonverbal clues in understanding and helping the people whom they treat. Observation of the person's behavior, individually and in interaction with others, together with careful attention to the use of language, particularly the use of "I" and the verb forms noted earlier, is something their structural approach and this structural approach have in common. Furthermore, they invoke Polyani's (1966) concept of tacit knowledge in order to help the person make explicit what he or she understands implicitly about self and significant others. This is also in line with the structural approach of this book, which draws upon the person's "implicit psychology" (Wegner & Valacher 1980) in order "to know what he (she) already understands."

Finally, Guidano and Liotti's concern with problematic patterns of attachment, of "failed distancing," and "pathology of attachment" is similar to a number of our central problems and themes of mid-life transitions, including issues of attachment, separation, loss, and reattachment. Their creative use of Bowlby's attachment theory throws a good deal of light on these issues.

PHENOMENOLOGICAL CONCEPTS AND METHODS

This section will not be an exhaustive treatment of the extensive philosophy and psychology of phenomenology. The focus will be on those concepts and methods that are relevant for this structural approach to the study of mid-life transitions. A number of these concepts and methods are very close to some that have already been covered in the perceptual and cognitive theories. However, the phenomenological approach and its particular perspective on the problems and issues we are concerned with here should add further depth to our understanding of mid-life issues. This will be an experiential dimension that is not quite captured by the other theories and methods.

There will be no attempt here to explicate a "pure" or procedurally "correct" method of phenomenology. Again, the intention is to utilize the phenomenological approaches that can enhance this multi-faceted approach. That means that this structural approach will be relying more heavily on certain phenomenological thinkers and orientations that seem particularly suited to getting at the structures of meaning in mid-life crises. Where these thinkers and orientations fit within the larger phenomenological movement will become more clear in the process of providing the following brief overview of phenomenology's central concepts and its basic approach.

The wide use and misuse of the adjective "phenomenological" in the behavioral and therapeutic literature has led to as much confusion about it as about the term "structural." There is question whether phenomenology is a theory. It is in fact much more; it is both a method and a system of epistemology, it is a conception of the nature and grounds of knowledge. From this perspective phenomenology becomes a whole science in its own right, and it has been formally defined as "the science of phenomena that manifest themselves in our consciousness" (Baker 1972, 305).

If we look at phenomenology as a basic method, it "begins with a kind of empirical observation directed at the whole field of possible experiential phenomena" (Ihde 1986, 31). As such, phenomenological method can be applied to such diverse areas as the natural sciences, the social and behavioral sciences, and even the arts. The contribution of phenomenology to the methodology and approach of this book comes primarily from phenomenological psychology, which "seeks to articulate explicitly the implicit structure and meaning of human experience" (Keen 1975, 19). It can be seen that this conception of phenomenology is in agreement with our essential purpose here.

One principle of phenomenological method that is important for our purposes is the requirement that all preconceptions and assumptions about the nature of phenomena have to be put aside when studying them. We have to look at the whole field of experiential phenomena with "fresh eyes" in a particularly open way. This is, in a way that will allow the phenomena to "speak for themselves," without the imposition of our own habitual, theoretical, or diagnostic preconceptions on them. This type of orientation allows for the kinds of "radical beginnings" in the study of phenomena which were called for by the founder of modern phenomenology, Edmund Husserl (1900/1970, 1936/1970 & 1962/1977).

Within this general stance of suspending our usual assumptions and ways of looking, Husserl proposed "a particular method of access . . . for the pure phenomenological field: the method of 'phenomenal reduction.' This method of 'phenomenological reduction' is thus the foundational method of pure psychology and all its specifically theoretical methods" (Husserl 1973, 52). The purpose of the reduction is to see the phenomenon in its own right and not as an example of a particular notion, concept, or descriptive category. The first step in the method is called an *epoche*—meaning to step back or suspend our ordinary way of looking. In order to do this we have to put our implicit assumptions "in brackets." Phenomenologists refer to this procedure as "bracketing," and it is intended to eliminate everything about the phenomena under analysis that is not given to us directly in our consciousness. This goes back to the definition of phenomenology as "the science of phenomena that manifest themselves in our consciousness."

Bracketing is one step in a system of observations referred to as eidetic analysis which seeks to identify the "essence" of the phenomenon (Ihde 1986). One way in which we can get at the essence of a phenomenon is to let the phenomenon emerge as a meaningful whole. In this sense, bracketing is used to prevent the common tendency of partializing, looking at parts rather than wholes. Thus, one brackets off the partializing tendency in the analytical mode of looking so as to let the whole, or the gestalt, emerge.

This is consistent with the emphasis in structuralism first on wholes and then on elements or parts. It is different from the approach of most scientists to phenomena, which is usually analytic. "Phenomenologists, on the other hand, prefer to work from experiences as a whole to its specifiable parts, each of which would have an already clear context and place in the whole by virtue of the general picture with which they begin" (Keen 1975). This is an important distinction to keep in mind as contributions from other theories to the structural approach are considered. These other theories were built and tested upon methods in which the analytic or partializing approach is preemptive. For the moment, suffice it to say that the phenomenological reduction should be carried out prior to the application of these other approaches.

One other major contribution of phenomenology to the foundation of a useful approach to the study of human experience is its emphasis on the central place of language in the structuring of experience. Heidegger (1927/1962) said that "language is the house of being and in that house man dwells." One phenomenological psychologist has said that "this implies that the meanings conveyed to us in the world of everyday experience are structured in language" (Kruger 1981, 183). Berger and Luckmann (1966) developed their sociology of knowledge on the foundational idea that the "social construction of reality" relies in large part on the shared meanings conveyed by language.

Thus, while Heidegger's concept of being-in-the-world (Dasein) represents a unity that is unique to each individual, it is not totally unique and personal to the individual. There are those commonalities among persons by virtue of the shared meanings of the language of their particular groups (whole cultures, nations, societies, and smaller groups). Given this pervasive influence and importance of language for human perception, procedures and instruments that utilize natural, everyday language will have a central place in the structural approach to be developed here. That is why the semantic-differential, Reptest, and semantic analysis, which use everyday language, were explained in such detail in the preceding section.

Throughout this chapter we have talked about the importance of perception, of how a person perceives his or her situation. Indeed, Merleau-Ponty (1964) insisted upon the "*primacy* of perception" for understanding human behavior and existence. However, it is important to note that the level of perception that Merleau-Ponty dealt with in his *Phenomenology of Perception* is much more raw and immediate than, for example, the "perceptual attitude" construct of George Klein (1970) which was mentioned earlier. Klein's construct includes both cognitive and precognitive phenomena. Merleau-Ponty's perception is the fundamental, raw perception of phenomena that one would experience prior to any cognitive structuring. It therefore consists of inchoate, unstructured sensations and feelings that are precognitive, pre-logical, and preverbal in nature. It is a sort of raw experiencing of phenomena in terms of any and all of the senses.

His approach basically represents something very close to what Husserl was aiming at with his method, to allow the "things (phenomena of raw perception) themselves" to emerge spontaneously before imposing any predetermined structure or interpretation on them. The main difference between the two phenomenologists had to do with how "pure" (free of prejudgment) the phenomenological reduction could be (Spiegelberg 1965). Merleau-Ponty felt that a complete reduction was impossible.

Another difference between the two thinkers is that the body is central to Merleau-Ponty's conception of human perception and consciousness. Not only is the body at the center of our being-in-the-world, it is a source of knowledge: "The ontological world and body which we find at the core of the subject are not the world or body as idea, but on the one hand the world itself contracted into a comprehensive grasp, and on the other, the body itself as a knowing-body" (Merleau-Ponty 1945/1962, 408). Through the vehicle of the "lived body" there is an accumulation and reservoir of experience at a nonconscious bodily level; the body responds and stores information (including habits, tensions, etc.) without our awareness. Some people are more attuned to their bodily states and how these are related to their emotions and behavior than are others. Additionally, the body can be the starting point of reference for developing an experiential sense of meaning in one's life situation.

Eugene Gendlin of the University of Chicago, who is an academic philosopher and psychologist as well as a psychotherapist, has been able to incorporate Merleau-Ponty's contributions about human perception and the body into a coherent method. In his book, *Experiencing and the Creation of Meaning,* he noted that "meaning is not only *about things* and it is not only a certain *logical* structure, but it also involves *felt* experiencing. . . . Besides logical schemes and sense perception we have come to recognize that there is also a powerful *felt* dimension of experience that is prelogical, and that functions importantly in what we think, what we perceive, and how we behave" (Gendlin 1962, 1). He operationalized, developed, and tested a method where the body is indeed a vehicle in the perception of the "felt dimension of experience" and in the formation of what he called "felt meaning." The method is known as "experiential focusing," and he has developed it to the point where it can be used to help people gain insight into their experiential states and to discern a sense of meaning and direction in their lives (Gendlin 1981). It has been used by individuals themselves, by psychotherapists, and by gerontological researchers (Lieberman & Tobin 1983). This author has used it in his own practice and research with older persons (Sherman 1984).

At the same time as he was developing the central ideas in his "experiential phenomenology" Gendlin (1973) was also able to contribute to psychotherapeutic research and practice. Carl Rogers (1980) credits Gendlin's concept of experiencing with helping him to develop his own "process conception" of psychotherapy and personality change.

Gendlin's conception of experiencing is that it is the basic felt datum of our inwardly directed attention which involves our preverbal, preconceptual, bodily sense of being in interaction with the environment. In short, it is a "guts-level" sense or felt meaning of things. This conception includes the feeling of having experience and the continuous flow of sensations, feelings, impressions, somatic events, reflexive awareness, and cognitive meanings that make up a person's phenomenological field.

Gendlin and Tomlinson (1967) developed and tested an Experiencing (EXP) Scale which was intended to measure the degree of direct inner reference apparent in the person's communication—the degree to which the person focuses on and expresses the subjective, personal meanings and experiences of events and his or her reactions to them. Early studies using the EXP Scales showed that experiencing and global process ratings of brief therapy were consistently and highly reliable, and that they provided a meaningful differentiation between more and less successful therapy cases as well as between less and more severely disturbed (diagnosed schizophrenic) persons (Gendlin & Tomlinson 1967; Gendlin, Beebe, Cassens, Klein, and Oberlander 1968).

At stage one of the EXP Scale, the person seems distant or remote from his or her feelings. Reported experiences have an impersonal quality in which feelings are avoided and personal involvement is absent from the communication. At stage four, the middle of the Scale, the quality of involvement shifts and the person is no longer concerned almost exclusively with external or remotely experienced feelings. Instead, the person draws directly from experience to describe feelings and personal reactions. Finally, at stage seven the experiential perspective becomes a trusted and reliable source of self-awareness, and it is the primary referent for thought and action.

Gendlin's conception of experiencing is that it is a process and not a fixed personality trait, and its measurement involves the quality of a person's *communicated* experience of her or himself at a particular moment in a given aspect of her or his life. Therefore, it is situational, flexible, and open to change by its very nature.

A somewhat more refined and tested version of the EXP Scale was later developed in which even nonprofessional but specifically trained judges can make ratings solely on the basis of *manifest* recorded content (Klein, Mathieu,

Gendlin & Keisler 1970). It is this form of the Scale which was used in a number of the case studies reported in this book.

It can be seen that experiencing is both a concept and a method. It should be noted that although the method begins with the bodily felt sense of things, a preconceptual and preverbal experiencing, it does progress to a conceptual level in which the person has to name the vague things he or she is experiencing in the body. Then there is a step called "resonating" in which the descriptive words (cognitive level) are checked with the precognitive and preverbal level of the bodily felt sense (Gendlin 1981). Indeed, Spiegelberg (1972) has said the main function of Gendlin's method of experiential focusing "is to integrate experiencing and conceptual reflection in a creative exchange."

There is an interpretive step in this phenomenological method which is a mutual process between practitioner and person as interpreter of the meaning of his or her own experience. The experiential approach just described begins with the bodily felt sense of meaning which is accessible to the person for the purposes of interpretation and understanding. It can be done with the practitioner facilitating the experiential focusing of the person through Gendlin's (1981) steps or the person can do it alone and then make the meanings uncovered in the process verbally explicit.

Another phenomenological way of uncovering meaning is directly through ordinary language. This has been called a "hermeneutic strategy," and it is the basis of what has been called "hermeneutical phenomenology" (Ihde 1986). Martin Heidegger was the most formative figure in its development and it continues in the more recent phenomenological work of Paul Ricoeur (1981) and the hermeneutics of Hans-Georg Gadamer (1976).

The use of everyday language, particularly names of persons, objects, and ideas is something we have already seen in devices such as the Reptest and the semantic-differential. These latter approaches from psychology were being developed almost simultaneously with the strong hermeneutical trend in phenomenology. Howard (1982) noted that by 1960 "the phenomenological movement was turning toward language as the key manifestation in the way in which a person constructs his world."

Hermeneutics is not unique to phenomenology, of course. In theology it has been defined as "the interpretation of the spiritual truth of the Bible." More recently Wilhelm Dilthey (1947/1976) used the term to denote disciplines concerned with the investigation and interpretation of human behavior, speech, institutions and so on—practically any discipline we currently call a social or behavioral science. However, Dilthey used the term "human sciences" to distinguish them from the natural sciences. He noted a fundamental difference in the two approaches: Natural sciences investigate objects from the outside ("objectively") while the human sciences rely on a perspective from the inside. It has been said that "the supreme category of the human sciences is that of *meaning*" (Atwood & Stolorow 1984). On this basis, the structural approach of this book is definitely in the human science and hermeneutical tradition.

STRUCTURAL CASE STUDY METHODS

How can all of this be put together: the perceptual, cognitive, and phenomenological concepts and methods? The foregoing discussion of theories and methods should enable the practitioner to add certain relevant approaches and methods to those that are already covered in the literature on the case study method (Bolgar 1965; Runyan 1982). The relevant methods, of course, are those that are particularly suited to getting at the structures of meaning in mid-life transitions.

First, in approaching an individual undergoing a crisis it is important to attempt to put aside one's preconceptions, to engage in the phenomenological reduction, and to allow the individual's experiencing of the critical event(s) to emerge in the course of his or her descriptive narrative of the experience. It is of paramount importance, therefore, that in the interview situation the practitioner listen empathically, in a nonintrusive and unstructured manner, to the person's narrative. The approach that is being proposed here is very similar to Joseph de Rivera's (1981) method of "conceptual encounter." He describes this as an encounter between the investigator and the person who has undergone a strong emotional experience in which the investigator allows the person to recall, describe, and even relive an emotional experience in his or her own words, after which the investigator shares his or her ideas about the essential characteristics of the experience.

One practitioner who first utilized this phenomenological approach in a study of anxiety described her experience as follows:

> During the first, comparatively unstructured interview, I listened in an empathic mode, experiencing in myself what the other was saying and deliberately inhibiting any critical thoughts I might have had. I found that this facilitated the fullest communication. After the person had clearly finished all that he had to say, I used the remaining time to ask questions that flowed directly from the material. My questions surprised me by coming from seemingly nowhere, yet they had a "right" feeling to them (Goodman 1981, 87).

In the kinds of case studies illustrated in this book, the practitioner does not stop at one conceptual encounter. Just as assessment is an ongoing process in clinical practice, the process of interpretation of meaning was an ongoing one in the cases to be presented here.

The process of interpretation can be complemented and supplemented by the use of the aforementioned instruments. Since any instrument necessarily involves prestructuring of the study process, it is important that the phenomenological reduction and the mutual experiential process of interpretation be carried out first in accordance with the procedure described above. Then it is possible to use assessment instruments or any other devices that fit the situation. In this sense, the assessment methods emerge from what is learned in the course of the prior unstructured process, in accordance with the epoche and other methods in the phenomenological approach.

A number of the instruments mentioned earlier in this chapter were developed as quantitative methods of measurement for research purposes and for generalization to populations based on data from samples (i.e., nomothetic analysis). However, that fact does not preclude use of these instruments to study the unique, individual aspects of a person's experience (i.e., idiographic analysis) for the purposes here. They can also be used phenomenologically in the sense that they can serve to schematicize relevant phenomena in a way that might provide a different and fresh perspective to the practitioner and person alike. In his influential article on experiential phenomenology, Gendlin (1973) noted that "any scheme can be employed as an open scheme—that is to say, it can enable us to refer directly to aspects of experience which may be formulated in a different, and possibly a better way, with many further aspects emerging."

The Reptest and semantic-differential can be particularly useful in this way. The emphasis in using them should be on understanding the *meanings* and intentional (structural) relations of key persons, objects, and ideas in the person's life space rather than a precise mathematical representation or measurement of those elements. The primary reason for the use of these and the other tests mentioned earlier is to enable the practitioner, and the middle-aged person, to gain a phenomenological understanding of the person's underlying subjective frame of reference and structures of meaning in the crisis experience.

Even after using these tests, the practitioner should continue to maintain an open, empathic approach in ongoing sessions. Background and developmental information have to be gathered and dealt with in the ongoing interpretation process. This was done in all of the study cases to be presented. The practitioner has to continue listening sensitively for the person's use of language as experiences are described, and also for the level of experiencing. If the level is superficial, say one or two on the EXP Scale, it will add little to an understanding of the structure of the experience and its meanings.

In summary, it is necessary to look for any signs—verbal, emotional, or behavioral—that provide insight into the structures of meaning inherent in the person's description of the experience of a mid-life transition or crisis. All of the cases to follow involve the use and interpretation of such signs and they all contain information about each of the three types of structure that are of particular concern in this idiographic study of mid-life transitions: the individual life structure, cognitive structures, and structures of experience.

Chapter 3

THEMES OF MORTALITY AND FINITENESS

Elliott Jaques's (1965) article called "Death and the Mid-Life Crisis" has become the classic piece in the adult development literature which proposes that the mid-life crisis begins with the recognition of one's mortality and personal finiteness. This recognition ordinarily brings about certain changes: "Life is restructured in terms of time-left-to-live rather than time-since-birth. Not only the reversal in directionality but the awareness that time is finite is a particularly conspicuous feature of middle age" (Neugarten 1968, 97). This has been referred to as "the personalization of death" (Datan 1980).

Whatever it is called, there has been a remarkable consensus that awareness of death and finiteness is a common theme for men in their middle and late thirties (Cath 1980; Gould 1978; Levinson et al. 1978; Tamir 1982). Fifteen years after his essay on death and the mid-life crisis was published, Jaques continued to maintain that "it is this fact of the entry upon the psychological scene of the reality and inevitability of one's own eventful personal death that is the central and crucial feature of the mid-life phase" (Jaques 1980, 11).

Jaques's initial essay was written largely on the basis of his study of men in creative fields, notably the arts, where he noted a marked tendency toward crisis in the work of great men in their middle and late thirties. The crisis frequently expressed itself in a drying up of creative work, such as writer's block. Jaques (1965) felt that the mid-life transition in women was somewhat obscured by the proximity of the onset of changes connected with the menopause. However, other authorities, particularly psychiatrists who deal with women in their middle years, have been clear that the phenomenon does take

55

place in women at about the same time as men. However, it might manifest itself in different ways. For example, Cath (1980) notes that there is often "a reconsideration of previous choices to remain barren" in women in the middle and late thirties. Yalom (1980) describes the case of a thirty-six-year-old professional woman he treated whose major symptom was death anxiety, but which was initially obscured or expressed by alcoholism and obesity. He notes that "the therapist who treats a patient in midlife must remind himself or herself that much psychopathology emanates from death anxiety" (Yalom 1980, 196).

The following case of Doris Pierson illustrates Cath's point about women reconsidering previous choices to remain barren. At age thirty-five she decided she very much wanted a baby, but when this dream was smashed in a confrontation with her husband, her basic death anxiety expressed itself very directly and forcefully. On the other hand, in the subsequent case of Allan Kahn, the death anxiety never expressed itself directly. Nevertheless, his acute attack of agoraphobia probably emanated from a basic death anxiety. Some of his prior behaviors were indicative of this. There was a good deal of manic activity in his work, which Jaques (1965) has noted as indicative, and he lost confidence in himself at work. Gould (1978) has noted that men "lose confidence in themselves and confuse their awareness of death with their situation at work." At any rate, the reader will be able to judge the validity of these interpretations after having had a chance to read the two cases, which follow.

DEATH ANXIETY IN A THIRTY-FIVE-YEAR-OLD WOMAN

This case illustrates a transitional process in which two events had profound meaning for a troubled woman. The two events were critical in the reappraisal and dismantling of Doris Pierson's existing life structure. The first event brought her into therapy, where it became clear that she was in a state of crisis and needed help in coping and making crucial choices about her life. The second event represented the loss of a life dream and the onset of a depression.

Although it was not an articulated problem or theme at the beginning of therapy, the issue of mortality and finitude arose later in conjunction with the depression. This theme remained prominent even after therapy. Thus, when the worst of her depression had abated and she had finished therapy, the nature of her problem at that time was consistent with Elliott Jaques's conception of the mid-life crisis and its underlying concern with death.

In terms of Levinson's developmental periods, she was somewhere between the end of the Age Thirty transition and the beginning of the Settling Down Period (ages thirty-three to forty). This was the time for commitment to choices which would form the basis of her life structure up to the mid-life transition at about age forty. It was clear that the major elements of her life structure were in disarray and she was in a transitional crisis when she started therapy at age thirty-five.

At that time, she was married and living with her thirty-two year-old husband, Bill, and her fourteen year-old son, Josh. She had been married to Bill for four and a half years, and it was her first marriage. Josh had been born out of wedlock and was raised by her alone until her marriage to Bill.

Doris Pierson was born and raised in a small town about twenty miles outside the northeastern city she was living in at the start of therapy. She had an older brother and sister and another sister who was two years younger than she. Her parents had an unhappy marriage, and her father left the family to live out of state with another woman. She thought her father had had numerous affairs with other women before that, and she said her mother always contended that the whole family was better off without him. Doris's parents both came of Scotch-Irish rural American backgrounds and her mother was described as a very religious and moralistic Baptist. She always seemed to be judging and lecturing Doris for her willful and rebellious ways. Additionally, she did not show much overt affection toward her children, although she tended to approve more of Doris's compliant younger sister, Carol, than of Doris and her older sister. Doris, therefore, experienced her childhood as full of disapproval and lacking in affection. When she graduated from high school, she immediately left home to come to her current city of residence.

She rented an apartment with another young woman from her hometown and got a job as a waitress in a diner. Before long she was involved sexually with a number of men, mostly truck drivers and construction workers who frequented the diner. Soon afterward she took a job as a waitress in a night club, and continued with what she readily described as a very open and promiscuous life style.

She said that she would sometimes be an "occasional call girl" for certain influential men who were passing through the city on business. She claimed she was never really a "steady hooker" or call girl, but she seemed always to be heavily involved with one man or another—"all bastards." In addition to the promiscuity, there was a good deal of drinking and drug abuse, although she never became addicted to any substance. However, she did become depressed with her lifestyle and attempted suicide with sleeping pills shortly after she had an abortion at age nineteen.

The following year she began an intense relationship with a local man who was married and had five children. He seemed "more steady and less of a bastard than the others." When she became pregnant with Josh he insisted that she should have the child and let him support her and the child. He did this for two years after Josh's birth, although he continued to live with his family.

Then he began failing to support Doris and Josh, which led to a bitter fight, and final breakup between him and Doris.

She applied for AFDC payments for herself and Josh from the Department of Social Services after the breakup. She claimed that Josh was her "whole life" at that time. He gave her a purpose for living and added some meaning to her life, which she thinks she would have ended if it had not been for him. She became determined to make something of herself and insisted that the Department of Social Services help her get training to become a professional nurse. She claimed that the Department did not want to do this, for it meant not only payments for tuition but also day care and other child care arrangements. She claimed she had to "fight the Department every inch of the way." They were always trying to get her off the AFDC rolls or refusing funds for various educational expenses. She finally did succeed in obtaining her RN, after which she quickly got a job and went off AFDC.

Her life changed considerably after that, since she felt she had accomplished something important (her profession) and she had something to live for (Josh). She worked hard at her profession and at her role as mother, so she never went back to her former lifestyle. She did have an extended, on-and-off relationship with a married doctor at her hospital. Then she met Bill and they got married within six months. He seemed accepting and even fond of Josh. She was thirty when they married, and she had already purchased a home of her own before the marriage.

This, then, was the nature of Doris's life structure at age thirty-five. It was a vast improvement over the structure of her early adulthood, but it was showing the inevitable strains of a transition, together with the resurgence of chronic, unresolved problems in her intrapersonal and interpersonal life. These factors all added up to a transitional crisis for which Doris sought professional help at that time.

Largely at the insistence of her husband, who had just completed work on his master's degree in counseling, Doris applied for individual counseling at a private center for psychotherapy where she and her husband had received conjoint marital counseling six months before. They had ended treatment after eight sessions, stating that they had gained a lot from it and that they needed to cut expenses. Ms. Pierson had requested brief, time-limited therapy at this time, too, which she understood the Center could provide. The case was referred to me on that basis, and I set up an appointment for two days hence.

Doris showed up for the first session in a crisp white nurse's uniform, explaining that she had just completed the evening shift at the hospital. She was small and neat in appearance, wearing no make-up, and looking eight to ten years younger than her thirty-five years. She had a girlish appearance, not only because of her small and youthful figure, but also because of an upturned nose and cleft in her chin. However, her manner of speaking completely belied the girlish appearance. She spoke in a rapid, clipped voice that could best be described as "tough." She freely used four letter words for emphasis, and it was clear that the tough-talk was not put on for effect. It was in fact her characteristic way of expressing herself.

When asked what brought her to the Center at this time she replied, "I must be a real mess, because I seem to have so many problems and I don't even know where the hell to begin."

She was encouraged at this point to just begin with whatever came to mind without worrying about any order of importance. She began by noting that her marriage was still in trouble, even though she and her husband, Bill, had several sessions of marital counseling at this Center with Dr. Markus some months before. She was convinced that she needed individual help at this time, because there were several things bothering her which she had to straighten out before she could even decide about her marriage, or whether it would be worth going back into marital counseling at all.

She said that the sessions with Dr. Markus had been helpful for awhile. She and Bill had learned how they were supposed to talk to one another by beginning with "*I* feel, etc.," instead of saying "*You* always, etc.," and then start blaming one another. They also learned something about working out contracts concerning household responsibilities, privileges, and so on, but before long they were having emotional explosions and bitter arguments over the matters they had contracted about.

Bill, who knew about contracting because of his training in counseling, always accused her of not living up to their contracts. She said that she had to admit that the failure of the marital counseling to help was probably mostly her fault. She just didn't seem to be able to communicate very well. Her husband kept telling her that she was "passive-aggressive" because she wouldn't say what was on her mind, and she would keep it all in until she couldn't control herself any more. Then, she would attack him, out of all proportion to what he might have done at the time.

She acknowledged with a characteristic shrug and grin that she could be "one real bitch" when she loses her temper. She wished she was better able to express her emotions. It was hard for her to express affection, especially in words. There was no problem in terms of their sex life. "I know how to please men, and Bill seems more than satisfied that way," she said. But, when it came to nonsexual touching, embracing, or verbal expressions of affection, she just did not seem able to do these things.

Bill, on the other hand, was very good at these expressions, and insisted that she learn how to show caring and affection. He would get outraged by her inability to provide him with them, saying he needed them, and that she was a "cold bitch" for not giving these expressions to him. She said that he "really goes off his nut" in these situations. He actually throws tantrums, beating his fist on the table, or throwing things. When he starts smashing her dishes, she really lays into him. She has even slapped him at such times, and she is "always a little surprised that he doesn't start beating on me." He never really had struck her, but she did get worried about his violent temper, which seemed to be getting much worse and more frequent lately.

She said she really needed to come to a decision about her marriage. Bill seemed to be "such a baby." He not only threw those childish tantrums but also spent her hard-earned money on his expensive hobby of flying model airplanes. Some of these planes cost over one hundred dollars apiece. She told him to wait until he got a job, since he had just received his master's degree, before buying any more of these planes. But, he went out and bought one the prior week, using their joint charge card.

Another thing that discouraged her about her marriage at that time was a basic disagreement over her desire to have a baby and to stop work. She said that she would like nothing better than to have a baby and stay home to care for the baby, at least until the child would be old enough for school. She claimed that she was sick and tired of working so hard, of "breaking my ass on a job I can't stand." She worked hard for the past three years to get him through his master's degree program and then when he got the degree he claimed that the counseling field was so glutted that he could only get a job for eleven or twelve thousand dollars a year—with luck. Here she had hopes that they could have a baby and she could quit work, but he claimed that even if he could make more money he would expect her to work as well. There were nurseries and day care centers to take care of children; that's the way "modern couples" lived, he told her. She said that maybe she was old-fashioned, but she felt that she was entitled to be a "live-in mother" after all these years of work and helping Bill to get his degree. In these past three years while working on his degree, he had not brought in any substantial money except for poor-paying, part-time delivery work.

She said they had a lot of bills, including his student loans, which amounted to several thousand dollars. So, money was a major problem for them. She had mortgage payments as well. She had bought the house two years before their marriage, and she said she intended to keep it regardless of what happened with their marriage. Bill did not "give a shit about the house." It needed all kinds of repairs and maintenance work done that he was capable of doing, but he just kept putting it off and not getting around to it. They would have terrible battles over this, and when she would get after him about it he would call her a "demanding dictator."

She said she really did not know whether she could continue with her marriage. Bill was such a child, had no sense of the value of money, but she was still very attracted to him. He was very good looking and intelligent—

"educated, and that's important to me." It was all very confusing, and she hoped that it could be straightened out in counseling.

She reiterated at this point that she wanted to keep the counseling time limited, as she had requested over the telephone. This was because she did not think she could afford long-term psychotherapy. Although she currently had medical insurance coverage for out-patient psychotherapy, she desperately wanted to quit her present job just as soon as possible and to do private nursing. However, she would then not have insurance coverage for the psychotherapy, as she did under her present job at a large local hospital.

She said that her current job was intolerable for several reasons. It all began when she was on the regular day shift and began getting criticism from the head nurse about inconsistencies in her recording of medication on certain patients' medical charts. Doris insisted to me that this was due to slip-ups by two nurses on the prior shifts who were responsible for the same patients. However, she did not feel right about reporting them. They, on the other hand, did not acknowledge their responsibility for the inconsistencies, and Doris ended up taking the blame for it. Her relations with the head nurse deteriorated rapidly, with the latter criticizing her more frequently. Doris, in turn, felt that her own established record for hard work and scrupulous care of medicines should have been evident to the head nurse. It finally came to a breaking point when the head nurse began to criticize Doris again, and Doris exploded, telling the head nurse "to go screw herself." Doris also demanded to be put on the night shift in order to get away from the head nurse. This was granted and she had been on the night shift now for several weeks, but she was worried that the head nurse was probably preparing some kind of personnel action against her.

Doris said she wanted to leave the hospital before any such action could be taken. Even if they did not fire her, or undertake any other disciplinary action, she simply could not stand the night shift anymore. This was because she could not sleep during the day. She found herself getting up during the day, "compulsively doing laundry and other housework." She was also suffering from migraine headaches much more frequently than she had in the past. She said that her nerves were raw, and that she just could not take it much longer. She added that she was a terror to live with and that she was making life miserable for Bill and her son, Josh. She would lash into them on the least pretext, and she was worried about what this would do to her marriage and her family.

Because of all this, she said she would take a private nursing job, which would be much less stressful. However, a private job would not have fringe benefits, such as insurance coverage for psychotherapy. It also represented a step down and was less challenging than hospital work. She would probably end up taking care of elderly patients in their own homes, and though it would be much less demanding emotionally, it would also be boring. She felt that she was a very good nurse and was recognized as such by others, with the exception of the former head nurse. Doris felt that she had the intelligence, the organizational skills, and the conscientiousness necessary to move into a supervisory position. She had been encouraged to do this by others in the past, and she would like to in the future.

The problem was that she was so sensitive to criticism and what other people thought about her and her work. Although she was very competent and conscientious herself, she would try to make up for incompetencies or laxness in others around her by working harder rather than confronting them and demanding that they do their share. Instead, she would "take on a slow burn in silence" and continue driving herself harder and harder. She recognized this in herself, and if she could get over it she would really like to move up into supervision and eventually even into administration.

She said that this issue of her career was something that she would also like to get straightened out in counseling. She added, though, that she had to get her head "screwed on straight" before considering any moves upward in her career.

At this point I mentioned that she had identified a number of problem areas, but I wondered whether there was any one thing that caused her particular concern. She thought for a moment and then said that something had happened about three weeks before, on Christmas Day, that frightened her very much. She never again wanted to experience such an emotional reaction in her life, and she hoped that psychotherapy could help her in this.

She said that although Bill had been prompting her to come for individual psychotherapy, it was this incident that made her decide to come for help. She, Bill, and her son, Josh, were just getting ready to leave for a Christmas dinner at the home of her younger sister, Carol. She said that she and Bill were both upset about having to go to the dinner and the fact that it was being held at her sister's house.

As far as Doris was concerned, she "had to swallow a hell of a lot of hurt and anger" in order to bring herself to go to the dinner. She explained that these Christmas dinners had become a tradition with her family, particularly for her mother, who used to prepare and hold the dinners at her home when she still had her own house. However, she had been living in a small efficiency apartment for the past four years and in each of those four years the dinners had been held at Carol's home, which Doris resented very much. She said that she had offered to have it at her house for the past three years, including this one, but her mother and Carol together always seemed to succeed in having it at Carol's. Four years ago, her mother broached the idea of having the dinner at either Doris's or Carol's house. However, at that time Doris was working extra shifts on her nursing job to pay for the house she had recently purchased, and she was trying to get the house itself into shape before having anyone over. She therefore declined at that time, and Carol ("Miss Goody-Two-Shoes") had it at her home.

Ever since then, when Doris would offer to have it at her house, her mother would say that Doris was working hard at her job, that it was easier for Carol to have the dinner because she didn't have a job, and it was more convenient for everyone concerned. Doris felt that her mother was "rubbing it in" because of the time four years ago when Doris said she was working too hard to have it. She said her mother was that way, "She always managed to remind you about things you didn't do for her—great at guilt trips—wouldn't let you forget them."

This particular time Doris was insistent that she have the dinner at her home but both Carol and her mother were finding reasons to say they were not sure they could make it. Her mother might decide to visit the older sister in New Haven, and Carol was not sure whether she and her family might not accept an invitation from some close friends to have dinner with them. They thought that perhaps this year they would not plan on having the dinner. Then, on the day before Christmas, Doris's mother and Carol decided that they would have the dinner at Carol's.

Doris's mother did not feel up to making the trip to New Haven, and Carol's husband had to be out of town on business during the holidays, so it seemed best for Carol to have everyone over to her place. They felt it was too short notice for Doris, who was working, to be able to prepare everything.

Doris became extremely upset when her mother called her to tell her this. She exploded at her mother, blamed this situation on her mother's life-long favoritism of Carol, and said that she would not come to the dinner. She also called Carol to "tell her off," but instead of saying she and her husband would not come to dinner she said she did not *think* they would.

She explained that as angry as she was at her mother, she was already feeling guilty when she put the phone down after berating her mother. She also was concerned about the fact that she and her mother were drifting farther and farther apart, and such explosions only made things worse. So, by the time she called Carol she was wavering in her decision not to go. Then, after a sleepless night of worrying over it she decided it was important that they go, for fear that it might make for an irrevocable break if they did not.

When she told Bill this he was furious. She said he always disliked her mother intensely and felt much the same way about Carol. He claimed that Doris was "insane" and a "masochist" for being willing to go to dinner at Carol's. He at first refused to go, and told her to go without him, but she persuaded him with great difficulty that if she and Josh went without him it would represent the kind of break in family relations she was trying to avoid.

Bill had a temper tantrum in the process and was very sullen throughout

Christmas Day. She noted that he had planned on the three of them going out to a matinee of a science fiction movie he very much wanted to see and that they would go out for dinner after that. She said that Bill had a way of spoiling anything *she* particularly wanted to do together with him, such as going to a movie more to her taste than his. Although he might make the initial offer to go to such a movie, as a special favor to her, by the time they were ready to leave for the movie he always managed to make it known how distasteful it was to him, how reluctant he was to go, and in general to "make himself obnoxious."

In this instance it was not only something he did not want to do, but it also involved his intense dislike for her mother, her sister, and the fact that it frustrated *his* plans for Christmas. Therefore, he not only was sullen and obnoxious all day but he was very late in getting dressed and ready to go. They were already past the specified dinner time, and he was still not finished dressing. She was feeling frantic because she did not want to be late, to be put in the humiliating position of having to apologize for holding up everyone's dinner when she felt so outraged by the whole situation to begin with.

Then she started yelling at Bill, telling him how much he was upsetting her in addition to all the other pressures she was feeling. By this time Bill had come downstairs and approached the vestibule to the front door where she and Josh had been waiting for him for a long time. He was livid about what she had been yelling up to him, and he yelled in her face "I don't give a shit for you and your goddam family, and you can all wait all goddam day for me."

At this point Doris claimed to have lost complete control of herself. She felt that she might black out, but instead she swung her fist through a small pane of glass in the vestibule partition. She cut her right forearm badly, and it started bleeding profusely, so that they had to put a pressure bandage on it and drive right off to the emergency room of the nearest hospital. The cut required a dozen stitches, but, more than that Doris was in a state of near shock over her reaction and the intensity of the emotion she felt during the incident. It was this that worried her more than anything else at this time. She said she felt completely out of control, and she did not ever want to feel that way again.

I said at this point that the loss of control seemed to have been the most frightening thing about the whole event. She responded very readily that it most certainly was. Then, since the session had already run over the allotted time, I indicated that it would be good to begin the next session by reviewing this event—what it meant, why her reaction was so intense, and what could be done to prevent this sort of thing in the future. We would also go over the list of problems she identified in this session, so that we could select two or three of them to work on for the duration of her therapy.

It is instructive to look at the foregoing anger event within the context of

Doris's individual life structure at this time. In a sense, this experience encapsulated the central issues and concerns of her life structure at that stage of her adult development. It should be clear that the major components of her individual life structure were in danger of coming completely unstuck as they were represented in this particular transitional episode.

What was in the foreground was her relationship to Bill, her marriage, but also her relationship to Josh, which was so important in giving her life meaning. Additionally, there was the fear of completely endangering or severing the relationship with her mother. At this stage of her life Doris was becoming interested in reversing her increasingly negative relationship with her mother. If we think of the two paramount elements of the individual life structure, the affiliative (love, marriage, family) and work or career, it is evident that a crisis in the affiliative elements was present in this event. Even the work element played a role in the incident, although it was more in the background than the foreground. The intense pressure Doris was feeling as a result of working on a night shift in a job she despised was certainly present in the phenomenal field of this experience.

At any rate, it seems clear that this even represented a crisis with respect to Doris's life structure at this stage. It brought to the foreground her need to make critical decisions concerning her marriage and related matters in order to build a viable life structure for the remainder of her thirties. Her attempt to obtain individual counseling indicated an awareness of her need to sort out matters and make the necessary critical decisions and commitments. It also indicated that she did in fact see the situation as a crisis, for she did not think her usual ways of coping were adequate to solve the situation without help.

It was clear that one of the problems that had to be worked on in her counseling would be to make a decision concerning her marriage. Therefore, it was not surprising that this was quickly selected from the list of problems we went over in the second session. However, her emotional reaction in the Christmas Day incident was in the forefront of her mind, and Doris was sure that gaining more control over her emotions was her first concern at this time. She was also aware that her emotional reactions were very much related to her lack of assertiveness at appropriate times—or, according to Bill, her "passive-aggressive behavior pattern."

Consequently, at the second session it was agreed that the remaining ten sessions of counseling under our short-term agreement would be geared toward working on her negative emotions—particularly anger, her assertiveness capacity, and decision making concerning her marriage. Doris was given therapeutic work and exercises to carry out at home in addition to her weekly office sessions. She also agreed with interest and enthusiasm to complete certain tests at home for assessment purposes. She was very much interested in getting feedback from these and learning more about herself.

The test results shed some additional light on Doris's view of herself, on the significant others in her interpersonal world, and on her sense of control over the events in her life. The semantic-differential test seemed to confirm a number of impressions I had obtained from the prior interview and on our mutual interpretation based on the conceptual encounter in the second session. The first component of concern was Doris's view of herself, and the results of the semantic-differential illustrated in Figure 3-1 showed a marked discrepancy between "ME" (self concept) and "IDEAL ME" (ideal self).

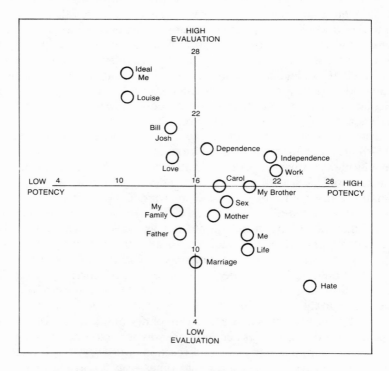

FIGURE 3-1. Doris Pierson's Semantic-Differential Graph

The ideal self was quite highly evaluated, whereas the self-concept was very low. On the evaluative axis, Doris described herself as "quite bad," somewhat "worthless" and "unfair," and "quite sad." This discrepancy between ideal and actual self was of course indicative of very low self-esteem. This was something we would have expected based on Doris's description of herself and her background. Another point of interest was the fact that her actual self concept was higher on the potency axis than her ideal self-concept.

This was explained largely by her description of her actual self as "quite tough," whereas on the test and in an interview she indicated that she did not want to be either tough or soft.

There were two other individual item responses on the self and ideal concepts which were noteworthy. First, she described herself as "extremely cold"—the "cold bitch" label used by Bill which she accepted as descriptive of herself. She checked the middle position on the hot/cold scale for her ideal self, which she explained by saying that she wanted to be a warm person but not a "hot-head." She also checked the middle position on the young/old dimension in describing her actual self, whereas she ideally wanted to be "extremely young." Although this concern with age and aging first showed up on the test results, it became very salient and thematic in her life at a later point when the issue of mortality and finiteness came to the forefront in therapy.

The most significant persons in her life at that time were her son and her husband, and it is noteworthy that they were both located in the identical spot on the semantic space grid. They were both described by her as "quite valuable" and "quite good" on the evaluative scale, and they were on the lower half of the potency scale. Bill was described as "slightly soft" and "quite weak," while Josh was described as "quite soft" and "slightly weak." It is worth noting by way of contrast that Doris described herself as "quite tough" and in the middle of the weak/strong axis.

This reflects the fact, which was borne out in later interviews as well, that she saw herself as the strongest person in her small nuclear family. The family itself was located on the low side of the evaluative and potency scales and was described by her as "quite valuable," "quite sad," and "quite weak." Her sister, Carol, was at the midpoint of the evaluative scale with her mother somewhat lower, but neither of them approached the low level of Doris's self evaluation. Her father was in the lower quadrant of the semantic space grid, and was described by her as "quite worthless," "quite weak," and "quite sad." She saw him as having failed her and as having been a failure in his own personal life.

Her brother was not at all salient in her life space. She had not been in touch with him from the time he left home when she was in her early teens, and she had never considered him to be significant in her life. On the other hand, her sister Louise represented something of an ideal and model of achievement for her. Louise had been rebellious and in conflict with her mother, and like Doris, had left home at the first opportunity. She also had a somewhat promiscuous and rocky late adolescence and early adulthood, but she seemed to have achieved a happy marriage and family. Although Louise lived in a distant city, Doris made a point of exchanging visits with her at least once a year. She said that Louise's life, and her marriage and family, offered some semblance of hope in her own life.

Apropos, both life and marriage were extremely low on the evaluative dimension of the semantic space in Figure 3-1. Both were seen as "quite sad," "quite bad," and "quite unfair." Life was also described as "quite old," which again was indicative of her concern with age and aging. Although the concept of love was much more highly evaluated than life and marriage, it was described as "extremely weak."

The related concepts of dependence and independence were of particular interest in Doris's case. It is usual for people in our individualistic culture to see independence as positive and dependence as somewhat negative on the evaluative scale. Rather than dependence being evaluated negatively by Doris it was slightly higher on that scale than independence. It was described as "quite good," "quite valuable," and "quite young," which was an interesting contrast to the description of independence as "quite old." This high evaluation of dependence was discussed with Doris, who confirmed that it was directly related to her desire to have a child and "to be cared for" in her marriage. She described her "dream in life" as having a strong, successful, and affluent man as her husband and father to her children.

At that time, of course, she saw her marriage as weak and her husband as somewhat less than strong. She was clearly depressed by this state of affairs but not really hopeless. On the Zung Depression Scale (Zung 1965), which she filled out at home between the first and second sessions, Doris scored just below the point at which she could be considered clinically depressed. She did not have somatic symptoms such as poor appetite, constipation, and psychomotor retardation, but items tapping feeling of worthlessness, indecisiveness, and incompetence were all at the high end of the scale.

Her responses to the Rotter Locus-of-Control Scale were also somewhat mixed. Her overall score was more in the direction of an external locus, but not exceptionally so. She demonstrated an external locus by checking off the following items: (1) "Many times I feel that I have little or no influence over the things that happen to me," (2) "Sometimes I feel that I don't have enough control over the direction my life is taking," and (3) "Most people don't realize the extent to which their lives are controlled by accidental happenings." On the other hand, she checked off the following internal locus items: (1) "In my case, getting what I want has little or nothing to do with luck," (2) "Getting people to do the right thing depends upon ability, luck has little or nothing to do with it," and (3) "Most misfortunes are the result of lack of ability, ignorance, laziness, or all three."

On the other hand, her responses on the Embedded Figures Test (Witkin et al. 1971) showed that she was clearly "field dependent" in cognitive style. This meant that she tended to look to others in her field or immediate social environment for cues, guidance, and support in situations requiring problem solving. Also, she showed a high intolerance for ambiguity; higher even than nurses in general, whom Budner (1962) found to have the highest average intolerance scores among the professionally trained persons he sampled in establishing norms for the Ambiguity Test. Doris's responses to the test indicated that she wanted simple and sure solutions to problems, and that she was very threatened by complexity in either the problems or their solutions.

These apparently contradictory responses seemed to be reflective of the confusion in her life at that time. Overall, she did not feel in control of the direction her life was taking, particularly in the area of her marriage and family. At the same time, she recognized that she had accomplished quite a bit in her life (obtaining a professional education, buying a house, raising a son, etc.) through effort and determination. These internal loci, the recognition of the importance of personal effort, were good indicators for the purposes of psychotherapy. The need for her to work at improving her situation was pointed out to her and reemphasized in the course of her therapy. Since therapy was time limited, it required extra work and continued practice on her part outside of counseling sessions.

Doris worked hard at the three problem areas that had been identified and targeted in the second session. The first two of these, control of anger, and lack of appropriate assertiveness, were handled by combined cognitive-behavioral techniques. In general, Doris did very well in following and practicing the behavioral procedures but had somewhat more difficulty with the cognitive elements. In dealing with the anger problems, Novaco's (1975, 1978) stress innoculation approach was used. This called for the identification and monitoring of: (1) the most frequently encountered events of anger arousal and provocation (insult, abuse, criticism, etc.); (2) internal factors including cognitive ones such as expectations, beliefs, appraisals, and self-statements and affective ones dealing largely with physiological manifestations of tension such as headache, chest pains, or "feeling wound up"; and (3) behavioral factors or responses to provocative events, such as avoidance, verbal antagonism, self-derogation, and various passive-aggressive strategies. Treatment of the anger involved the use of Ellis's ABC technique (Ellis 1962, 1973, and 1977) to dispute irrational ideas concerning the events. These events were organized into a hierarchy of anger scenarios which were handled by desensitization techniques utilizing progressive relaxation (Jacobsen 1938) as well as by the rational disputation of the ABC technique. Role playing and practicing of appropriate communication of feelings and assertiveness were to provide her with a better behavioral repertoire for dealing with anger-provoking events. Much of the work on the anger problem was linked to her assertiveness problem, so there was a synergy of effort with respect to work on those two problems.

A self-directed assertiveness training program for home use (Rakos & Schroeder 1980) was used because of the time limitations. It involved taped instructions on audio cassettes together with written guides and a workbook for specific exercises at home. It also included the ABC approach for the cognitive element of the program together with relaxation techniques and exercises for learning "how to say no" and other assertiveness skills. Doris took to the approach very readily and began practicing it in her interactions at work as well as at home. She clearly made identifiable progress in learning the skills, and she exclaimed at one session, "This is the greatest thing I ever learned! It's what they should be teaching in school!"

Despite this enthusiasm, she did have some problem in identifying, monitoring, and changing her cognitions. She insisted that she was "taken over" by her emotions when angry and therefore unable to identify or dispute her irrational thoughts and self-statements. Nevertheless, she was happy with the behavioral gains she felt she was making.

The third problem of arriving at a decision concerning her marriage was handled by Janis's (1982) balance sheet procedure in which Doris was asked first to consider the divorce option and then list both positive and negative possible outcomes in the following areas: gains and losses for self, gains and losses for others, self-approval or self-disapproval, and approval or disapproval from others. When this was completed she was to list possible positive and negative outcomes of remaining married.

Doris had fairly extensive lists of both positive and negative outcomes in the event of divorce. Among the possible positive outcomes she saw herself as having greater freedom of association (possibly with other men) and movement, as well as more free time. She said that "there would be one less mouth to feed" and she could keep a neater house with Bill gone. She thought she would have more energy if she did not have to cook, clean, and do laundry for him. The most positive possible outcome would be if she met another man, interested in marriage and children, who would be a "more mature and a stronger male figure than Bill." She also thought there would be less emotional turmoil in her life if Bill left, regardless of whether she found another man to marry or not.

On the other hand, she saw negative outcomes in the form of loss of Bill's companionship, loss of sex, and a fear of drawing more into herself and going into a real depression. She would also have total responsibility for the care of Josh. Bill was, after all, a male figure who spent time with Josh, played with him, and was certainly fond of him.

Another factor that added to the negative side of the balance sheet in the event of divorce was the fact that shortly after the start of her therapy, Bill obtained a job in a personnel department of a large manufacturer of data processing equipment. Although his salary was initially only $12,500 per year, he was told he had the chance of considerable improvement in both salary and position. At any rate, this additional income was important because of their indebtedness. Doris was quite sure she would lose her house without Bill's added income because of the size of the mortgage and their other indebtedness.

In purely quantitative terms, the balance sheet procedure turned up almost equal positive and negative outcomes under both contingencies— divorce or remaining married. Therefore, in order to bring out consequences that might have been ignored and to clarify the relative importance or emotional salience of the identified consequences, an outcome psychodrama procedure (Janis and Mann 1977) was used. This required Doris to project herself into the future and to act out a scenario that was to elaborate on the consequences of choosing each of the two alternatives. In this procedure Doris was asked to imagine that one year had gone by since she made her decision. First, she was asked to go through this as if she had decided to obtain a divorce, and then she was asked to go through it as if she had made a sustained effort to keep the marriage going. In both instances she had to imagine that she had come back to the therapist for a follow-up interview and to tell what happened in the interim year.

The enactment of the divorce scenario provoked a great deal more emotion and especially anxiety than the one in which she remained married. The thing that came most to the forefront was the turmoil that would be created by such a major change at this stage in her life. Furthermore, the likelihood of extreme loneliness and a more profound depression became a more salient and immediate threat in the psychodrama procedure than it had been in the purely cognitive balance sheet procedure. As a result of this, Doris was quite sure that she wanted to continue trying to make her marriage with Bill work.

After Bill obtained his job, Doris changed jobs and started private nursing duty. Although she had a few patients at first, she was soon involved entirely in the daytime care of a well-to-do elderly woman who resided in her own home with round-the-clock private nursing care. The woman quickly developed a strong preference for Doris over the other nurses assigned to her. She saw Doris as both a caring and competent professional, so Doris had the choice of working the regular day shift.

This arrangement turned out to be very satisfactory because Doris no longer had the sleeping problems related to evening work. In general, there was a great reduction in the amount of work-related stress. Her patient did not require extensive or involved nursing procedures, so her work was largely geared toward management of multiple medications and providing companionship. Although Doris found the work rather boring from time to time, she felt much better in terms of the time and energy available to her for other things—notably her home and family. The migraine headaches had been reduced markedly, and she was feeling good about the development of her assertiveness skills.

Toward the end of her scheduled therapy sessions she requested a joint session for herself and Bill. She said that Bill had been asking and then demanding to have one, and she laughingly added that she thought he was being "pushed out of shape" by her increased assertiveness. She noted that she, too, would like to have the session to see where they were as a couple and decide what they would do next, since she had worked on some of her main individual problems.

The joint session was held the following week, and during most of it Bill exploded with pent-up anger against Doris. He began by saying that although there had been some improvement in Doris's behavior in terms of her assertiveness after the first few sessions, things had gone from bad to worse. He claimed that she had become terribly self-centered in the process and that "everything with her now was me, me, me." He noted that she would say, "Now, I have to look out for myself—number one—for a change," but he added that this was "a lot of bullshit because she always *had* looked out for herself first."

He went on to say, "You talk about wanting a baby, but there's no way I'll have a baby with someone as selfish as you." He added that he wanted something out of the marriage for himself, but all she wanted to do was have him care for her and the baby. He would have none of that.

Doris appeared completely taken aback by the intensity of his outburst. She said practically nothing, except for one or two muted attempts to defend herself and contradict some of the things he was saying. Because of this it was necessary for me to intervene directively in the process so as to reduce the potentially destructive aspects of Bill's harangue.

I commented that there seemed to be nothing redeeming in what he had said about their marriage, which he referred to as a "farce" and a "shambles." I asked him whether this meant he did not want the marriage to continue. He responded to my inquiry as follows: "Not at all! I found this session very helpful. I think we should plan on having a few more of them."

At this point, I asked Doris what she thought of the session and the idea of having a few joint sessions. She appeared dazed and replied slowly that she did not know what to think about any of it, and she added that she needed some time to sort things out. I said that this made sense and suggested that we could spend her next regularly scheduled session to go over these things. She readily agreed to this, and the session was ended with that understanding.

At the next individual session Doris began by discussing her reaction to the session with Bill. She said that she was stunned by his onslaught, and that she was unable to contend with it despite her assertiveness training. She likened her restrained silence during his outburst as being like her reactions to her mother's frequent "lectures and tongue lashings." Her mother would accuse her of selfishness and willfulness while she would remain mostly silent and unprotesting, but feeling alternatively hurt, angry, then guilty, worthless, and hopeless. As we explored her feelings about the joint session in some depth, she identified the fact that she was "just about devastated" by Bill's attack. She had first been hopeful that the session would begin to lead to gains in their marriage, much like the gains she felt she had made in her own behavior. However, these hopes were dashed by Bill. She thus found herself in a state of almost complete hopelessness at the end of his diatribe.

She said that she must have been particularly affected by Bill's comment about not wanting a baby with her, because she had a dream two nights later that upset her extremely. It was a very short dream in which she was holding her stillborn baby and Bill was walking away from her and the baby. She said that the dead baby meant that her "dream" of another baby was dead. Bill had left her with this dead dream/baby. She felt utterly "lost and abandoned" in the dream, and she had been feeling deeply sad ever since.

Doris went on to discuss other feelings that seemed to be brought on by the dream. The outstanding one was a clear and oppressive awareness and fear of death. It felt oppressive because she saw herself as dying and not having what she wanted most in life—another baby and someone to take care of her and the baby.

She went on to note that it was ironic that she was afraid of death and at the same time she was thinking about suicide. She would like "nothing better than to take an overdose of sleeping pills and never wake up." She said she could not do this, though, because of Josh. However, she thought it was a real possibility when he was older and he no longer needed her. She could simply not see herself living beyond that point. Yet, just thinking about her death at that time made her very fearful. Therefore, at this point she was not only concerned about her feelings of sadness and depression but also her recurrent thoughts and anxiety about death and aging. What was noted earlier in her semantic-differential responses became explicit at this time, when she claimed she had dreaded aging and growing old for as long as she could remember.

Although her time limited therapy was to end with the next session, Doris requested, and certainly needed, further help to cope with these feelings and with her current life situation. She was given another Zung test at this time and it revealed a higher depression score than the first one and, although not indicative of a profound depression, it was indicative of a clinical depression.

We agreed upon additional counseling sessions to deal with her depression and with her current life situation. This second course of treatment would also be time limited due to several factors. One was that I would be gone on an extended leave of absence within four months, and another was that Doris no longer had medical coverage of her own since going into private nursing. Bill's medical coverage for her psychotherapy was questionable in the light of their troubled marriage and the percentage of cost coverage was considerably less than under her prior policy. Therefore, it was agreed that there would be a total of fifteen sessions this time, which would be sufficient to implement a course of cognitive therapy for depression based on the system developed by Aaron Beck and his colleagues (Beck, Rush, Shaw, & Emery 1979).

Before going into any discussion of the clinical work and subsequent developments in Doris's life, it is important to assess the impact and interpret the meaning of the two experiences Doris had just undergone—the joint session with Bill and the extremely upsetting dream. Doris claimed to be continuously "haunted" by that dream for the next several weeks.

It can certainly be said that these two related events marked a critical episode in Doris's life. It seemed to represent a setback in terms of her recent gains in morale and coping skills, as well as a derailment of her carefully-arrived-at decision to try to make her marriage work. Indeed, it can be said to have transformed her life, her being-in-the-world, at that particular time. An excellent phenomenlogical description of this transformational experience has been provided by Keen (1975) concerning an episode that occurred with his own young daughter, but it fits very well the experience Doris underwent:

> Simultaneously, her sense of herself changed from that of an incipient planning adult to a little girl. Her world changed from a set of meanings that supported her growing up to a set of meanings that supported her understanding of herself as a little girl. The meanings of the immediate field, of time and space, of objects and people, of herself and the world all changed at once (Keen 1975, 106).

The dream itself represented the specific transformational event within the larger context that included the traumatic joint session with Bill. It was experienced immediately, with intense emotion, and it left an aftermath of depressed mood, explicit death anxiety, and a view of herself as less competent, less able to cope, less *adult* than just before it occurred.

In order to understand this transformational quality, it is necessary to look at the meaning of the dream itself from several perspectives. The first perspective employs the type of cognitive therapy used in dealing with Doris's depression: "the dream needs to be understood in thematic rather than symbolic terms, and the thematic content of the dream is idiosyncratic to the dreamer and must be viewed within the context of the dreamer's life" (Freeman 1981, 228-229). From this perspective, Doris's dream was an intense, dramatic and encapsulated representation of the dilemma and loss she was faced with as a result of Bill's rejection of the idea of fathering her baby and of supporting her and the baby. This loss, then, could be seen as the precipitant of her depression; following Beck's (1976 & 1979) emphasis on the central theme of loss in his theory of depression.

From the perspective of structural psychology, it has been noted that "the structure of meaning of the dream and the unconscious dynamic of the personality are one and the same thing" (Mucchielli 1970, 160). In this sense, the meaning of the dream was much more pervasive, and the baby in it represented more than the baby she so desired. That desire, of course, had great meaning in its own right and was indeed a major factor in the ensuing depression. However, from the structural psychological viewpoint the baby also represented Doris herself, or that part of her that desired to be cared for, to be nurtured, and to be dependent. This interpretation was quite consistent with the semantic-differential findings which found the concept of dependence to be so potent and highly valued in Doris's semantic life space. As Moss (1970) has noted, there is often this clear correspondence between semantic-differential responses and dream content.

The dream was also transformational in that it triggered off the manifest death anxiety as well as the depressed state in Doris. Elliott Jaques (1965) sees such anxiety and depression as inseparably related to one another in the type of adult transition Doris was facing. Using Melanie Klein's (1948) object relations theory, Jaques emphasizes the importance of the prior working through of the infantile depressive position for the later handling of the mid-life encounter with one's own mortality. He outlines this importance as follows:

> The infant's relation with life and death occurs in the setting of his survival being dependent on his external objects, and on the balance of power of the life and death instincts which qualify his perception of those objects and his capacity to depend upon them and use them. In the depressive position in infancy, under conditions of prevailing love, the good and bad objects can in some measure be synthesized, the ego becomes more integrated, and hope for the reestablishment of the good object is experienced; the accompanying overcoming of grief and regaining of security is the equivalent of the infantile notion of life (Jaques 1965, 507).

However, under conditions of maternal deprivation or "prevailing persecution" the working through of the infantile depressive position will be inhibited and there will be a failure of reparation and synthesis, making the ego itself feel as though it were in bits. "The chaotic internal situation thus experienced is the infantile equivalent of the notion of death" (Jaques 1965, 507).

In early childhood, Doris claimed to have experienced emotional deprivation because of "an ungiving mother,"who was also seen as persecutory in
terms of her rigid fundamentalist ideas and strictures. According to the Klein-
ian theory, the infantile dynamics for dealing with such felt deprivation and
persecution "lead to feelings of intolerable helplessness through dependence
upon the perfect object" (Jaques 1965, 507). This interpretation would tend to
fit with the earlier structural interpretation which identified Doris with the
baby in the dream. Her need as the baby was for the good object, "the
idealized and bountiful primal object," who would provide her with the
sustenance and nurturance she craved. In the adult counterpart or fantasy, the
good object would be the loving and giving man (husband) who would care
for her—(and) the baby. The dream, of course, annihilated that fantasy as far
as her current life structure was concerned, and probably for good.

Irwin Yalom (1980) has given a somewhat different theoretical interpretation to the conscious type of death anxiety exhibited by Doris. Rather than
seeing the chaotic internal situation as ". . . the infantile equivalent of the
notion of death" he would see many of Doris' problems, including manifest
death anxiety, as having "roots stretching back to primal death anxiety." In this
interpretation all Doris's "needs" for dependency, nurturance, and the good
object were really ways of defending against primal death anxiety. In describing his work with a young woman similar to Doris, he made the following
observation: "To me, an existentially oriented therapist, these clinical phenomena—the wish to be loved and remembered eternally, the wish to freeze
time, the belief in personal invulnerability, the wish to merge with another—
all served the same function for (the patient): to assuage death anxiety"
(Yalom 1980, 47).

Regardless of the somewhat different theoretical perspectives represented in these two interpretations of death anxiety, they have common elements
associated with the same theme—mortality and finiteness—a theme that
certainly pervaded Doris's life at that juncture. Even her concern with aging
was consistent with this theme, and that concern contained many of the same
elements.

Levinson (1977) has said that the "young/old polarity" is the central one
to all developmental change. In Doris's case, at this transitional stage of life
this polarity took on some rather special and concrete meanings. For one
thing, she was acutely aware of and mentioned repeatedly in therapy the fact
that the passage of time was reducing her chances of having the baby she so
wished for. If she could not have the baby with Bill, then it would have to be
with a different man in another marriage. She could not see herself having a
baby out of wedlock and bringing it up herself as she did before. The only
circumstances under which she would consider having a baby would be in
marriage to a man who would support and care for her and the baby. She said,

"I'm too old to take care of a baby all by myself. I just don't have the kind of guts and energy I had when Josh was born." Furthermore, by the time she could separate from and divorce Bill, if she decided to do that, and then found the "right man" to marry, she felt she would be too old to have children.

Another way in which the young/old polarity manifested itself at this juncture was in her semantic-differential responses. It will be recalled that in those responses she identified her *ideal* self as "extremely young." It would not be stretching the point too much to say that this could be interpreted to mean that she would ideally (in her fantasies) wish to be a very young child again. In fact, this interpretation was presented to her as a possibility in one session in which I remarked that it "sounded as though you might like to be a very small child or infant again." She responded to this in an animated way, despite the general depressed tone she presented in sessions at that time. The substance of her response was that, indeed, she often thought that she would like to have her early childhood and infancy to live all over again, but under different circumstances. She felt strongly that she did not get what she needed and wanted at that time—"love and real caring." She was quite aware and conscious of the connection between this feeling and the high evaluation and potency scores shown by the concept of "dependence" on her semantic differential score as well as in her idealized version of the (dependent) wife/mother role.

The reason for emphasizing the infantile elements in this analysis is not to propose or favor a deterministic interpretation based on early childhood experience. In this regard, I am in agreement with Kegan and his "constructive-developmental" approach when he states that "the phenomena of infancy are better understood in the context of the psychological meaning of evolution, a lifetime activity of differentiating and integrating what is taken as self and what is taken as other" (Kegan 1982, 76). From this perspective, Doris can be seen as living through an adult version of the same underlying issue with respect to self and others, rather than a reenactment of the earlier experience, because of an earlier failure to resolve the issue. These elements are being emphasized in this analysis because they were salient and phenomenologically present for Doris after her dream. Furthermore, understanding these elements as they affected Doris's perceptual world provided some sense of empathy, of being with her in her world. As a result of the dream and the preceding events, Doris's view of the world was transformed, much like Keen's daughter, from that of an adult to that of a dependent, frightened child. To use Jaques's words again, "the infant's relations with life and death occurs within the setting of his survival being dependent on his external objects . . . , and this leads to feelings of intolerable helplessness through dependence on the perfect object" (Jaques 1965, 507). Bill's walking away in the dream represented loss of the object in this sense, and therefore brought the threat of personal extinction—hence the concern with death and the depressing sense of loss. This had to be a most frightening and demoralizing experience and resultant world view. It is the kind of experience that could lead to some demoralization and sense of hopelessness in the therapist dealing with it as well. What does one do with this?

The answer lies in understanding the role of intentionality and the underlying belief structure within the disorder. This understanding has to be made cognitively explicit for both the therapist and the depressed person. Given this understanding in Doris's case, the formulation of and strategy for dealing with such a depression was very well put by Arieti:

> . . . the fit of depression comes as a result of the following conscious or unconscious sequence of thoughts or their symbolic equivalents: "I am not getting what I should—I am deprived—I am in a miserable state." The patient is guided to stop at the first stage of this sequence, "I am not getting what I *should*," because these words mean "I would like to go back to the bliss of babyhood. I do not want to be a person in my own right, with self-determination." Can the patient substitute this recurring idea and aim for another one, for instance, "What ways other than aggressive expectation and dependency are at my disposal in order to get what I want?" In other words, the patient is guided to reorganize his ways of thinking so that the usual clusters of thought will not recur and will not reproduce the old sequence automatically and tenaciously (Arieti 1978, 224).

The general strategy of treatment, then, was to emphasize that she was competent to take care of herself and run her own life with or without Bill. She had done it in the past when she raised Josh and at the same time obtained an education and a profession. From the viewpoint of cognitive therapy, her infantile yearnings in the form of irrational thoughts, beliefs, and self-statements had to be made explicit and dealt with in clinical sessions.

This process was begun in the very next session after it was agreed to extend her therapy. However, in line with cognitive therapy procedures, the process had to be carried on at home as well as in clinical sessions (Beck 1976). One such homework assignment or bibliotherapy given in the first session was to read a booklet entitled *Coping with Depression* (Beck & Greenberg 1974). This provided her with an explanation of the various techniques that would be used in clinical sessions and at home. These included the "mastery and pleasure method" in which she had to identify and record on a daily activity schedule those activities or events of the day that gave her any sense of mastery or pleasure. This was done, of course, to contend with her pervasive sense of incompetence and lethargy as well as her anhedonia, i.e.— her inability to feel any pleasure at that time.

The booklet also described the ABC method of changing feelings and how she could review and correct the negative depressogenic and irrational thoughts that were associated with her sad feelings and moods. This entailed the use of the "double column technique" in which she would write down the unreasonable automatic thoughts in one column and her corrective answers to those thoughts in the adjoining column. All of this was incorporated into one form; the Daily Record of Dysfunctional Thoughts (Beck et al. 1979, 403). This form was set up in five columns. The first column, entitled "Situation," required Doris to briefly describe the actual event or stream of thoughts, daydreams, etc., she had which led up to unpleasant emotions. The second column was entitled "Emotion" and in this she had to specify the type of emotion experienced, such as sadness, anger, anxiety, and so on. The third column, entitled "Automatic Thoughts," required Doris to write down the automatic thoughts that preceded the emotion(s). The fourth column was entitled "Rational Response" and in it Doris had to write down her rational response(s) to the automatic thought(s) In the fifth and last column, entitled "Outcome," she had to reevaluate her belief in the automatic thought(s) and then to specify the subsequent emotions.

Using an example Doris experienced during her depressed stage, she identified a situation in which she failed to use her assertiveness skills in saying no to a sales person and then ended up buying an article she did not really want. This was followed by an immediate feeling of anger at herself which quickly changed to another emotion, a feeling of sadness. Her automatic thoughts associated with this were that she was both incompetent and helpless. Interestingly, she claimed to be convinced much more of her helplessness than competence. Her rational responses to this were that she was not incompetent in the general sense, because she had been quite competent as a nurse. Also, she corrected her automatic thought about general helplessness by noting that she had gotten her professional education, raised a son, bought a home, etc. Her belief in this rational response was weaker than her rational responses to incompetence, reflecting the stronger pull of her feelings of helplessness than her rational recognition of evidence of autonomous functioning. However, when she reevaluated her belief in the automatic thoughts under "Outcome," her belief in her incompetence and her helplessness were both reduced, and her subsequent emotion of sadness had been reduced to a more tolerable level—thus making her feel less hopeless for the time being.

This type of process had to be repeated many times as she experienced her recurrent moods of sadness, helplessness, and so on. She was able to implement this process much better in clinical sessions than at home, and her main stumbling block was in being able to identify and monitor the automatic thoughts associated with her emotions. Again, she claimed her moods tended to "take over" her capacity to think. However, she got better at implementing the process on her own, and this in conjunction with changes and developments in other areas of her life allowed her to overcome her clinical depression. At the end of the fifteen sessions or three and one half months of the second round of therapy, her Zung depression rating had dropped to a point below what it had been when she began her first round of therapy.

The problem of death anxiety was handled by much the same procedure. In its more acute form when we began the second round of therapy, the anxiety would express itself as an emotion in relation to an event, such as nearly having an auto accident, or in a stream of thoughts about a sudden terminal illness. The automatic thought(s) she had were that these things not only could, but would happen to her. Then she would experience great sadness in conjunction with the anxiety by ruminating about all the good (pleasurable) things in life she would miss out on and that she would be "short changed" by never being able to compensate for all the early deprivations and things she missed. She would correct and dispute these automatic thoughts and beliefs in the same way she did her moods of sadness.

One of the first procedures in the cognitive therapy of death anxiety is to determine the meaning of death to the person (Beck & Emery 1979). Is it seen as painful? As unfair? Or, is it the uncertainty of it—of needing to know when it will happen? In Doris's case death was seen as predominantly unfair. Also, there were elements of magical thinking in her case: "If I stop worrying or being anxious about death, I will die," and "If I keep making myself unhappy I won't die." In addition to correcting these irrational thoughts by the dysfunctional thoughts procedure, she was encouraged in sessions to live in the present, to enjoy the time that is left. She was made aware of the fact that she tended to focus so much on the past (deprivation and persecution) and the future (worrying about it or fantasizing a "Prince Charming" husband) that she was effectively denying herself an enjoyable present, and this would indeed deprive her of pleasures and satisfactions she could enjoy before dying. A general existential approach was also used to help counteract some of this magical thinking (Yalom 1980). Thus, no matter how much she worried, death would be inevitable, and it is better to accept this reality and *live* rather than engage in rescue fantasies and other irrational thinking.

Doris was able to reduce her earlier acute symptoms of death anxiety by the above procedures and by techniques of blocking (saying "Stop!") and diversion (purposely thinking of unrelated matters). However, her concern with death was more pervasive and recalcitrant than her depressive episode. That is why her case was placed in this section of the book, under themes of mortality and finiteness. This concern emerged and remained salient throughout this transitional episode of her life.

A few other points need to be made about her general cognitive style and her particular cognitive structure in the second segment of therapy. It was characterized by dichotomous thinking. In effect, she basically saw solutions to problems and questions as simple rather than complex—so simple, in fact, that just about everything could be reduced to yes or no and right or wrong dichotomies.

This general style was borne out in a Repertory Grid Test which was given to her at the beginning of the second segment of therapy. The Reptest showed that the predominant construct in her cognitive structure was "emotionally unbalanced." Further, it was strongly correlated with the construct "unhappiness" when the two were applied to the significant persons in her life. Thus, the following persons were all identified on her grid as both "unbalanced" and "unhappy": she, Bill, Josh, her mother, her father, her sister Carol, Bill's mother, and her former boss (the hated head nurse). Conversely, the following persons were all identified as balanced and happy: her "counselor" (me), a girlfriend, a "successful person" (a surgeon whose work she admired), "the person I want to be" (ideal self), and Ralph (a man she became intimately involved with just before she took the test). Figure 3-2 provides a graphic representation of the Reptest results.

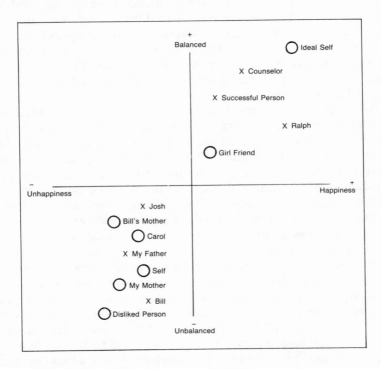

FIGURE 3-2. Doris Pierson's Repertory Analysis Graph
(Gender is indicated by O = female, X = male)

This tendency to classify people on different dimensions and characteristics in terms of one or two overriding constructs is indicative of a rigidly simple cognitive set (Wegner & Vallacher 1977). As we explored her use of the terms "unbalanced" and "happy" it was clear that the world was broken down not only into people who were both balanced and happy vs. unbalanced and unhappy, but also (the same) people who were successful vs. unsuccessful and those who could provide care (helpers and saviours) vs. those who needed help (victims). Just about every one of the persons on her grid had the same constellation of positive or negative characteristics. It is worth noting Doris's comment when she discussed the grid that at one time in the beginning of her marriage Bill would have fallen into the positive group—as a "balanced" helper. At that time Bill was training to be a professional counselor (helper) and that, according to Doris, had a definite bearing on her attraction to him. Thus, he was originally and potentially a balanced helper or "sane saviour" in her life, but was clearly no longer so.

Ryle (1975) found this same pattern in Reptest results in his clinical practice with patients who demonstrated an underlying splitting mechanism in their object relations—those who divided their worlds into "good" and "bad" objects. He also noted in Reptest results from experimental studies that patients in psychotherapy judged themselves and others in a simpler, one or two dimensional construct system than did controls. This suggests some further consistency with the object-relations interpretations made earlier about Doris's depression.

Bill had truly become the "bad object" in her life when he told her in the joint session that he did not want a baby with her, and further played the bad-object role by withdrawing even more from her physically and emotionally. He began cooking and eating his own meals, and cleaning his own dishes and clothing by himself, even though he continued to live in the same house. This was experienced by Doris as further punitive behavior on his part, as her need for nurturance and support had vastly increased as a result of her depression. The irony in all this was that shortly after feeling utterly hopeless and helpless following the joint session, she began feeling greater anger toward Bill, thus allaying some of the oppressive sadness she first felt. This, together with the planned emphasis in therapy on her demonstrated capacity to make it alone, if necessary, provided a motive force for change.

A complicating factor in this process was the fact that she met and dated a man within two weeks of the joint session with Bill. This man, Ralph, was the service manager of the place she took her car to for repairs. Although she had not paid any particular attention to him before, and he had made no overtures, she accepted his invitation at this time for a drink at a local bar after she picked up her repaired car. He was a married man in his late thirties who appeared to be very interested in her but not in an aggressively sexual way. In fact, the thing about him that appealed to Doris was that he was interested and solicitous for her without being demanding for himself. She found him to be mature and "balanced," in marked contrast to Bill.

Given her responses concerning Ralph on the Reptest, it became apparent what role he was playing in her life at that time. Further, the more Bill withdrew from her the more she turned to Ralph. Whereas at first she withheld any sexual involvement with Ralph, she actually initiated it as it became evident that Bill was literally not sharing her bed with her anymore at home. She said, "He's acting like he's not living in the same house with me, and he's making noises like he wants to leave, so screw him—let him go!"

She kept her relationship with Ralph a secret, but Bill began to suspect she was not going out with girlfriends (something she rarely did in the past) as she said. He became angry and accused her of her old "whorish" behavior from before their marriage. Although she vehemently denied this, she told him that if he was as dissatisfied with their marriage as she was he might just as well leave. She would just as soon have a divorce, since he showed her no attention or affection anyway.

It would be instructive at this point to look back on the sequence of events from the joint session and its aftermath of the depression to this expressed willingness of Doris to have Bill leave the house and end the marriage. It shows a remarkable relationship between the emotions of anger and depression in the entire process. In a structural analysis of the two emotions, Joseph de Rivera (1981) gave the following formulation, which shows an uncanny correspondence to Doris's situation:

> From our perspective, depression is not simply a passive reaction to a situation of loss. On the contrary, a conceptual encounter by Kane (1976) has shown that depression may be regarded, like anger, as transforming the person's situation. In fact, we may understand depression as an emotion whose structure is the reverse of the emotion of anger. That is, whereas anger instructs the person to remove the challenge, the instructional transformation of depression is "remove the self." Just as anger works to strengthen the person's will so that he or she can remove the challenge, depression works against the person's will so he or she *can't* fight against the challenge. Thus, part of the experience of depression is that one cannot do anything about the situation one is in (de Rivera 1981, 45).

Thus, while Doris was depressed she felt she could not do anything about the situation, but when her anger came to the fore again she was able to use it to "fight against the challenge." For what happened when she became angry, and was willing to end the marriage because it was not what it *ought* to be, was that Bill became shaken and frightened. The full impact of having to move out and live alone had not hit him until Doris began threatening him in her anger with "removal." His behavior toward her began changing quite dramatically thereafter. It can be said that her anger served the function of transforming their relationship.

It should be noted that at no time in her therapy did the issue become one of removing Bill and replacing him, in marriage, with Ralph. Early on in the relationship with Ralph she gave the following explanation: "He shows me a good time. He gives me what I need and want *right now.* He makes no demands himself, but I'm afraid that he might want to leave his wife and kids for me. I don't want that—ever—but I really need him now." She seemed oblivious to the potential danger of the situation, given Bill's explosive temper and his evident jealousy. The thing that did create a growing dissatisfaction with the situation, according to Doris, was her increasing sense of guilt about it. For when Bill was shaken by the threat of his removal and his behavior toward her began to improve so markedly, she began to feel increasingly more guilty. "The nicer he gets, the more guilty I feel," she said.

At any rate, Bill became very attentive to her and made a point of going to her and comforting her when she appeared sad. Further, he did not demand immediate feedback from her when he showed her affection. He also held his temper in check and rarely spoke in anger to her. As his behavior continued to improve toward her, she began to believe that a different life, one without a baby, would be possible with Bill. She said she didn't have any illusions about Bill. She saw him as immature and self- indulgent—"A baby in many ways— but so am I!"

As Doris attempted to make sense of all this in therapy she came to the conclusion that she knew all along that Bill was not the kind of man who could be the strong protector and supporter she imagined as father of her wished-for child. She said she probably knew that even before the joint session when Bill rejected the whole idea. She added that with the kinds of needs and demands they both had it would not be fair or realistic to bring a child into their world. She came to the conclusion that it would probably be best that the two of them continue working, as Bill had wanted all along, but without a child. Their combined income would enable them to have some of the things they wanted as well as to pay off their debts and to keep the house that meant so much to her. She could not begin to keep up mortgage payments on just her own income.

As her relationship with Bill improved, Doris began to withdraw from her relationship with Ralph. She said she was very grateful to and fond of Ralph, but that she never loved him as she did Bill. Although he was more mature than Bill, he never excited her sexually and emotionally as much as Bill did. She thought that something in her was attracted to Bill's childlike and dependent qualities. At any rate, by the time she left therapy, Doris claimed that the intimate sexual and romantic relationship with Ralph had ended and that they were just good friends who would meet occasionally just to have a drink and talk. She felt that he had been the best possible person for her in terms of her self-esteem because he cared for her as a person and never saw her purely as "a sex object."

She and Bill had gone on to use the negotiating skills they had learned in the earlier marital counseling. With her increased assertiveness and the more supportive tone of their relationship, they were able to work out their plans for mutual enjoyment as well as to resolve differences in a way they had not been able to do before.

However, not everything had been resolved through these negotiations. The issue of the baby was not closed, as far as Bill was concerned. As their relationship improved he came to believe that it might be good for them to have a baby, but Doris appeared convinced that it was not feasible. She felt there was no way she would agree to having a baby, holding a job, and keeping up a home—to being a "superwoman." Although Bill insisted he would carry his share of the load, Doris was not assured about how equitable it would be, or even that she would want it if it were. There had been one major flareup over this in which Bill accused her of making a unilateral decision about an issue (the baby) that was central to their marriage. Doris was worried at that point that she might waver in her decision, but she was able to persuade him to some extent that there were many things they could have or do if they were not tied down by a baby. This worked for the time being because Bill somewhat sheepishly admitted to being "a bit selfish" in wanting "a few more things"—some model planes and a new car.

One of the few blowups in their marriage at the end of Doris's therapy occurred over the issue of a new car for her. She had a badly rusted old car that was becoming quite dangerous because it was always saturated with exhaust fumes. Bill also had an old car, but it was in much better repair. Doris wanted a brand new car, but Bill disagreed with this because of their large outstanding debts. There was a heated statement on this until they negotiated an arrangement that was mutually satisfactory—they both bought new cars! The cars were the same make, from the same dealer, and the same colors, with only slight variations in trim.

This new "togetherness" also extended to other activities. They both became avid joggers, he running six miles and she running three miles a day. Doris felt that the running had been instrumental, along with the therapy and improved marital relations, in overcoming her depression.

Thus, at the end of therapy it could be said that her clinical depression had ended and that her marriage was markedly improved. However, while these criteria might be said to indicate success as far as short term, goal-limited psychotherapy was concerned, they did not indicate whether the adult transition Doris had just gone through was "successful." Success in this instance had to do with how sound and viable her individual life structure was at the end of the transitional process.

As Doris entered the structure-building stage identified by Levinson as the Settling Down Period, she was faced with the developmental tasks of making crucial choices, creating a structure around them, and pursuing her goals within that structure. She had indeed made some critical choices in the course of therapy and there were still others waiting to be made.

Let us look at the major elements of her life structure: the affiliative (love) and career (work), and see whether the choices made within them provide a viable structure for her to live and grow in.

In the affiliative area, it appears that Ralph served the purpose of a transitional man (object) in the critical juncture between the sundered emotional relationship between Doris and Bill immediately after the joint session and their later reconcilation. Doris had made her decision to stay and work on her marriage with Bill in the first segment of therapy. It was the issue of the baby and her choice not to have one that determined what the structure of their new relationship would be. The choice appeared to be a sound one for the immediate future. The question is whether it would be sustained. Bill never was an active party to the decision, and he gave every indication that he would renew the issue. Doris, in fact, was somewhat fearful of this possibility, and the question remained as to how stable and enduring a choice it was. She felt at the end that she still had until her early forties to change her mind.

The physical and emotional aspects of their marriage showed considerable improvement by the end of therapy. They appeared to be willing to give to one another, whereas earlier they were both essentially in a taking position. Their sex life was much improved and they were engaging in more mutually pleasurable things together. In fact there was a decidedly hedonistic, if not narcissistic, style to their life together. This was perhaps more realistic and closer to their emotional capabilities at that time than having a baby would be, but the stability of such a lifestyle under adverse economic and emotional conditions would have to be questioned.

Doris's relationship with her mother was also a significant part of the affiliative element in her life. She wanted a better relationship, but she seemed to be unable to work at changing it. Although at the end of therapy her mother made offers to meet with her to straighten out their differences, Doris backed out. She said, "I have too many angry and hateful things to say to her about the past, and I just know I would not be able to stop myself from saying them if we get together." This was certainly an unresolved area of her life. In fact, her relationships with women were either poor (in the case of her mother and sister, Carol) or nonexistent (no real friends, only acquaintances). I had referred her to a woman's therapy group to work on this at the end of her individual therapy, but she backed out of it, saying "I guess I just can't picture myself in the middle of a bunch of women. I much prefer men." This was, in fact, one of her long-standing problems. Unlike most women she had no potential support network of women friends and relatives for possible crises involving loss or separation. One important aspect of her (affiliative) self was not being realized under the existing life structure.

The second element of work and career had an uncertain future when she ended her therapy. Her decision to go into private nursing was only an interim one, designed to reduce stress for the time being. She was still interested in hospital work at a supervisory or administrative level, which she thought she would probably take a try at now that her family life had settled down. She admitted, however, that her career had always been "a poor second to the dream of having another baby with Mr. Right." She frankly admitted that she was not really emotionally ready to take the added stress of a supervisory job. Although she was better at asserting herself, she was still "supersensitive to every little sign of disapproval, rejection, or lack of recognition." She felt her sensitivity in these areas was so inordinate that she could not realistically assert her rights to any of these personal needs or demands. She certainly had a good deal more work to do on these cognitions or irrational beliefs after therapy.

As far as living within her new life structure was concerned, Doris was certainly living more in the present than the past at the end of therapy. There was not as much conscious ruminating and resentment about past slights and injustices. Her attitude was summed up in the following way: "I'm going to get all I can now. I'm entitled to it." Of course, the past was quite salient beneath the surface of this new attitude. There was the feeling of entitlement due to past deprivations and injustices. In other words, the basic depressive formula according to Arieti (1978), was still essentially in place: "I am not getting what I should—I am deprived—I am in a miserable state."

Given the continued presence of this essential depressive position, we would say according to Jaques (1965) that the basic theme of death and aging remains in this case and could be reactivated to crisis proportions in the future. In fact, Levinson (1978) claims that the Young/Old polarity is the major pressing one in the Mid-Life Transition (forty to forty-five), so one could expect it to be reactivated with special force when Doris enters her forties.

There is another polarity of the Mid-Life Transition that we could expect Doris to have a great deal of difficulty with. It is the Destruction/Creation polarity in which the person has to learn the following:

... about the heritage of anger, against others and against himself, that he has carried within himself from childhood. He has to learn, also, about the angers he has accumulated over the course of adulthood, building on and amplifying the childhood sources. And he has to place these internal destructive forces within the wider context of his ongoing adult life, setting them against the creative life-affirming forces and finding new ways to integrate them in middle adulthood (Levinson, et al. 1978, 225).

Doris certainly had great residues of anger and hatred from the past, as attested to by her continued sensitivity to any sort of slight or injury from others and particularly her almost uncontrollable rage against her mother, which she was fearful of reactivating in dialogue between them.

As we look at Doris's overall life structure at the end of therapy, we would have to say that it was viable for the time being, but that there were important aspects of her self that were not being realized in it. She still had a long way to go toward individuation, for her marital relationship was still a symbiotic and narcissistic one. A number of dormant issues and conflicts could be expected to come to the fore in her Mid-Life Transition. The creativity side of the Destructiveness/Creation polarity would be apt to express itself in a reawakened desire to have a baby, which would have all sorts of conflictual ramifications in its own right. Thus, it would be reasonable to expect further storm and stress in Doris's middle years.

A PANIC ATTACK IN A FIFTY-TWO-YEAR-OLD MAN*

The case of Allan Kahn illustrates how increased stress in both the work and love components of his individual life structure led to a crisis which was expressed in the form of a panic attack. Much of the stress emanated from changes in the real world of his marriage and workplace, but much of the pressure for these changes came from a faulty, outmoded life structure. Some of the stress he experienced at work was probably due to his own internal needs and workings which were projected onto the workplace. Through the coping mechanisms of projection, denial, manic activity, and other defensive maneuvers he attempted to shore up his existing life structure and fend off the underlying death anxiety. His internal assumptive world became very dissonant with the changed real world, thereby increasing the stress he was experiencing. This was evidenced in his agoraphobic condition in which his increasing irrational fears of leaving home became symbolic of his dilemma and also precipitated a panic attack. How this was handled and how it came about will be recapitulated below.

Allan Kahn was a fifty-two-year-old white male with no prior history of panic attacks. He was referred to the center in which I practiced by his family

---

*This case was published earlier in slightly different form in Sherman, E., *Working with Older Persons*. Copyright © 1984 by Kluwer-Nijhoff Publishing, Boston. Reprinted with permission.

physician who could find no apparent medical basis for the "fainting episode" (panic attack) Allan had experienced the day before. The physician claimed that Allan was in an "extremely anxious state" and needed to be seen as quickly as possible. Therefore, he was seen the very next day by me at the center. In addition to the request for psychotherapy "to contain his anxiety," Allan's physician referred him for a full battery of medical tests to an outpatient clinic to be sure there were no cardio-vascular, neurological, hormonal or other physical reasons for the episode and related symptoms.

In his first session at the center, Allan described the fainting episode as follows: He was waiting in a group of about twenty people for an elevator to take him up to his office on the fifteenth floor of a large downtown office building. He found himself "losing control" of himself in that he began feeling short of breath which then seemed to lead to a feeling of suffocation as his heart began to beat heavily. He became faint and began to tremble until he became so dizzy and unsteady that he felt himself falling. He must have blacked out because he did not remember hitting the floor when he fainted. He was also acutely aware just as he fell that he might be dying from "a heart attack, a stroke, or something."

A fellow worker who was waiting at the elevator with him picked him up, got him out of the crowd, loosened his collar and had him sip some water. Allan came to, almost immediately, and he chose not to go to the emergency room of a local hospital. He preferred instead to call his physician, an internist, who had just recently given him a complete checkup, including an electrocardiogram. After discussing the episode and related symptoms on the phone, his physician gave him an office appointment early that same afternoon. A friend and coworker drove Allan to his suburban home, from which his wife took him to the internist's office. The doctor's findings were negative, and he indicated to Allan that he probably had suffered an anxiety attack but that he would refer him for a complete medical workup as well as to the center for his anxiety symptoms.

He claimed to have had no previous fainting spells in his life. He also claimed that he was never really frightened of elevators or of closed places like elevators. However, he was feeling "very much closed in" by the crowd while waiting for the elevator. He had noticed that over the past month he was becoming increasingly more "tense, irritable, and nervous." He seemed to be more fearful about a number of things. He used to drive his car from his suburban home to a train station from which he would take a train to the city and then a bus to his office, but he was becoming anxious about taking the train and bus. Therefore, he began driving to work, parking the car near the office and walking the rest of the way. Lately, in the past two weeks or so, he had even become fearful of leaving his home alone and driving the car. His eighteen-year-old daughter, who just left home to start college last week, would drive him to his office and pick him up after work. On the day of the attack, his wife had taken him to work and was to pick him up after work. He noted that "things seemed to be closing in" on him, because he knew he could not continue this sort of arrangement. His wife had to take time off from her work as a legal secretary in order to drive him to and from work. She was feeling so pressured and angry about it that they had a big argument over it on the way to his office that same day.

Allan provided the following developmental history and background information leading up to the time of the attack. He was born in 1931 and was raised in the same northeastern city in which he currently works. He was an only child of a Jewish couple who did not practice the religion they were born into. His father, now retired, had been a shoe salesman and then manager of the women's shoe section of a large, fashionable department store in the city. Allan described his mother as having been a "housewife" all her life and that she was always considered to be physically somewhat fragile, although he does not know of any specific physical disorder she had. At any rate, he was led to believe that this was the reason she and his father did not have any more children.

His childhood memory of his mother was that she was "a Jewish princess" in that his father catered to her and that she would let it be known that Allan would be considered a "bad boy" if he was too wild, or reckless and a "very good boy" if he behaved nicely toward her. She also constantly warned him about being careful with strangers and outsiders, that "only family could really be trusted." Despite her presumed fragility, she seemed to him to be in much the same physical condition at age 74 as she was when he was a child.

Allan felt more positive toward his father, although his father backed the mother in warning against all sorts of things—being extra careful about crossing the street, about leaving the immediate vicinity of the home, about strangers, about not exerting himself too much, and so on. As a result, Allan claimed he had always felt kind of frail and physically weak himself. On the other hand, he seemed very sure that he was "the apple of their eyes." He would actually be embarrassed when his parents, especially his mother, would carry on about what 'a darling boy" he was in front of acquaintances and relatives.

Allan lived with his parents until he went into the Army at age twenty during the Korean War. He apparently received very high scores in general intelligence and certain aptitude tests, so he was trained for office and stenographic work and assigned to military headquarters in Seoul, Korea, for the remainder of the war. Consequently, he never got close to combat and never experienced any episodes of undue fear or anxiety in the service.

Before going into the Army, he had worked as a copy boy in a city newspaper office following his high school graduation. His "secret dream" at that time and for years earlier had been to be a sports writer. He had a way with the written word, and he edited the high school paper one year, but since he did not like school work he did not consider going on to college after high school. However, on the basis of his high test scores from the Army he knew he had more than enough intellectual ability to obtain a college education. Furthermore, he had the G.I. Bill, and that would enable him to give college a try without any undue expense to his parents.

He went to a local university while living at home with his parents and majored in journalism. He still did not like academic work, but he managed to get his bachelor's degree. Although he did not get a job in journalism, he was able to get a job as an advertising writer in an up-and-coming ad agency. He began by writing lines for magazines and newspaper ads, then spot commercials for radio, and finally scripts for some major television commercials.

He became quite successful at his work and after several years went with a much larger, nationally known advertising agency, at a much higher salary. His work was so much in demand that he was able to make quite a bit of additional income by doing some free-lance writing of advertising copy and scripts. He went on to note that he was becoming increasingly unhappy with his current job. The agency had a new director who was very ambitious and aggressive in his plans for the agency and in his handling of its employees. Despite Allan's excellent reputation in the field, he, along with other highly-regarded professionals in the agency, were being pressured and judged in much the same way as beginners in the field.

Allan claimed that the atmosphere of intense competitiveness, tension, and "back-biting" at the agency had led him to seriously consider leaving it. He would very much like to go into business on his own, to do free-lance work right out of his own home. He already had more offers for such work than he could begin to handle, and with his reputation and the contacts he had in the field he felt quite sure he could do well. He said that he felt as though he was at a "crossroads" in his career, that just as soon as he could get "this (anxiety) problem under control" he would make a decision about what to do.

When asked whether he thought the increased tension at work and his growing dislike of the place played any role in precipitating the attack, he said he doubted it, that he knew he could "hack it" at the agency, even if he did not like it very much. It was just a matter of getting himself "under control again." In fact, he said he wanted to be sure he "had this thing licked" before he made any decision about remaining there or going on his own.

As far as his marriage and family was concerned, Allan noted that there were some problems, but these too he thought he could handle once he got himself under control again. At the time of the attack, his family consisted of his wife, a fifteen-year-old son, a twelve-year-old daughter, and eighteen-year-old, Myra, the daughter who just left home to begin college. Allan admitted that she was always his favorite and that there was no doubt he missed her. He was able to talk to her in a way he had not been able to with his wife for quite a while.

Allan and his wife had been married for twenty-two years at the time of his attack. She was twenty-three when they got married and had been working as a legal secretary prior to their marriage. He was thirty when they married, and he claimed that he did not marry earlier because he had worked very hard putting in extra hours, in order to get ahead in his field. He lived at home with his parents, "plugged away," and did not seem to have as much time to date and enjoy himself as other young men. That is, until he met his wife. By that time he was well established professionally, and the two of them were able to afford a good time and still put some money aside as a working couple for over three years prior to the birth of Myra. He said his wife did not seem to mind leaving work in order to have children and raise a family; she was actually looking forward to it.

Now, however, it was a very different matter. She was pressing very hard to work on a more full-time basis. For the past year she had been working just about two days a week in a local law office in their suburban community. At first, she was even able to spend much of those two days typing legal briefs and other materials at home. Now, however, the law partners wanted to have her work full time at the office, both as an office manager and to coordinate the work of other part-time secretaries. They were very impressed with the quality of her work, her intelligence, and what they saw as her good managerial and human relations skills.

Allan was resistant to this. He claimed to be bothered by the fact that their two younger children would have to come home to an empty house just about every day of the week. His wife countered by saying that they were old enough to handle it, but more than that she resented that she had to be the one to be at home for them. She, too, had a career that seemed to be taking off and was providing her with a lot of satisfaction. She said that she now felt that she was appreciated by someone for the first time in a long time.

Allan intimated to me that their sexual relations had not been good for some time and that she had accused him of not showing her enough affection. He noted, however, that now when he makes it a point to show her more affection she claims to be too tired or too caught up in the overflow of work from the law office. This has not only hurt Allan but has made him suspicious of his wife's fidelity. All three of the law partners in her firm are men in their forties and fifties and she is "still a very attractive woman who looks much younger than her (forty-five) years."

Recently, Allan expressed his suspicions, "but not as accusations," to his wife, and she exploded. She was shocked that he had such little faith in her, and she added that it was ironic he was accusing her when she had more grounds for suspicion on the basis of his previous lack of attention to her and the availability of women in his office. Allan denied that there had ever been any infidelity on his part. However, he did confide to me that there was a thirty-eight-year-old divorced commercial artist at his office who openly expressed an interest in an affair with him. In fact, she was the coworker who brought him home after his attack, a fact which his wife threw up to him despite his distress over the attack. At any rate, Allan was very concerned about his relationship with this coworker, for he admitted to being very attracted to her and he was very concerned about the effect of such an affair on his marriage and his life at that time.

I commented that there seemed to be some areas needing attention in the marriage and wondered whether Allan would like to consider working on them in couple's counseling in the course of therapy. He replied that he did not see how he could work on that until he got himself under control. He felt that he would be able to work things out with his wife, once he got his "act together." He said that he had just requested three weeks of accrued vacation time in a phone call to his boss, and it had been granted to him to get counseling help for his problem. He was prepared to come in as many times as necessary in those three weeks in order to get over his excessive anxiety and fear of another such attack. He requested time-limited individual psychotherapy for the next several weeks in order "to conquer this anxiety state and get back some of the old self control."

Allan was given several assessment tests, one of which was an anxiety score inventory. This showed that he was indeed in a highly anxious state. He was also given the Rotter (1966) I-E Scale, which indicated that he had a high internal locus of control. Allan therefore perceived himself as *usually* being able to control his environment and its rewards largely on the basis of his own initiative, effort, and behavior. However, in his current state of anxiety he was feeling less in control and he was eager to re-establish his usual sense of control and mastery. It is crucial to add, however, that his cognitive style was highly field dependent, as indicated by the results of the Embedded Figures Test. It can truly be said that he was in a curious and conflicted frame of mind. He felt that he was in control of his environment, and yet he was unusually dependent upon it for support, safety, and happiness.

In the course of treatment, Allan also filled out a semantic-differential instrument. On the basis of this test, he saw himself as follows: good rather than bad, superior rather than inferior, a success rather than a failure, and quite valuable rather than worthless. In short, his self-esteem was quite good as far as the evaluative items in this test were concerned. On the other hand, he saw himself as somewhat weak rather than strong, extremely tense rather than calm, somewhat sick rather than healthy, and somewhat delicate rather than rugged. Overall, then, Allan saw himself as an intelligent valuable person who was quite sociable and likeable, and who saw himself as competent and successful even though somehwhat weak (physically) and characteristically nervous.

It is both interesting and pertinent to note Allan's description of his wife according to the adjectives and dimensions of the same test. In contrast to himself, he did not see her as smart. Although he did not say she was "dumb" (he identified her as neither smart nor dumb), he did indicate she was "somewhat dull" rather than sharp. He also saw her as a follower rather than a leader, but he saw her as "steady" in contrast to shaky (like himself) and more rugged than delicate. He explained these comparative descriptions of his wife and himself by noting that she was always the steady one who could be counted on to be the consistent one, to be physically strong and durable in contrast to his nervousness and tendency toward frequent minor physical ailments. Since he was the "somewhat sharper" ("at least more educated") one and since he was the primary worker and breadwinner, he tended to take the lead in decision making concerning money management and investment.

He saw his wife as having changed in a number of ways recently. She was described as now being very dissatisfied rather than satisfied and happy, as she used to be. She was now seen as much less steady, much less available for support and comfort, than she had characteristically been. Now that he needed her old qualities to help him in his present state of anxiety, she seemed unavailable and unknown to him. He felt, however, that the two of them could work out a better relationship once he got himself under control.

From a phenomenological perspective, his perception of self and situation was probably quite discordant with what his wife's perception of him and their situation would be. There appeared to be a discrepancy between his description of the current situation and his current internal experiential state. Although he was very anxious and described himself as such, his reported experiences had an impersonal quality to them in the sense that these were things which were "happening" to him, as though they were visited on him from outside—most certainly from outside his current perceived range of control. His ratings on the Experiencing (EXP) Scale were always in the range of one or two. Although there were self-references, they tended to be somewhat abstract and objective in that he did not focus on or express the subjective, personal meanings of the problematic events and his reactions to them. He seemed quite unaware of his own aging processes and how they might be impinging on his behaviors and attitudes in marriage and at work. His attitude toward the decision he had to make about his current employment had a driven quality to it. It was based on immediate, contingent external conditions rather than a more long-term developmental change in needs, motivations, capacities, and implicit (intentional) preferences.

Given Allan's emotional and physiological distress in his anxious state, treatment began in the very first session and was concurrent with clinical assessment. It was based largely on Beck's (Beck & Emery 1979) model of cognitive therapy of anxiety, which is brief and time limited. Ordinarily, there would be from five to twenty sessions according to this model, depending on the nature of the anxiety. Certain specific performance anxieties or mild anxiety states might require only five sessions, whereas chronic cases of anxiety might take up to twenty sessions. Since Allan's was a case of acute onset (a panic attack with no prior history of such attacks), I felt that nine to ten sessions, which could fit into the intensive three week time frame Allan had allowed for, would be adequate to handle the most distressing and debilitating symptoms related to the problem.

I began by using relaxation procedures to demonstrate to Allan that he did have some control over his symptoms. He was advised to sit quietly as I described how he could bring about a feeling of relaxation by the use of breathing. He was told to take slow deep breaths and exhale slowly because of the direct effect breathing has on heart rate and on the rest of the body. He was also instructed in how to deepen the relaxation and relax away feelings of tension by thinking silently to himself the words "relax" and "calm." Somewhat later a positive imagery technique was used to deepen the relaxation even further. The most relaxing scene he could imagine was to be at a peaceful, sunny seashore with his family safely and contentedly around him. By evoking this image, he was able to relax even more.

I also described the nature of anxiety to him and indicated that it is an unpleasant feeling state and physiological reaction that occurs when fear (an awareness or appraisal of danger) is provoked. He was also told that the anxiety symptoms not only interfere with the coping process, but they become a serious threat in themselves by being fed back as a new source of fear. Thus, there is a vicious cycle in which anxiety reinforces fear and anxiety. Allan seemed very enthusiastic about this explanation, which he said made a great deal of sense. He was also enthusiastic about the relaxation techniques, because he wanted to gain control over those physiological symptoms.

Allan was given an explanation of the cognitive theory of emotions and the role of automatic dysfunctional thoughts and beliefs on emotional states such as anxiety (Beck 1976). He was then asked to monitor his dysfunctional thoughts in conjunction with anxiety-provoking events and experiences by using the Daily Record of Dysfunctional Thoughts Form (Beck et al. 1979). However, he had a lot of difficulty monitoring his cognitions in this or any other form. It seemed as though the attempts to monitor and dispute the underlying cognitions, in contrast to the relaxation control measures, created more distress and anxiety for him.

Given the response to the cognitive approach, we explored the possibility of using systematic desensitization (Wolpe 1973). Allan was particularly agreeable to this because of its clear emphasis on control of physiological symptoms. In collaboration with me, he was also readily able to develop a hierarchy of steps based on Subjective Units of Disturbance Scale (SUDS) ratings going from "least anxious" to "most anxious." The thing which made him most anxious was fear of another panic attack, and the most fearful situation he could imagine was going back to the same spot where he had his attack and then going up to his office on a crowded elevator.

Therefore, the treatment strategy that was devised was an *in vivo* desensitization process which would culminate in his successfully going up to his office under those circumstances. Since he was fearful of leaving his home and of going anywhere, particularly on public transportation, the following kinds of steps were included in the hierarchy: leaving home and being transported to the clinic by his wife, then by taxi, then by driving alone by car, then by public transportation, then taking public transportation to his office building, then standing in front of the same elevator after working hours when it would not be crowded, then standing there in a crowd, and finally going up to the office in a crowded elevator. Given the number of sessions available, it was anticipated that the last step could actually coincide with Allan's going back to work after his three weeks vacation.

He progressed well, with practically no slippage, according to the hierarchy and timetable. The relaxation techniques, together with the positive imagery, seemed to give him a sense of control that increased his optimism and effort. In fact, he was able to go back to work by himself on public transportation when his vacation ended. Thus, what began as essentially a cognitive treatment approach ended up as largely a behavioral one through systematic desensitization. However, before assuming that this was a fully successful form of therapy in Allan's case, it is important to look at several troublesome remaining questions.

First, it should be noted that on his last clinic visit, two weeks after he had returned to work, he notified me that he had decided to quit his job and go into free-lance ad writing. He had done this on his own, without any advance discussion or indication to me. This was also somewhat true with respect to discussion with his wife. He reported later that she did not seem to be able to make up her mind when he broached the subject to her. She saw some positive things to it and some negative ones, such as the lack of fringe benefits paid for by an employer. However, he reasoned that he could do quite well financially and could compensate for that loss in terms of savings and more private insurance coverage. Furthermore, he would be working at home and would be available for the children when they return from school or are on vacation. This would mean less pressure on his wife, and therefore, less resentment from her.

It is possible that this might have been something of a pseudosolution for his problems, but only time would tell. For one thing, it has been noted that the anxious person is "governed by an internal imperative or admonitory image to avoid the anxiety situation because of fear that it will have dreadful consequences" (Beck & Emery 1979). Allan's anxiety was essentially agoraphobic in nature and, to the extent that this represents fear of leaving home for the fearsome competitive world outside, this "solution" of free-lancing at home might mean that he is being governed by the "internal imperative" to avoid.

To leave that issue for the moment, it is clear that Allan's anxiety episode represented a transitional crisis point as well as a more circumscribed panic attack. There were unresolved adult development issues which most men would have worked through by their forties, but were breaking through on Allan in his early fifties. This phenomenon has been described as follows:

> There is an Age Fifty Transition, which normally lasts from about age 50 to 55. The functions of this period in middle adulthood are similar to those of the Age Thirty Transition in early adulthood. In it, a man can work further on the tasks of the Mid-Life Transition and can modify the life structure formed in the mid-forties. It may be a time of crisis for men who changed too little in their Mid-Life Transition and then built an unsatisfactory life structure. ... It is not possible to get through middle adulthood without having at least a moderate crisis in either the Mid-life Transition or the Age Fifty Transition (Levinson et al. 1978, 62).

Some of the mid-life issues which Allan had not yet faced with any insight or deliberation were those pertaining to waning physical, competitive, and sexual energies. Although he was always attuned to his "somewhat delicate" physical functioning, he expressed no feelings of change from aging. The sexual issue has to be inferred in the light of his largely abstinent behavior and his wife's resultant dissatisfaction. Yet, the appeal (actually, the threat) of an affair with the divorced woman at his office might represent the "last chance" for the exciting and forbidden sexual expression for which many people in mid-life seem to reach. He did not have an exciting erotic life before his marriage, so there might be something of that nature at work here.

Allan might be experiencing a degree of the disenchantment with competitiveness and achievement in the workplace that men his age tend to feel in the normal course of development. However, there is no evidence that he was aware of such an experience by making his decision to leave his increasingly competitive place of work.

Finally, he had not even begun to work through the unsatisfactory patterns or "conspiracies" that Gould (1978) claims need to be broken in midlife. For example, he still seemed to be operating on the following old assumptions in his relationship to his wife when he finished treatment: "I'll be the smart one—you be the dumb one"; "You be the healthy one—I'll be the sick one"; "I'll be the leader—you be the follower"; and finally, "I'll be decisive—you be wishy-washy" (Gould 1978, 279-280). Indeed, this last pattern had been perfectly enacted when he made his decision to leave his job in the face of his wife's indecision. This did not seem to bode well for the future of their marriage in the light of her obvious efforts to break these old patterns and assert her own identity. Clearly, Allan and his wife could have benefitted from marital counseling when he completed treatment for his anxiety attack. However, it is not known whether this came to pass, although it was strongly recommended to him by me when his case was closed at his insistence.

Collusions such as these carry all the earmarks of a symbiotic type of union in the marriage. Allan's wife was emerging from this fused or embedded union but Allan was not. We can say, in line with Kegan's (1982) formulation that Allan was unable to develop a more mature, adult relationship with his wife because of his embeddedness; his emotional need for fusion in the marriage. His wholesale use of the mechanism of denial would be indicative of this psychological state. Indeed, intense anxiety related to the possibility of losing embeddedness is no more graphically portrayed than in cases of agoraphobia such as Allan's.

The prognosis for Allan could not be considered good. He did not seem at all attuned to the realities of his deteriorating marriage. He even refused the offer of marital counseling without consulting his wife. Although he gained somewhat in therapy, it was entirely in terms of the instrumental behavioral (relaxation) techniques he had learned. He actually described them as "tools" and "handles." However, even the rather superficial cognitive monitoring techniques represented a threat to him in that they could have led to some insight into his internal state, which was chaotic and fearful. Jaques (1965) described this type of state as a profound abandonment anxiety which characterizes the death anxiety beneath the mid-life crisis.

Gould (1978) claims that work is often "a magical protection against death" for men. Allan's decision to go into free-lance work might have represented a desperate and magical maneuver on his part, according to the following formulation:

> Faced with this intense anxiety, some of us redouble our efforts at work and reinvest in its illusions with a passion. The relentless pressure to make a quantum leap into the world of fantastic success, to end death with one major stroke of achievement, increases . . . (Gould 1978, 231).

Allan did express high hopes of huge success in his free-lance venture, believing that it could change the direction of his life. However, since the maneuver played directly into his agoraphobia it is doubtful that it could have been a successful coping strategy, even if it turned out to be a commercial success. In summary, we would have to say that Allan was ill-prepared to see this transitional crisis through successfully in terms of expressive coping and insight.

Chapter 4

GENERATIVITY, STAGNATION, AND CRISES OF IDENTITY

The nuclear conflict or crisis for the ego in the seventh developmental stage (middle adulthood) of Erik Erikson's (1963) theory of ego development is generativity versus stagnation. Crises of identity in his theory are most clearly associated with the nuclear conflict of the fifth developmental stage (adolescence), which is ego identity versus role confusion. However, there are frequently crises of identity in the middle years involving a reactivation of earlier issues around the nuclear conflict of ego identity versus role confusion, as will be illustrated shortly.

Erikson (1963) has noted that "mature man needs to be needed, and maturity needs guidance," so generativity "is primarily the concern in establishing and guiding the next generation." This does not refer only to one's own offspring, for "the concept of generativity is meant to include such popular synonyms as *productivity* and *creativity*" (Erikson 1963). If there is not this gradual expansion of "ego-interests and . . . libidual investments" there is apt to be a regression to a state of self-preoccupation, "often with a pervading sense of stagnation and personal impoverishment." There, individuals will begin to indulge themselves and "early invalidism, physical or psychological, becomes the vehicle of self-concern."

There appears to be an inconsistency, or at least a dilemma, in the developmental literature on the middle years. On the one hand, Erikson talks about the preoccupation with self in the state of stagnation when a balance in favor of generativity is not achieved. Yet, gerontological research has found that an increased sense of self and "interiority of personality" seems to be a general or almost universal development in middle age (Neugarten et al. 1964). If this self-concern is so pervasive in the middle years, does this mean that most middle-aged persons are stagnated? The answer lies in the fact that the locus of problems shifts in the middle years. As one gerontologist put it: "In the rooms where the middle-aged live, quarrels are not between people but deep within the self, and the aggression of youth is turned inward, to become the depression of middle-age" (Datan 1980, 4). However, most of these problems do not end up in depression, or even chronic stagnation. The whole issue of generativity versus stagnation has to be seen in the context of an ongoing dialectical process, as follows:

> In every stage, developing is a process in which opposite extremes are to some degree reconciled and integrated. Both generativity and its opposite pole, stagnation, are vital to a man's development. To become generative, a man must know how it feels to stagnate—to have the sense of not growing, of being static, stuck, drying up, bogged down in a life full of obligations and devoid of self-fulfillment (Levinson et al. 1978, 30).

Needless to say, this process is true of women as well as men. Indeed, the case of Linda Craft in this chapter illustrates how a sense of stagnation leads to a powerful desire to change and to become generative.

As noted earlier, crises of identity are not at all uncommon in the middle years, even though they are more commonly identified with adolescence. Identity has been defined as the "accrued confidence that one's ability to maintain inner sameness and continuity . . . is *matched* by the sameness and continuity of one's meaning for others" (Erikson 1959, 97). Thus, there has to be a match between the person's individualized way of maintaining continuity and sameness and the external definitions based on the community's perceptions of the person. Problems of identity in mid-life are frequently those arising from a mismatch between the person's sense of self and his or her role(s) in life. Therefore, in cases of middle-aged men whose primary identification has been with their work roles or careers, mandatory retirement or unemployment can indeed lead to an identity crisis. This is brought on by the break in sense of sameness or continuity of self and its mismatch with the external reality of unemployment and loss of a major social role by which the community tends to assess or validate one's identity. The consequent feelings of aimlessness, alienation, and low self-esteem are strikingly similar to those of adolescents in a state of role confusion as a result of failing to achieve ego identity.

The same sort of issue can arise with women. Not only does the "empty nest" represent a threat to her identity as a care-giving nurturing mother, but it calls for development of alternative roles for the purposes of ego identity.

Divorce or disillusionment with the role of being a wife becomes a precipitant for a crisis of identity in many middle-aged women.

A number of these factors were operative in the case of Linda Craft, who in a sense represents a mixture of the generativity and identity issues. As will be seen, she is compelled by her sense of stagnation and need to express denied aspects of her self, and to reach toward totally new social role alternatives in order to attain a sense of ego identity and generativity. The case of Steve Gornecky in this chapter represents a more clear-cut crisis of identity, whereas the case of Ralph Kane is a clear illustration of a crisis in which stagnation and lack of generativity is the predominant problem.

THE EXPERIENCE OF STAGNATION IN A FORTY-FOUR-YEAR-OLD MAN

Ralph Kane came to me to inquire about participating in a men's therapy group I had just started. He appeared much younger than his forty-four years, perhaps because of a rather boyish face and full head of reddish brown hair. He was of medium height and build, and he spoke with an intense, almost studied, earnestness. He would speak in a very frank tone of voice while looking directly at me in order to gauge my response. He was frank in saying that he had tried to go into group therapy with a Gestalt therapist who practiced in the same community. However, she was going to be out of the country for the whole summer and would not be starting a new group until the fall. He said that it was "absolutely necessary" that he get into a group now, because he felt he would either "suffocate or explode" in his current emotional state.

He went on to explain why he wanted a group experience rather than individual therapy. He explained that he was feeling "all bottled up and emotionally isolated," and the only way he could seem to deal with that feeling was in a group situation where he could express his feelings in "a free give-and-take encounter with others." Ralph was quite articulate in his use of the terminology and jargon from various types of group therapy. Not only was he intelligent and well educated, having a law degree, but he had already "shopped around the therapy circuit." He said that he had been in a Transactional Analysis group the year before and although he gained some insights in the process it had been "too much of a head trip." He found the structural analysis of personality in TA, which uses the conceptual terms of "parent," "adult," and "child," to be too analytical for his purposes because he wanted more direct experience and expression of his feelings. That was why he wanted to participate in a Gestalt group, which would be much more experiential and confrontational.

I indicated that most of the men in the group he wished to join were in individual therapy with me or with some other therapist in the same center for psychotherapy. Although it was not necessary to be in individual therapy to join the group, the men who were in it were all dealing with problems like divorce and separation. Therefore, the emphasis was on a lot of mutual support and understanding rather than confrontation, at least in this early stage of the group's development.

Ralph said that he could appreciate this, and that he felt he was a sensitive and empathic person who could fit well into such a group. He added that he also had problems in his marriage, although probably of a somewhat different nature. He then went on to explain some of these problems, and they all added up to a strong sense of dissatisfaction with his current life structure.

Although he claimed to have a stable marriage and family, he was currently feeling a "lack of connectedness or strong attachment" to them, and this was very distressing to him. He said that marriage and family were extremely important to him, but he seemed to be "unable to reach and connect emotionally" with them. He was sure it was mostly his problem, especially in relation to his children. He could express his interest and concern in their school work and social activities to them, but he had difficulty expressing his fondness and love for them directly. Even when he was angry with them, which seemed to be more frequent lately, he expressed it in indirect forms of irritation instead of confrontation.

There was even less direct expression of feeling between himself and his wife. He said that there used to be more, and he was fearful that their relationship was drying up. He was getting more irritable with her and she more resentful about his irritability and dissatisfaction. Their sexual activity had dwindled down to intercourse about once a month and even then it was far from satisfactory. He said, in short, that he ws having "severe problems with intimacy" in his family life.

His work had also become boring and routine. He was a division head within the State Labor Department, and for all intents and purposes, he felt like a "bureaucratic functionary." He had studied labor law and had earlier visions of becoming a lawyer for some industrial union with a strong interest in social activism as well as the welfare and working conditions of its members. He mentioned that he had been active in the peace movement during the 1960's, organizing a group of Catholic laypersons in the area to make them a more viable part of the larger peace movement. He remained active in Catholic lay activities, but it was "of the Knights of Columbus variety" which he felt put him right in the mainstream of conventional social and political thought (at least overtly) in his community.

Since he originally thought the state job would be a temporary stepping-stone into a union position, he now saw his retention of the job as a betrayal of his ideals. He now had 18 years with the Labor Department as well as a good salary, together with the security of substantial retirement and other fringe benefits. In the light of his family responsibility, he did not see how he could leave his job. Yet, he was feeling "suffocated" by the job as well as by his current family situation. He used the word "suffocation" repeatedly in describing his feelings, and it had all the earmarks of a state of mid-life stagnation. "Suffocation" was his subjectively felt experience of the state of stagnation.

There was no question in my mind that he was experiencing this as an intense personal crisis in his mid-life. He was in fact in the forty to forty-five year age range which Levinson identifies as the mid-life transition and describes as follows:

> For the great majority of men—about 80 percent of our subjects—this period evokes tumultuous struggles within the self and with the external world. Every aspect of their lives comes into question, and they are horrified by much that is revealed. They are full of recriminations against themselves and others. They cannot go on as before, but need time to choose a new path or modify the old one (Levinson et al. 1978, 199).

There was no question that Ralph Kane's individual life structure was no longer viable in terms of its two major components of love (marriage and family) and work in their existing forms. He either had to break out onto a new path or modify the existing structure.

Since it was evident that he was experiencing a crisis in the sense that his usual ways of coping were inadequate, and since he was very clearly in distress, he was added to the men's group.

The group was in its formative stages, and Ralph joined the initial group of seven men at the start of its third meeting. He became an active group participant in his very first session and in every one thereafter. A few of the men discussed some of the insights they were gaining from individual therapy and from the assessment test results that were shared with them. Ralph became intrigued by this and, given the kind of self-concern and preoccupation he was going through, he asked if I would be willing to see him individually for what he termed "testing, evaluation, and personal consultation." It was interesting that he preferred to identify this as an individual "consultation" rather than "treatment" process.

This was, of course, perfectly acceptable and advisable, for I felt that he might benefit from a consultation or mutual "conceptual encounter" concerning himself in his current life situation. In the course of his individual contacts with me he gave considerable background information about himself as well as engaging in the testing and interpretation process. His childhood family background did indeed provide a number of insights into his current perceptual attitudes and assumptive world.

Ralph was born into an Irish-American, working class family consisting of his parents and seven children. His father was an iron worker and a staunch union member. "We were a strong union family, and that's where I got the desire to be a labor lawyer," he said. His family was also very religious, especially his mother, and it looked for a while as though he was going to be a priest. However, in the middle of his seminary studies he decided he did not want to be a priest and transferred to a Catholic college in his hometown, where he did exceptionally well, graduating summa cum laude. He was the only member of the family of three boys and four sisters to go to college, and as noted earlier, he went on to obtain a law degree.

He said that he somehow always felt "responsible" for his family. Although he was only the second oldest (his brother, Joe, was two years older), he had the feeling that he had been "selected" to be the responsible one, "a sort of second father figure," in the family. He thought that was why he was the one who was encouraged to be a priest and the only one to get a professional education. As a result of all this, and even earlier childhood experiences, he felt that he "never had a childhood." He felt his mother was more demanding of him than giving or nurturing, and he always felt "this burden of responsibility" in his family.

He lived at home all the time he went through college and law school, usually working part time and contributing his financial share to the family. When he graduated from law school he stayed on and contributed even more to the family until he married at age twenty-seven. He still felt very responsible for his parents, who were having some difficulty as a result of his father's recent stroke. He was the one who had to work out the arrangements for his father's return home from the hospital, obtaining home health care and support, as well as having to contribute financially to ease the burden on his parents' modest resources.

He admitted to feeling very resentful toward his siblings because he was the one left with total responsibility. He was especially angry at his older brother, Joe, who "never did seem to give a damn—just let me do it all." Although he and his family got together with his siblings and their families several times a year, Ralph found himself getting more angry at them. He was concerned about the growing bad feeling between himself and them, which he felt might lead to a blowup.

His wife, Betty, was the first woman he ever became "really emotionally involved with." He was "somewhat shy and backward" after leaving the seminary and only dated sporadically in college. Consequently, his first sexual experience was on his honeymoon, and he looked forward to a life of intimacy with his wife and raising a family of his own. They had three children: Carol, age sixteen; Chris, age fourteen; and Elizabeth, age nine. Ralph noted that it was ironic that he had so looked forward to this marriage and these children, comparing this to the sense of burden and responsibility he felt in his family of origin. Now he was having similar feelings about his own family.

The semantic-differential test gave some indication of the place of these significant others in his current life space. Figure 4-1 gives a semantic space portrayal of the test results.

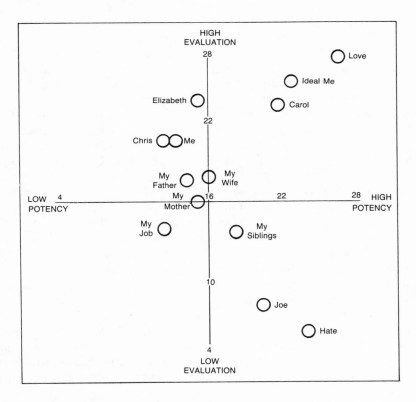

FIGURE 4-1. Ralph Kane's Semantic-Differential Graph

Ralph described himself as "extremely tense," "extremely soft," and "slightly weak," which reflected his current state of tension in the transitional crisis as well as his feeling of weakness or lack of capacity to deal with it. In response to "Ideal Me" on the test he checked off "extremely strong." Thus, he felt less potent than he would ideally like to be, so there was some discrepancy on the potency dimension between self-concept and ideal self. There was also some discrepancy on the evaluative dimension, mostly because he reported himself to be "quite sad" when he would like to be "quite happy." On the other hand, he described himself as "quite good" and "extremely fair," which is what he would like to be ideally. So, his self-esteem was not unusually low. However, there were some questions raised in my mind about possible misconceptions he might have about himself, particularly in seeing himself as "extremely fair." That was indeed an extreme self-evaluation, which is often a useful clue to finding problem-producing misunderstandings of the self (Raimy 1975).

In contrast, Ralph described his wife as "quite unfair," which he explained by saying she was not understanding or supportive of him in his current state. In fact, Figure 4-1 shows her to be rather neutral or nondescript on both the evaluative and potency dimensions of his semantic space. Ralph was not surprised to see this in his test results, because he felt that she and their relationship had become rather cool, distant, and neutral.

Ralph's daughters, Carol and Elizabeth, were both highly evaluated by him. So was his son, Chris, but he was somewhat lower on the evaluative dimension because he was "quite sad" whereas the girls were both "quite happy." Actually, Chris was remarkably close to Ralph in Figure 4-1, and Ralph did acknowledge that he saw Chris as "regretfully" like him. He felt that he was not getting close enough emotionally to his son, who was therefore feeling somewhat like he did in his family at the same age.

The relatively low or neutral evaluations of his mother, father, and siblings speak to this feeling in Ralph. Joe, in particular, has a low evaluation, and his close proximity to the concept "hate" in Ralph's semantic space speaks to the anger he was feeling toward his older brother. The extreme diametric distance between the concept of "hate" and the concept of "love" is also of interest. This often suggests a denial or failure to integrate actual feelings of hatred into one's self-awareness and self-concept, and this will be discussed somewhat further in Ralph's case. In the meantime, it is important to note the extremely high evaluative and potent place "love" has in Ralph's semantic space. This he explained by saying that love, intimacy, and relationship were all closely associated in his mind, and he felt these were all acutely lacking in his current life.

Ralph's participation in the group was at first quite positive. He appeared sensitive and supportive of the other men in terms of their experiences of separation, loss, and depression resulting from the breakups of their marriages and families. After about two sessions, however, he became quite insistent and even demanding about the need for greater catharsis and emotional expression and confrontation in the group. This went beyond the appropriate expression of anger on the part of the men toward their wives in their separation experiences, and he was expecting and promoting undue confrontation and expression of negative emotions between members of the group. Since this was not appropriate in terms of timing or the makeup of the group, I had to discuss it with him in his individual sessions.

There was a distinctly moralistic flavor to the way Ralph would say in group sessions: "You *must* express your emotions"; "You *ought* to let it all out"; and "It isn't *right* to keep your feelings bottled up like that." There was almost a religious fervor to the way Ralph felt about catharsis and confrontation in the group process. Consequently, the group experience was too "mild and bland" for him, and after twelve sessions he left it to join a new group being formed by the Gestalt therapist in whom he was originally interested but who had been out of the country.

Before he left I had been able to share with him some of the test results and my observations in a mutual process of conceptual encounter. He had insight into some of his problems but not others, and there were certain kinds of change efforts he was prepared to engage in, but not others. The one thing that was clear and that there was mutual agreement about was his stagnation and dissatisfaction in his current life structure. He was unhappy with his family life, especially his marriage, and his work. He was afraid he no longer loved his wife, and he did not know what to do about their stagnated relationship.

Just before coming to me, he had a brief sexual episode with a woman lawyer at a conference in another city. They had met at an afternoon session and had a number of drinks and dinner together, after which they went to her motel room. This had been his first and only sexual contact with a woman other than his wife. Whether for this reason, or the alcohol he had consumed, or both, he found himself impotent with this woman. He said she was "very nice about it" and attempted to satisfy him by fellatio. Although he achieved orgasm, this made him feel worse—"guilty, sorry that I couldn't satisfy her, and inadequate."

This experience, added to his strong Catholic beliefs, convinced him that divorce was out of the question and that he simply had to continue with his marriage and his current family structure. He also felt locked into his job because of its security and his responsibility to his family. Consequently, he was not able to "choose a new path," as Levinson would put it, and what he was prepared to do to modify the old one was of doubtful value, in my mind. For one thing, he did not care for my suggestion that he go into marital or family therapy since he was so dissatisfied with this aspect of his life. His response to this was that it was too early. He had to "unfreeze" himself first in the Gestalt group, and then he might feel capable of handling the marriage and family problems.

As far as his job was concerned, he felt that he could learn some good Gestalt techniques in the group he was joining which would be helpful in his job as well. He had been wanting for some time to use organizational development group methods with the staff under him in the Labor Department. He felt that the Gestalt approach might help him to make his work environment more lively and productive for his staff and himself.

I had some doubts that the Gestalt group he was joining could accomplish all these things, particularly in his personal life with his wife and family. It seemed like an attempt at a "quick fix." Yalom (1980) has observed that "psychotherapy with the affect-blocked (feeling blocked, like Ralph) patient is slow and grinding." However, because it seems so evident to everyone, including the patient, that if blockage holding back the affect could be "dynamited away" by dramatic affect-generating techniques all would be well. Unfortunately, some research has shown that when powerful encounter and Gestalt affect-arousing techniques have been used in intense group marathons, that although "many patients had intense emotional breakthroughs, these were not sustained: there were no discernible effects on the subsequent course of individual therapy" (Yalom 1980, 307).

Regardless of these research findings, there are aspects of Ralph Kane's functioning that suggest he would need some of the "slow and grinding" work to which Yalom referred. First, even though he talked a great deal about his feelings and he could use descriptive words like "suffocation," "tension," "anxiety," being "bottled up," and so on, he did not have a strong experiencing rating on the EXP Scale. He was consistently at the lower levels of the Scale, with ratings of two or three, instead of the fours, fives and sixes which indicate real experiential involvement and movement in psychotherapy and personality change. This is perhaps made more understandable in the light of the following:

> It is also important to point out that experiencing is not synonymous with expressiveness or emotionality, nor is it related to tone of feelings. The continuum deals with the manner in which feelings are experienced, not whether they are uncovered or expressed. Indeed, someone who is completely immersed in strong feelings of anxiety, guilt, or depression may be so involved *in* the feeling or its situational or behavioral details that he has no grasp of his experiencing of it (Klein et al. 1970, 7).

A rating of three on the EXP indicates that "feelings come into clear but limited perspective" in the sense that the person refers to feelings and owns them, but bypasses deeper ramifications concerning the self. To go beyond this would call for more internal communication and exploration of the meaning of certain feelings. It was at this level that Ralph was not in tune with his feelings and was feeling "stifled" and "suffocated." It was not simply a matter of expressing his feelings, or exchanging feelings with other persons in a Gestalt or encounter situation. It was a matter of exploring the feelings and gaining connection and insight into various aspects of himself in a more internal, ongoing process.

There was considerable evidence to show that he was not aware of or not experiencing certain aspects of himself. For example, in group sessions his behavior would often not be congruous with his beliefs about himself. Although he characterized himself in the semantic-differential test as "extremely fair" and "sensitive" in his relations with others, he often appeared rather judgmental toward others—especially if he felt they were not expressing or "owning-up" to their feelings in the group. Also, he felt his wife was "unfair" for not understanding or supporting him in his state of distress, without recognizing the negative impact his own testy and withholding behavior was having on her. Another aspect of his self he was not exploring was his anger. He was quite willing to express his anger in the group but not to expose its sources in himself. The extremely low evaluation but potent place of "hate" in his semantic-differential test (Figure 4-1) indicates this was not well understood or integrated by him. Thus, he was not coming to terms with the destruction/creation polarity Levinson (1978) identified as so stressful in midlife. The destructive end of the polarity has to do with the anger and hatred accumulated over the years by the middle-aged man who "may be utterly immobilized by the helpless rage he feels toward parents, wife, mentors, friends, and loved ones who, as he now sees it, have hurt him badly" (Levinson et al. 1978, 223). He was feeling the anger but was not really in touch with its sources, except for his older brother, Joe. Toward his parents there was probably a great deal of anger which he was not fully aware of, and which would be related to the demands he felt they made on him and what he felt they did not give him. The demands for responsibility, achievement, premature adult behavior, and the felt absence of a free and enjoyable childhood could well have left considerable anger and rage that needed to be worked through. This same legacy could have been displaced onto his own wife and children in later life as he experienced his responsibility toward them as an onerous continuation of his earlier life.

Erikson (1963) has noted that when adults do not achieve generativity, "the reasons are often to be found in early childhood impressions; in excessive self-love based on a too strenuously self-made personality." Indeed, Ralph Kane gave the impression of a "too strenuously self-made personality." He gave the impression of having been a careful, responsible, and even moralistic individual all his life. If this does not change, if enrichment through new forms of generativity does not take place, a "regression to an obsessive need for pseudo-intimacy takes place, often with a sense of stagnation and personal impoverishment" (Erikson 1963).

This did seem to be where Ralph Kane was when he went into Gestalt group therapy, which could have been indicative of his "obsessive need for pseudo-intimacy." However, it could only be hoped that he might gain enough insight and get in touch with the sources of his feelings as a result of the Gestalt experience so that he then might be prepared to undertake the "slow and grinding" work in psychotherapy which Yalom feels is necessary for his type of problem.

ISSUES OF GENERATIVITY AND IDENTITY IN A THIRTY-SIX-YEAR-OLD WOMAN

Linda Craft was a participant in the mid-life study I was conducting in several self-help organizations in 1981 and 1982. She was a member of a Parents Without Partners group, which she had joined a year earlier. At the time of her participation in my study she had been divorced for three months, although she had been separated from her former husband for approximately two years. She had a son who was ten years old, and a daughter who was seven years old.

Linda was a slim, vivacious woman who had a lithe, athletic appearance about her. She was, in fact, a tennis and ski enthusiast as well as a regular jogger. She was friendly but also tense and business-like in the first research interview with me, and it quickly became apparent that she wanted to discuss her current life situation. She readily gave the following background information on her marriage and the events leading up to her divorce.

She originally met her husband in the Albany, New York, area where she had come to study for her master's degree in education. He was a native of the Albany area, and he was in the same master's program as she. Her hometown was in western Pennsylvania where she had lived until she graduated from college. She knew she wanted to be a teacher from the time she was in high school, and her husband had also known early on that teaching was his career choice.

They seemed to have so much in common that they quickly formed a relationship and became engaged while still in their master's programs. Their plans were very clear. They would begin teaching as soon as they received their degrees—he in a high school, she in a grammar school. They would get married, save some money, and in about two years they would have their first child. They would have two children, and she would stay home with them until the youngest was ready for kindergarten, at which time she would go back to her teaching career.

It all seemed idyllic, and it appeared to be working out that way until two years ago when she discovered her husband had been heavily involved with another woman for about six months. Linda was thoroughly shaken by the discovery, and when she confronted him with it he first tried to deny it. When it was evident she knew beyond a doubt about the affair, he broke down and admitted it. He actually broke down sobbing, saying he was confused and conflicted and unable to know what to do. She said to me, "Can you believe it? He actually asked me to help him, because he was so confused!"

The other woman was single, in her late twenties and anxious to get married, so she was pushing him to get a divorce. Linda was appalled that he would even consider doing this, but here he was confused about whether he should or not. She said she had never been and hoped she would never again be so disillusioned in her life. Here the man she had loved, respected, and married turned out to be a "gutless wonder." She went on to say she had many occasions in their later contacts to see just how weak and passive he was and how wrong she had been about him.

At the time of the confrontation she had very little hesitation, after overcoming her initial shock, in telling him he would have to leave their home. She would not take him back until he broke off his relationship with the other woman, and even then she was not sure she would want him back. As it turned out, he left to take a furnished apartment but continued to see the other woman while continuing to visit Linda and the children. Before very long Linda decided that she wanted a divorce and began making plans for carrying it through.

Within that same crisis period she sought professional help while getting considerable support and understanding from her family, including both parents and her siblings. Here she was with all of her life plans, and even her identity as a wife and mother in an intact family, gone asunder. She first sought help from her parish priest, and he provided her with some counseling, after which he referred her to a Catholic family agency for ongoing counseling.

Turner (1980) has noted that this type of separation/divorce crisis calls for both identity and personal reorganization, and he describes the process as follows:

> Identity and personal reorganization are established as new life goals and priorities are developed. New values may be formed or modified from prior values. Weiss (1975) estimates that a personal recovery time may range from two to four years. Establishment of a clear pattern of life, less frequent mood swings, establishment of a new set of emotional and social support networks, as well as stable employment are all signs of personal reorganization and stability. In addition, some seek psychotherapy for help in clarifying identity issues and facilitating personal growth in a subjective jumble of old and new emotions (Turner 1980, 162).

Just about all of the above processes of reorganization had been undertaken by Linda in the course of two years of separation. For one thing, she immediately began questioning her prior values with respect to marriage and family. Her prior commitment to being a wife and mother first and foremost was the initial value to be challenged. Now that she was divorced, she had strong doubts about ever marrying again. It would be against her religion, and that was a definite consideration, but more than that was her desire to be an autonomous individual. That seemed to override everything else at this stage of her life.

She was committed to motherhood and her children, but she was feeling a strong compulsion to set out on an entirely new path by moving to a different part of the country and even beginning a new career. Since her divorce was finalized three months earlier, the desire to relocate and possibly change careers had become more urgent. There was a distinct opportunity for such a move at the present time, and she was sorely tempted but conflicted about taking it. She seemed poised for a major change in her life and was far from having established a clear pattern of life or even stable employment in terms of Turner's earlier description.

She had sought counseling early in the separation process, and she had moved on from that to join Parents Without Partners. From this grew a whole new support network, and she even progressed to becoming a support-group leader. She had taken workshops in communications and human relations skills and was getting a great deal of personal satisfaction out of her group leadership. One of her mentors in this regard was a psychologist, a divorced man, who was also a PWP group facilitator. She felt that he had taught her the most about interpersonal relationships, and the kinds of skills and sensitivity these relationships required. The two of them had developed an intimate relationship, and it was now quite intense and exclusive. However, she was far from feeling the need for more permanency in their relationship, although he was beginning to. So, even though she had established a new set of emotional and social supports, she was now at a point where she might have to give it all up.

Linda had been intrigued with some of the self-report instruments she had filled out as part of the research process, and she asked if I had any instruments that might help her in coming to some conclusions about herself, her relationships, and what she should do about relocating and developing a new career. She said she was not asking for full-scale counseling or psychotherapy, such as she had received at the family service agency after her separation, but she did feel she could use some brief help in sorting things out in her mind. The internal pressure she was feeling at this point was intense, and she felt she needed to get her "emotional bearings" in order to make some critical decisions in her life.

Given the nature of the mid-life study, involving interviewing and testing individuals in mutual support and self-help organizations, it was anticipated that some individuals would be in distress, perhaps in a crisis or near crisis state that might require brief intervention and/or referral. It was possible that the research process itself might bring certain unresolved conflicts and problems to light. Therefore, it seemed quite appropriate that I should respect such a request and assess the nature of the problem and the need for either brief or more extended professional intervention. The valuable information provided by the participants in the study also argued for the provision of some service by me in return. Therefore, I did see Linda in four subsequent sessions for the purposes of assesssment and brief help with her decision-making problem.

Some of the instruments completed by Linda in the study provided some useful information for assessment purposes. For one thing, she showed a very strong internal locus of control—she really believed that she could achieve what she wanted by way of effort and self-improvement. The results of the Intolerance of Ambiguity Test were more mixed. On the one hand, she was apparently quite tolerant of diversity in culture and ideals, but she showed intolerance of ambiguity through a high degree of "phenomenological denial" on one component of the Test. What this means is that she had a definite tendency to deny the complexity involved in many aspects of human activities and relations. She was the sort of person who believes there is a right way and a wrong way to do things. She strongly disagreed with the statement, "Many of our most important decisions are based upon insufficient information." There could have been good reason for strong denial on her part in response to this, given the critical nature of the decisions she had to make at this point in her life. However, she was a person who generally tended to believe that there is no such thing as a problem that cannot be solved, and solved correctly.

Most of the results on the values part of the research instrument she filled out were consistent with her strong internal locus of control. For example, on the existential values part (Yalom 1980), she responded "strongly agree" to the following statement: "No matter how much or how little support or guidance people get from others, they must take ultimate responsibility for the way they live their lives." There was, however, one response by her in that part of the instrument that ran counter to this general stance on her part. It was her "strongly disagree" response to the statement: "I have to recognize that no matter how close I get to other people, I must still face life alone." In fact, she added the following written comment on that response: "I find the closer I get to people that I'm not alone in times of crisis or trouble, as well as good times." This response turned out to have a great deal of significance for her as she went through this particular transitional stage in her life.

Whether she was going through an actual mid-life crisis at this stage is open to question. She was indeed stressed and in a state of disequilibrium, which at least meets that part of the definition of a crisis. Despite the stress, however, she seemed to look at the situation as a challenge. This, of course, was a good indicator of her potential capacity to overcome the crisis situation. Her internal locus of control was also a good indicator (Rabkin 1977).

Nevertheless, she was quite anxious as a result of the situation. She was given the State-Trait Anxiety Inventory in the first of our assessment sessions, and the results showed that she was in a state of high anxiety relative to the norms of the Inventory. There was a sharp discrepancy between the state score and trait anxiety scores in her inventory. She was experiencing far more anxiety than she usually did. Some of the reasons for this came out in our discussion of the results of her semantic- differential test, which she filled out between our first and second assessment sessions. These results are displayed in Figure 4-2.

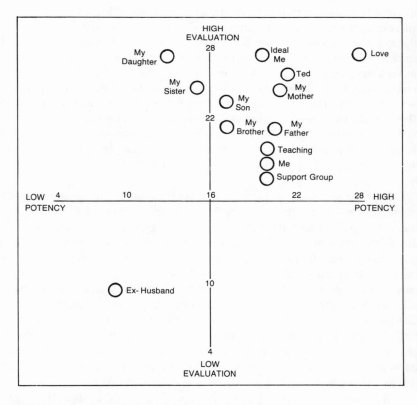

FIGURE 4-2. Linda Craft's Semantic-Differential Graph

It can be seen that Linda had a good self-concept. She had a relatively high self-evaluation and was on the strong or potent side rather than the weak side of the potency axis. She did have a highly idealized self on the evaluative axis, but her basically good self-concept prevented her from having a very low self-esteem because there was not a large discrepancy between the ideal and the self-concept.

Another positive aspect of the test results was the high evaluation of all her close relatives: daughter, son, sister, brother, mother and father. Ironically, the positive closeness she felt toward all of them was in part responsible for her current dilemma and stress. This was because of the geographic separation of her family. Her married sister was living in Tampa, Florida, with her family, and now her brother had taken a job there where he was a pilot for a national airline. In addition, Linda's parents had moved down to an area of Florida which was only about eighty miles from Tampa. She was being urged by all of them to move down there, and added to this were some good job opportunities for her there that her sister had told her about—opportunities for a new and challenging career.

Opposed to this was her son, Denny. He definitely did not want to leave the Albany area. She said he was "strong willed" like she, and this is attested to by Denny's location in Figure 4 on the potency axis and as compared to his sister. Linda agreed that her daughter, Janice, was quite compliant and easy to get along with. Janice would not resist the idea of moving and would go along with whatever her mother said. However, Linda was worried about her relationship with her son. They seemed to be having more and more arguments lately, and she felt he would very much resent any effort on her part to move them to Florida.

She felt her ex-husband, Stan, was adding a great deal to this difficulty with Denny. He was "Mister Good Guy" to Denny. He would take him out to fast food places, feed him "junk," take him to ballgames—all the good things from Denny's perspective. However, Stan was not very responsible or helpful in the pinch when she needed him to take care of the kids because of some unusual pressures or outside commitments on her part. It was clear that she was still quite resentful and now disdainful of him. This is evident in Figure 4-2 in which Stan is evaluated quite low ("quite bad" and "quite worthless") as well as weak ("extremely weak" and "extremely soft"). She also described him as "extremely passive," and she wondered how she could ever have seen him as strong or decisive. She had found out that she was by far the stronger and more decisive of the two, but this perception had not been clear to her because of her prior beliefs and values concerning marriage and the relationships between husband and wife.

She said that one of the reasons she wanted to move had to do with Stan and her former marriage. He was from Albany and that area reminded her of him and that part of her life. She said she wanted to leave and "wipe the slate clean." She was sure he would not resist her leaving and taking the children with her, because of his "extremely passive" attitude, which extended to his children.

Among the reasons for not leaving Albany was her carefully developed support network. The strong positive valence of the PWP support group in her life space can be seen in Figure 4-2. So, too, can her current male friend and lover, Ted. She said he was a far cry from her ex-husband, Stan. He was "extremely valuable," "extremely good," "extremely strong," "extremely fair," and "extremely active." Indeed, her responses to him on the semantic-differential test put him closer than any other person (including herself) to her idealized self. Given this high evaluation of Ted and the extremely high and powerful evaluation of "love" in the test results, I asked if she loved him. She hesitated and struggled with the question and then said she thought she loved him "as a person," but she had grave doubts that she loved him "as a husband." She felt now that she could never go back to that kind of relationship, regardless of how good Ted was at intimate human relationships.

She said she could not bring herself to commit herself to him even though he seemed to want such a commitment, which he was prepared to give to her. This she also felt was pushing her somewhat toward the move to Florida, because she did not feel ready to make such a commitment. She added that there were some differences in lifestyle, as well. She was well organized, business-like, prompt, and so on, whereas he tended to be somewhat disorganized and quite casual in almost all respects. She admitted that this irritated her from time to time and led to some testy exchanges between them.

At the end of the second assessment session Linda was asked to go through the "Balance Sheet Procedure" used in decision counseling (Janis 1982; Janis & Mann 1977). This required that she go home and carefully develop a list of utilitarian gains and losses for herself and significant others as well as possible elements of self-approval and self-disapproval and elements of approval and disapproval from significant others in making a decision to move to Florida. She was asked to do the same thing for making a decision to remain in the Albany area. This procedure also involves having the person think out possible negative scenarios in which it is recognized that for every set of risks in making a change there is also a set of risks in not making a change.

This last aspect of the procedure seemed to make a great impression on her because when she came to the third session she was "absolutely convinced" that there were too many risks in not making a change. She felt that she would regret it the rest of her life if she did not make a move now.

Furthermore, she generated many more positive reasons on her "balance sheet" for moving to Florida than she could for remaining in Albany.

She was not only convinced that she should move to Tampa but that she should also change her career. She said her sister had told her of opportunities in personnel work with a number of businesses in the Tampa area. Linda felt that her interests and increased knowledge and skills in human relations and communication would equip her well for personnel work. Further, she thought that her own personal characteristics of ambitiousness, being well organized and business-like, would stand her in good stead in the corporate world. She found school systems too bureaucratic and unresponsive to new ideas and initiatives to her liking. For this reason she was sure she would find the business world more exciting and challenging.

Her enthusiasm helped her decide that she was sure she would make the move to Florida. She would regret it too much if she did not. She was going to contact her sister about making a trip to Tampa with the children during the next school vacation period so that they could look over possible places to live as well as employment opportunities for her.

It would be helpful at this point to look at the meaning of all this from the perspective of Linda's individual life structure at this particular stage of her life. Levinson (1978) says that the "second adult life structure" takes shape between the ages of thirty-three to forty. This is called the "Settling Down" period in his developmental paradigm, and it represents the culmination of early adulthood. It follows the "Age Thirty Transition" which extends roughly from twenty-eight to thirty- three when the individual has the opportunity to work on the flaws and limitations of the first adult life structure and to create a foundation for a more satisfactory structure. Thus, the Settling Down period is a structure-building one when the person makes key choices, forms a structure around them, and pursues goals and values within that structure.

Linda had clearly been engaged in structure changing in her Age Thirty Transition, with the breakup of her marriage and her ensuing activities. In one sense, the establishment and cultivation of her new support network represented the beginning of her Settling Down period. However, here she was intensely involved at age thirty-six in making key choices that would pull her away from that network and the new love relationship she had found with Ted. This appears to be somewhat at odds with the idea of settling down.

Levinson's paradigm was developed out of research on men, but he was convinced that the same developmental periods applied to women as well. He claimed that a successful outcome of the Settling Down period was by no means assured, and he made an observation about some men in this period that applies equally well to Linda: "He may have a sense of being held back— of being oppressed by others and restrained by his own conflicts and inhibitions" (Levinson et al. 1978, 145). There was indeed a quality to Linda's description of her current dilemma which indicated her sense of being held back by others and by her own inhibitions. She felt that she was being held back by Ted and by her son, Denny, who was being influenced by his father's "irresponsible and indulgent" behavior toward him.

There was also a kind of driven quality to Linda's description of the new world that would open up to her in Tampa. There was too much "hype" to it, as though she was trying to convince herself. Perhaps this was her way of attempting to overcome her own inhibitions and conflicts.

These were some of my concerns about her when I had the good fortune of being able to consult with Daniel Levinson about some of the case material at this particular point in my mid-life study. He observed that Linda's rushing off into a new career as well as a new location seemed to reflect what he sees as a greater impatience in women during the Age Thirty Transition and the Settling Down period. Dr. Levinson and his colleagues had just completed the field survey part of research on women that replicated his earlier study of men, and they were preparing for a comprehensive analysis of the data. On the basis of this he felt sure that his paradigm of developmental periods did fit women as well as men, but there were certain differences of salience and intensity within the periods between men and women.

His impression was that women might feel more oppressed and held back by husbands and other significant others in their lives because of the common early life experience of girls of being held back from aggressive participation in the outside, nonfamily world by their parents, particularly their mothers. Therefore, when they do come to realize their own achievement potential as compared to men during the Age Thirty Transition and the Settling Down period, there is apt to be a built up sense and legacy of oppression that is displaced from the past and added to the real constraints of the present. This creates a greater sense of urgency and oppression among women in the transition from the first adult life structure to the second. Dr. Levinson's observations tended to validate some of my concerns about the possible precipitous nature of Linda's recent choice.

When I met with her for the fourth and final session, I attempted to identify some of the potentially stressful consequences of her choice by taking a look at the stress quotients attached to various kinds of changes according to the Holmes and Rahe (1967) Social Readjustment Scale. Although it was not my view that the Scale could be used in a simple cumulative way to predict probable breakdown, it could at least give a crude idea of the possible additive impact of stressful changes. Among those that had to be considered in terms of Linda's choice were the following, in descending order of impact or stress quotients: business readjustment, change to a different line of work, change in residence, change in living conditions, change in schools, and change in social activities, as well as a possible change in financial state, depending on her job situation in the new location.

Linda gave these matters some thought, but she remained convinced about the rightness of her decision to move to Tampa. After more exploration and discussion of the various options, Linda said she might reconsider the idea of starting a new career at this time. She could check out teaching opportunities in the Tampa area, which she felt should be quite numerous. However, she was convinced she wanted to begin making plans for the move to Tampa, and she was not interested in any further exploration or counseling around these issues. She was very appreciative of the sessions we had together, because she felt they enabled her to come to a clear decision.

This might have been the end of this case study if it had not been for an unexpected meeting she and I had about a year after that last session. She had attended a workshop and panel in which I was a participant and came up to talk to me afterward. We were able to find a place where we could talk in privacy for a lengthy period of time. She explained that she was still living and working in the Albany area as the result of a number of things that began happening shortly after our last session. First, her sister and her family moved back to the Northeast because of a change in her husband's job, and she was now only a three hour drive away from Linda. Shortly after that, Linda's brother was transferred to the west coast by his airline, and although her parents would remain in Florida, they would be making more trips up north to visit their daughters because of their proximity to one another.

She said that these events drastically altered her attitude about relocating. For one thing, she had not realized how important moving to her family in Florida had been to her in the formulation of her plans. It would have been a homecoming, but she did not recognize this in her urgency to get away from Albany and all the things it represented. She also came to realize she was running away from her relationship with Ted, which was too threatening in its implications for her. She had to admit that he meant a great deal to her. She said he had a number of qualities that she wished she had herself and was trying to develop—a kind of tolerance and openness to others and new ways of looking at things. She said she knew she was too judgmental and rigid in many of her attitudes, like her parents, and she would like to be more like him. She was still somewhat bothered by his casual and somewhat disorganized approach to the details of daily living. However, she realized that in part this was due to some of her own rigid attitudes.

She was still very, very cautious about the possibility of overestimating or idealizing him and to the possibility of the kind of disillusionment she ran into with her husband. There was also the issue of her Catholicism and restrictions on divorce and remarriage. However, she was sure she loved Ted and that this was a much more mature kind of love than she had ever had with her ex-husband. She said this was unlike her, because she was usually a very planful person, yet here she was willing to let her relationship with Ted go wherever it would. This was something she had never experienced in her life before, being willing to let go and follow her feelings rather than mentally and planfully trying to control things.

She was more content in her work, as well. She continued to teach in the same school but she had become active in the teachers union, which provided an outlet for her organizational abilities and interests. She was also more active in faculty meetings and school affairs, working toward changes she felt were necessary. She also continued her work as a group facilitator at Parents Without Partners and continued to get much satisfaction from it.

Toward the end of this meeting Linda said that she had often thought about contacting me after her plans to move had gone awry. At first she did not because she felt a "little guilty or ashamed that I didn't go through with all my brave plans." Later, she continued to hesitate because she remembered that I was concerned she might be acting too precipitously. Finally, she came to realize that she had a number of things to resolve here in Albany, especially her relationship with Ted, and that she really did not want to leave the good and strong networks of friends and supports she had built in the area.

Given this additional bit of life history it is now possible to take a further look at Linda's life structure in her Settling Down period. In several respects the affiliative (family, lover, friends) component of her life structure had begun to settle. She did not have to move in order to be closer to her family of origin. In effect, that choice had been taken away from her, for her sister was now closer to her and that insured that she would be seeing more of her parents than she had since their retirement.

She had been concerned about her relationship with her son in the event of a move to Florida. Fortunately, that problem was avoided, and her son was delighted that he could stay in the area of his birth and continue in the same school with his many friends. Also, she was able to keep her same circle of friends and associates at her school, while continuing her valued friendships and activities in Parents Without Partners.

All of this seems to lend considerable substance to Gilligan's (1982) contention that relationships and caring are primary in the evaluative dimension of women's lives. Although Levinson might be correct in stating that more than men, women tend to feel held back in their middle years by significant others, this could be attributed to the greater sense of responsibility for and weight given to relationships by women in their lives. At any rate, even though the final form of Linda's relationship with Ted was not yet evident, what did seem clear was that it was with Ted that the love dimension of her life structure would have to be worked out.

As far as the work/career component of her life structure was concerned, a number of things had begun to solidify. She dropped the idea of going into personnel work and decided that she would stay with teaching. She had entertained that idea even though she still loved teaching because teaching had become associated in her mind with her ex-husband and their former life plans for mutual careers as teachers. Since she was trying to jettison as much as possible of her past life with her husband, teaching almost became a casualty of that process. That could have been a serious loss, for teaching was a potent and highly valued aspect of her life space (see Figure 4-2).

Teaching was also important for the issues of generativity at this stage of her life. In addition to raising her own children she felt she obtained an additional sense of meaning and purpose in her life from her work with her students. Not only was she educating them, but she felt they were still in a formative stage and that she might be providing a role model for some of them.

Linda's case was presented to illustrate the issue of identity as well as generativity. In this regard, it is important to note that her drive for individuation was a powerful and compelling force in the background. After her disillusionment with her husband and marriage she not only wanted to carve out an identity independent of the role of wife, she also wanted to become as autonomous a person as possible. This desire to become independent and to shed her former marital identity was so strong that she was prepared to make some drastic changes in her life—including her teaching career and forfeiting a new love relationship. Fortunately, this did not come to pass.

It is doubtful that the relationship with Ted represents any diversion from her development in the direction of greater individuation. The only commitment he wanted from her was that of an exclusive relationship in which neither of them would become involved in other relationships for as long as theirs lasted. He was not proposing marriage, but she had bridled against anything resembling a conjugal relationship when she was so urgently trying to throw off her old identity as wife. Therefore, she would experience a great deal more autonomy in her relationship with Ted than she had with her ex-husband and there would be more room for further individuation and differentiation, but this differentiation would not be at the expense of integration (Kegan 1982) in her life.

AN IDENTITY CRISIS IN A FIFTY-FOUR-YEAR-OLD MAN

Stephen Gornecky became a participant in my mid-life study as a result of his association with an organization called "Sharing-and-Caring," which is a mutual support group of former heart patients and is affiliated with the

American Heart Association. When I first met him he made a strong, positive impression on me. He was of medium height but husky and powerfully built, with light brown hair, grey-blue eyes, and strong facial features. Although he gave the appearance of physical prowess and presence, it seemed contained, natural, and reassuring rather than bristling or threatening. The tone and content of his speech also gave the impression of an integrated and mellow strength, if not contentment. As I found out, this attitude and aura of quiet strength was something that did not come about until after he was well recuperated from a massive heart attack that he had suffered two and a half years earlier.

Steve had been recommended to me as one of the most admired and successful "graduates" of the local Sharing-and-Caring support group. Although he was not a current member of the support group, I selected him for inclusion in the study because of the fact that he had gone through a dramatic and clear cut identity crisis in mid-life as a result of his near fatal heart attack. Furthermore, he had weathered the crisis, not without difficulty, but successfully and at a much higher level of psychosocial functioning than before the heart attack. I felt there was something to be learned from him and his experience.

Steve was interviewed and tested like other members of the study, although his experience of a mid-life crisis was not as recent as most of the other participants. This meant that his responses to the self-report instruments were based on his current, post-crisis functioning. What we did was to engage in a mutual exploration—and conceptual encounter—of what his frame of mind and responses to the instruments would have been prior to, during, and immediately after his crisis. It therefore represented something of a retrospective re-experiencing of the crisis and its aftermath.

At this point, it would be best to give background information about Steve and the events leading up to and following the crisis, so that the reader can relate to the comparative analysis of differences in Steve's responses to the research instruments and questions based on this retrospective approach.

Steve was of Polish-American extraction, the oldest of eight children from a blue collar family in a Northeastern industrial city. Although working class, his family was industrious and achievement oriented. He, his parents, and the older siblings were proud of the fact that they were able to send the two youngest children in the family through college, and the youngest through law school, as well.

Steve left school before finishing high school and went to work at a large airplane factory in his home city. There he was found to be a quick learner and he soon became a toolmaker apprentice. He continued working there until he was drafted into the Army at age twenty-two in 1950 during the Korean War. Although he saw some heavy ground action as a member of the infantry, he came out of the war unscathed. He got married at age twenty-four, while home on leave from the Army, to a young woman he had met and dated before his induction into the Army. He was discharged from the service shortly after the armistice was signed in July of 1953, and three months later his first child, a son, was born. His other child, a daughter, was born three years later. Both children completed college, got married, and were raising their own families in neighboring Eastern cities at the time I first interviewed him.

Steve returned to the aircraft plant after his discharge and did very well. He became a toolmaker, obtained a high school equivalency certificate, and went on to take certain technical and managerial courses at the university in his city, with the encouragement of his superiors at the plant. He moved up to foreman, assistant general foreman, and then general foreman of his section of the plant. His abilities came to the attention of a man who had dealings with Steve in the course of obtaining subcontracts from Steve's plant for a toolmaking firm in which this man was Vice President and General Manager. He, Walter, persuaded Steve to take the position of plant manager in his firm at a substantial raise in pay and full payment for Steve's move to a city which was about three hundred miles from Steve's hometown.

Since Steve's children were grown and living away from home, he and his wife had no great hesitation about his taking the job and the opportunity it seemed to represent. Actually, they would be living somewhat closer to their son as a result of the move and still only a few hours drive from their daughter. However, the new job, which he took in 1979, turned out to be a nightmare. Steve soon found that the firm's plant was seriously understaffed, particularly in skilled toolmakers, for the amount of subcontracting it had been doing with larger firms. The machinery was also beginning to break down as a result of the heavy volume of production and the use of double shifts.

This all necessitated Steve putting in long hours, often ten to twelve hours a day, in order to correct mistakes, deal with breakdowns, and instruct the inadequately trained and relatively inexperienced workers. He was working himself into a state of exhaustion while pleading for more staff and better equipment, but to no avail. To add insult to injury he found that Walter had been taking credit for the high rate of productivity that was being maintained under the trying circumstances. In the midst of all this, just shy of a year after taking the job, Steve suffered a massive heart attack.

He almost died, and his life was hanging in the balance for eight days in the hospital intensive care unit. He was not aware of being conscious during those eight days, but when he awoke one day he saw a person hovering over and peering at him through his oxygen tent. He then realized it was a priest saying prayers over him. He claimed he almost died of fright at that moment, thinking the priest was giving him the last rites of the Church. Actually, the priest was on duty at the hospital and was checking routinely on all patients when Steve's very distressed wife requested that he say a few prayers for her husband. However, Steve became enraged by the fright he received and he began to yell and curse at the priest for "sneaking up" on him in that way. It took his wife and several nurses, as well as a sedative, to calm him down after the startled priest left.

Later in our research interviews, Steve identified the fact that the only time in the course of his crisis experience he was acutely aware of the possibility of his death was at that frightening moment with the priest. After that he was only conscious of being enraged—first at the priest, then at his wife for having asked the priest to pray for him, and then "at the whole world." He said he was in a steady state of rage for days, weeks, and months after that, with an interval period of depression.

He said that he was aware, even before his doctor told him, that he would never again be able to take a responsible managerial job without endangering his life. This realization threw him into a depression, for he felt that all his life's dreams and work had been shattered. He had worked so hard to advance to the point he had achieved without much formal education. Now he felt that all sense of who he was and who he had become was gone. He was acutely aware of the "ache" of the gap between what he had achieved and what he was now—"a nobody, a nothing."

The more he thought about this the more his anger began to focus on Walter and the toolmaking company. They had exploited him, used him, had not given him what he needed to do the job, and they had broken him. They had not even come to see him at the hospital after his attack. Actually, he had been angry at them before his heart attack, and his wife, fearful about his possible reactions, had wisely advised Walter and the president of the company not to visit. At any rate, Steve's anger became more and more focused on Walter, who had enticed him to take the job, to move himself and his wife, who had exploited him, and who then took the credit for the fruits of that exploitation. He said that if Walter had crossed the street in front of his car at that stage in his life, he would gladly have "run over that son-of-a bitch until he was dead."

There was, of course, substantial reason for Steve's feeling the way he did toward Walter and the company. He actually had a good case for claiming his heart attack was job related, as attested to by both his physician and his lawyer. Consequently, he began proceedings to obtain compensation benefits for his heart attack and condition. However, as he described it, he continued "to stew" about his life situation and the litigation concerning his compensation claim.

In the course of all this, he had a bitter fight with his youngest brother, who just happened to be a compensation lawyer for a large insurance company that handled industrial compensation claims. At first his brother was concerned and sensitive to him as a result of the attack he had suffered, but as Steve continued to rail against his employer and the resistance to his compensation claims the brother became defensive, then ideological, and finally aggressive toward Steve. He even went so far as to call Steve "paranoid" because of his attitude and behavior. The bitterness that ensued between them spread to other members of his family, with a number of his brothers and sisters siding with the younger brother in his claim that Steve was irrational and overreacting. Of course, Steve did not see his reactions as irrational at the time, and he deeply resented the failure of his relatives to see his point of view and to support him under the circumstances.

Steve's wife was becoming very concerned about his virtual isolation at this point and about his "stewing in his own juices" in such an anti-social way. She was the one who found out about Sharing-and-Caring and urged him to attend. He was very resistant to the idea at first, and he attended only because of her. She had been supportive of him throughout all of the travail, and validated his feeling of outrage at Walter and the company. Since she was literally begging him to at least try the group, he could not bring himself to refuse her. He planned to attend just a few sessions as a kind of token to her.

To his surprise, he found the group that was made up predominantly of men, to be understanding and supportive of him in his attitude toward his former employer, his compensation claim, and above all, his anger and rage. A number of them had experienced intense rage in the wake of their heart attacks, and they could connect directly with his feelings. He was not only able to ventilate his feelings, he was understood. In fact, his group came to seem more like a supportive family to him than his own brothers and sisters.

Some of the group members talked about their near death experiences in association with their heart attacks and how this affected them with respect to their attitudes toward their work, their families, and their lives. These discussions got Steve to thinking about his own near-death experience. He became aware that he had not really thought about how close he had come to death since the episode with the priest. All of his concern about the position he had attained, his status in life, and so on, had paled in the light of the reality of death. This attitude was something he also noticed in one or two others in the group. He did not want to die; he did not want to leave his wife and children; and he wanted to enjoy the life he had left. This was not out of a desperate feeling of limited time left, but out of a realization of how much of the pressure to achieve in work and career is self-imposed. He slowly came to recognize that he now had the opportunity to get off the treadmill, to slow down, and to savor life.

This emerging change in attitude and perspective was aided by the fact that his compensation claim was ajudicated about six months after his attack, and he was awarded a substantial backpayment as well as ongoing compensation. He felt vindicated, and this helped him to turn toward other matters. He began engaging in repair and remodeling activities around his house, enjoying getting back to the pleasures of skilled manual work after all the mental pressure he had experienced in his managerial role.

Steve went back to work as a toolmaker in a large local industrial firm just about one year after his heart attack. He was soon back "in the groove" in terms of his toolmaking skills, and his aptitudes were again noticed by his superiors. Before long they were asking him to take on a foremanship, which he firmly declined. However, he received a great deal of satisfaction from helping and instructing his coworkers, particularly the younger apprentice toolmakers. In addition, he was winning prizes of as much as three hundred and fifty dollars for ideas he put in plant suggestion boxes for improving operations in certain aspects of the plant's functioning. This gave him a sense of accomplishment similar to his prior managerial initiatives, but without the lethal burdens and responsibilities of such a role. Consequently, two and a half years after his heart attack, he could say to me that he truly felt much better about himself and his life than he did before the attack.

A number of his test results reflected this change in perceptual attitude. His locus of control was basically internal at the time he was tested. However, he was sure his responses before his attack would have been entirely internal. He really believed that he and he alone was responsible for all the things that he achieved in life, particularly in his work. Thus, on one item in the test he would have agreed with the statement, "There is really no such thing as luck."

On the other hand, immediately after his heart attack, he would have agreed with the alternative to the above statement: "Most people don't realize the extent to which their lives are controlled by accidental happenings." Thus, his locus of control had become more external as a result of his heart attack, and that of course is understandable. Although he returned to a more internal locus of control, it was not so pervasively internal. This would be reflected in his rejection of the statement, "Most misfortunes are the result of lack of ability, ignorance, laziness, or all three," in favor of its alternative, "In the long run the bad things that happen to us are balanced by the good ones." Although he did not agree entirely with this statement, it was more acceptable to him than the other.

His Intolerance of Ambiguity Test, too, would have been quite different in its results before his attack than after it. He used to believe strongly in the following kinds of test items: "An expert who does not come up with a definite answer probably doesn't know too much;" and "A good job is one where what is to be done and how it is to be done are always clear." His later tolerance and mellowness was reflected in his more moderate and doubtful attitude toward those items.

This more accepting and open attitude toward life was also reflected in his "agree" response to the statement, "I find that I am not much bothered by the fact that there are now many things in my life over which I have no control;" and his "strongly disagree" response to the statement, "I feel very bad when there are things I want to have or want to change and I am unable to do so." Before his heart attack his responses would have been "strongly disagree" and "strongly agree," respectively, to the above statements.

In the values area, his ranking of Rokeach's (1973) terminal values at the time of my study were quite different than they would have been before his attack. At the time of the study the top three were ranked as follows: Happiness (contentedness), Wisdom (a mature understanding of life), and Family Security (taking care of loved ones). Before his attack they would have been: Social Recognition (respect, admiration), A Sense of Accomplishment (lasting contribution), and An Exciting Life (a stimulating, active life).

House (1974) has reviewed the relationship of coronary disease to occupational stress and from this developed a model of social stress that fits a number of the features in Steve Gornecky's mid-life crisis. Central to the model is the idea that the perceived importance of the event (in this case a heart attack) and the amount of behavioral disruption generated by it will be important components of the *meaning* of the event as experienced by the individual. As Tamir (1982) has observed, "perhaps no other role is more integral to the identity of the male than the work role." This was certainly true of Steve at the time of his heart attack. According to House's model, the meaning of the heart attack for him was that it threatened his very identity and precipitated a crisis of identity. There was no longer a "match," as Erikson (1963) would put it, between Steve's former sense of continuity and maintenance of self and his primary social (occupational) role.

Steve was able to make the changes in his assumptive world to meet the drastic changes in his life space. Parkes (1971) has identified this as necessary for persons experiencing the kind of psychosocial transition that Steve did. Steve's changes in psychosocial functioning were also consistent with Parkes's contention that traumatic situations such as Steve's attack can actually be turning points for better psychosocial adjustment.

In addition to his handling of the identity crisis, Steve Gornecky also showed a clear shift in the direction of generativity. Troll (1975) gives the following indicators of successful resolution of the generativity versus stagnation issue: "to have plans for future that require sustained applications and utilization of skills and abilities; to invest energy and ideas into something new; and to have a sense of continuity with future generations. Steve showed evidence of all these indicators. He was, of course, continuing to use his skills and abilities as a toolmaker. He was investing his energy and ideas into something new with his creative suggestions for improving plant operations, and he did have a sense of continuity with future generations as a mentor to his younger coworkers.

Overall, Steve accomplished a great deal and overcame what Gould (1978) identified as the "disillusionment with work as a magical protection against death." In Gould's words, he reached the point at which "the life of inner-directedness finally prevails."

Psychologist Robert Peck (1968) has proposed that a closer look at the second half of life according to Erikson's psychosocial developmental scheme would suggest that there is a Middle Age period in which there are more distinct substages and tasks than Erikson had so far delineated. They are: Valuing Wisdom vs. Valuing Physical Powers, Socializing vs. Sexualizing in Human Relationships, and Cathectic Flexibility vs. Cathectic Impoverishment. The first and third of these are of particular relevance to the cases covered in this chapter.

The first is most pertinent for Steve Gornecky. His physical powers were dramatically assaulted and diminished by his heart attack, so that he was no longer able to engage in the kind of career he had felt was so meaningful and essential for his identity. However, he was able to achieve the task required to overcome this crisis and did come to value wisdom more highly than his physical powers, as evidenced by his responses on the Rokeach values instrument.

The issue of cathective flexibility versus cathectic impoverishment applies to all three cases of the chapter. "The phenomenon for which this label is intended might equally well be described as 'emotional flexibility': the capacity to shift emotional investments from one person to another, and from one activity to another" (Peck 1968, 89). Steve Gornecky was able to shift his emotional investments back to the activity of toolmaking and away from management. Linda Craft was able to shift her emotional investments from her marriage and former husband to new friends and support persons in Parents Without Partners, especially Ted. Although she was initially wary about her emotional investment in him, she finally was able to allow herself to become more emotionally involved with him. If there was any one of the three persons who demonstrated cathectic impoverishment, it was Ralph Kane. He did not seem to have enough cathectic flexibility to break through his sense of stagnation and cathectic impoverishment.

Chapter 5

CRISES OF ATTACHMENT AND SEPARATION

Separation-individuation becomes a particularly important mid-life issue for women because of the separations that have to be managed. This observation was made by psychiatrist Malka Notman (1980), whose primary clinical and academic interest is women in mid-life. She is careful to distinguish between separation and loss in making her observation. This is an important distinction. Mid-life phenomena such as the empty nest represent separation rather than loss experiences, and management of separation is a different matter than coping with loss. Given that distinction, she goes on to say that women are particularly vulnerable to separation "since they define themselves strongly and consistently in terms of their relationships with others and seem sensitive to and dependent on the opinions of others" (Notman 1980, 89). She is in agreement with Gilligan and Rubin that women's lives tend to be characterized by greater involvement in personal relationships from the beginning, and she adds that girls will tend to have more problems with separation and individuation than boys, who are more apt to have difficulties with intimacy and attachment. This suggests that men will have greater difficulty with issues of attachment and intimacy when they reach mid-life.

Levinson and his colleagues (1978) identify the issue of "attachment/separateness" as one of the key polarities in the mid-life development of men. Levinson is careful to distinguish "separateness" from separation, isolation, or aloneness. A person is separate when he or she is primarily involved in the inner world, in "constructing and exploring an imagined world" rather than adapting to the "real" world outside. Therefore, separateness fosters individual growth and creative adaptation, although it can be carried to a harmful extreme as in schizoid behavior or even schizophrenic states.

Attachment, on the other hand, "is to be engaged, involved, needy, plugged in, seeking, rooted" (Levinson et al. 1978, 239). Actually, this description is more in line with what has been identified as attachment *behavior* in contrast to attachment per se (Ainsworth, Blehar, Waters, and Wall 1978). Attachment behavior includes all the action systems and strategies used for maintaining contact with the attachment figure, whereas attachment is the "representation model" of the attachment relationship plus the affective bond that the person establishes with his or her attachment figure. This author favors the definition of attachment given by Guidano and Liotti (1983) as "a cognitive structure that is constructed during the course of development, starting from inborn dispositions shaped by experiential data and directing the child's search for physical proximity and affective contact." They note that even infants are able to form representational models of their attachment figures, of themselves, and of the surrounding environment, in a developmental process through which the models become more articulated and complex as one moves into adulthood.

This definition is very compatible with concepts such as "constructive-developmental," "assumptive world," "perceptual attitudes," and others that were identified in the structural approach of this book. Such a definition allows for the complex and interrelated meanings that are inherent in any attachment situation. The applicability of this definition of attachment should become evident in the cases of John Raymond and Gary Robertson, which will be described in this chapter. The applicability of Notman's observations about the problems of separation-individuation in the lives of middle-aged women should also become evident in the case of Joyce Kurland.

AN ATTACHMENT CRISIS IN A THIRTY-SEVEN YEAR-OLD MAN

This clinical case represents a crisis where the fragile life structure of a man in his late thirties was threatened by his wife's demand for a separation. He experienced this as a threat to his "whole world," and in describing the experience he used words that were very congruent with Parkes's (1971) delineation of breakdown in an adult's assumptive world. Since the meaning of this development was so threatening to this man and his assumptive world, he responded with a great deal of anxiety as well as a depressive reaction which grew as the inexorable reality of his situation became more apparent to him. As will be seen, he initially struggled intensely to remain attached to his wife and to the precarious life structure to which he had been so committed. The structures of meaning within this total experience became evident in the initial interviews and from his responses on the cognitive assessment instruments.

John Raymond was close to thirty-eight years old when he was referred to me by a colleague in the same center for psychotherapy. That therapist had been seeing John's wife, Christine, on an individual basis for about two months prior to this referral. She had also seen John and Christine jointly just prior to the referral to determine whether it would be possible for them to salvage their marriage. On the basis of the joint session and her prior work with Christine, she felt it was highly unlikely that the marriage could be salvaged, largely because of Christine's strong insistence upon separation and her long-standing emotional problems. The therapist felt that John was in great distress and in need of help to cope with the current situation and to come to terms with the likely separation.

She provided the following background information on the situation and on Christine prior to my initial contact with John. The situation began with a recent affair Christine had with a man she had met in the U.S. Army Reserve. She had become very active in the Reserve within the past six months. The affair came to John's attention when he had seen Christine in a parked car with the man near the Army Reserve Station, and after answering a number of telephone calls for Christine from a man who would not identify himself. John confronted Christine with his suspicions, and she admitted to the affair. She went on to say that it was just as well that he knew the truth because she was convinced the marriage would not last. She said she wanted a separation now and would probably want to begin divorce proceedings before very long. She told him she did not want to hurt him because she still cared for him, but she did not "love him like a man and a husband." He was good to her and to the two children, but she was feeling "stifled and bored" in their marriage. She said she needed to "realize" herself and to become her "own person."

The therapist said that Christine had identified herself as something of a feminist, as a woman who had become aware of how much she was feeling oppressed in her marital and domestic roles. That was one reason she had become actively engaged in the Army Reserve six months earlier. Initially, the therapist had taken these feelings of oppression at face value and referred Christine to a women's group in the center which engaged in mutual support, consciousness raising, and peer problem solving. However, after attending two sessions Christine stopped attending and told her therapist that she found the women in the group to be "a bunch of man-haters." She claimed she liked men; it was just the oppressive marital and domestic roles she hated. She went on to explain how well she got on with the men she worked with at her office and the men she interacted with in the Army Reserve.

It became evident that she had become sexually involved with more than one man in the Reserve. Although she claimed to be serious about the man she had the affair with, he was a married man who gave no indication that he would seriously consider leaving his marriage and family. He also seemed to be avoiding Christine after the first few weeks of heavy sexual involvement. She claimed that in retaliation she went out with "a couple of other men" in the Reserve. The therapist was concerned that Christine was engaging in promiscuous sexual activity as part of an almost manic, desperate search for satisfaction and for fending off a possible impending depression. Christine was saying that she had been deprived and felt deprived most of her life, so she was "entitled to a little fun and satisfaction while I still can."

Christine did have a history of some deprivation and of depression. She was alienated from what was left of her family, except for one married sister with whom she remained in regular contact. Her mother had died when she was eight years old, and she did not get along with her stepmother after her father remarried. After completing high school, she joined the Army, in large part "to get away from home and be independent." She was trained and served as a clerk-typist for three years. After her discharge she took a similar job in business and then married two years later. She had her daughter, Melanie, a year after the wedding. Her husband, whom she described as a gambler and drinker, simply left within a few months of Melanie's birth. He never attempted to contact them or support them, so Christine had to go back to work to support herself and Melanie.

Nine years before her current therapy she had become clinically depressed. This was about three years prior to her marriage to John. During this depression, she had been hospitalized and received shock treatments. She became clinically depressed a second time two years before her current therapy. That depression lasted for over a year, and she received out-patient treatment consisting largely of antidepressant medication. She tended to blame John for her depression during that time, claiming "he did not know how to keep me happy."

When the depression lifted, she decided to join the Reserve and later to get help (therapy) in order to begin making a life of her own. This, then, was the situation John was faced with at that particular juncture in his life. The love component of his life structure was disintegrating, and the work component was also suffering somewhat as a result of the deterioration in the marriage.

John appeared very distraught at his first session. He was a clean-shaven, sandy-haired man of medium height and build who looked about five years older than his actual age. This was probably due to the fact that he was balding and he wore a conservative business suit. He wore these suits during most of our sessions, since he came to them from his civil service job as an actuarial accountant in the state insurance system.

He was experiencing a very mixed array of emotions which came tumbling out as he brought up various aspects of his current situation with practically no prompting. He said that he could not understand why his wife wanted a separation. He was willing to try to work at the marriage despite her affair with "that man." When he began suspecting she was being unfaithful to him, he was afraid of what he would do. He said he not only thought of killing the man, but also of killing himself. The only thing that would keep him from doing that was his children. He said he felt very responsible for Melanie, whom he had come to accept as his own, and his eight-and-a-half year-old son, Billy. "Didn't she feel responsible for them? How could she do this to them?"

When he discussed his numerous thoughts about the other man, John made it clear that it never entered his mind to retaliate against Christine. He said he could not kill her or even harm her because he still loved her. He also felt responsible for her and said that he blamed himself that he could not bring her out of her prolonged depression during the latter part of their marriage. When asked if he thought this was her first depression, he answered that he knew she had a prior period of depression. However, he felt that as her husband, he "should have been able to pull her out of it." As he discussed this, it was evident that he accepted much of his wife's criticism that he did not know how to keep her happy.

He then went on to say that he would probably not be able to make any other woman happy, either. He simply could not stand the idea of having to start dating again, if they separated or got a divorce. He said that as an adolescent and as a young man, he was "terrible at dating and making out." In fact, he claimed that "for all intents and purposes," he was "a virgin" before he met Christine nine years earlier. He went on to emphasize that he was twenty-eight years old at the time, so that should show how backward he was when it came to sex. He never felt he had the right to be aggressive or assertive about sex with the girls and women he dated during his adolescence and young adulthood.

He was actually surprised at "how easy it was with Christine" on their first date. In fact, he wondered in retrospect whether she was the aggressor in the beginning and noted that he suspected her of being "loose." However, he found sex with her intensely exciting, and he was ecstatic over that state of affairs. When she became pregnant early in their relationship he did not hesitate to propose marriage, even though he admitted to lingering thoughts that she might have been "somewhat loose."

He went on to say that he did not regret it, that he was very happy being married. He loved her, he loved the children, he loved their home, and he could not stand the idea of this all coming apart. He said that he hoped his willingness to enter therapy would induce his wife to try to keep the marriage alive, because it would show he was willing to work at being a better husband.

This was not forthcoming. In fact, he came to his third session looking haggard, unshaven, and red eyed, stating that his wife had written a note to him earlier in the week demanding a separation. She had just gone off for a two week camp with the Army Reserve and had left the note for him rather than discussing it before she left. In the note she had said she was sure she wanted a divorce but that she would be willing to have a separation for the time being, if he could not face the idea of divorce so soon. She wrote that she did not love him as a husband anymore and that the marriage was "dead." She also asked that he move out of the house. She noted it would be a lot easier for him to find a place on his own and for her to maintain the house and take care of the children in it.

John was extremely upset during the session and broke down sobbing several times. It was evident that he needed a good deal of support at this juncture in his life, but he claimed to have no close friends or relatives he could go to for it. His mother had died two years earlier, and she was the only person he could really confide in except for Christine. I suggested that he might want to attend a men's group in the center which consisted of men who were going through many of the same experiences as he. Since I was the group facilitator, he agreed to give it a try, but added that he most certainly would not cry in the group as he had in this session.

John attended the men's group two nights later, and although he was somewhat reticent at first, he did start talking about his current situation after hearing some of the other men talk about their own concerns. He soon became the focal point of the group's attention at that session, and there was a good deal of support given to him. However, when some of the men suggested that it was not right or fair that he should have to leave the house when it was his wife who wanted the separation, he came to her defense. He said that he really was better able to go on his own and take care of himself than she would be. He went on to note how he was not able to help her when she was depressed, and one of the men asked him, "Do you think you're her psychiatrist?" John was somewhat taken aback by this, but after some thought he went on to say that although he was not a psychiatrist, he should have been able to help her. The other men did not dispute this at the first session but when it came up again in later ones they began to confront him with the grandiosity of some of his beliefs about what he could do for his wife when it was evident that she had some long-standing emotional problems.

When Christine came back from Reserve camp, a joint session was arranged in which she, her therapist, John, and I met. With quiet insistence, Christine emphatically held out for at least a separation. She again stated that she was almost certain that she wanted a divorce but that she would settle for a separation for the time being. John tried to convince her that they would be better off trying to make the marriage work, but he became shaken and withdrew when she said she no longer loved him and that he was stifling her.

In his next individual session, John claimed to be somewhat resentful that neither Christine's therapist nor I had tried to convince Christine to keep working on the marriage. Then he said he realized there was nothing we could do to make her work at it. He said that he came to the conclusion that if she did not want him he did not want her. On that basis, we mutually agreed that a major goal of therapy would be to enable him to separate from her and to establish a new home and life of his own.

It would be helpful at this point to discuss some of John's assessment test results from the initial sessions in order to get an idea of his cognitive construction of his current life situation and of the significant others in it. Figure 5-1 gives a graphic portrayal of his semantic-differential test results.

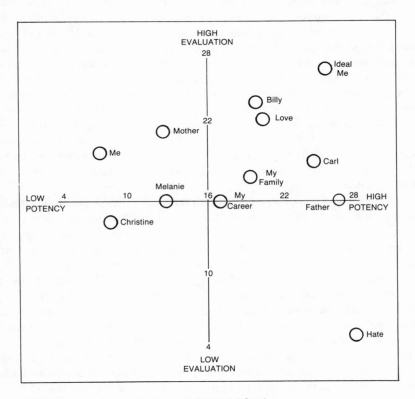

FIGURE 5-1. John Raymond's Semantic-Differential Graph

The most prominent concept in John's semantic space is "Ideal Me," or his self-ideal. This was the most highly evaluated concept, and it listed as highly potent. It is in marked contrast to "Me," which represents John's self-concept. Since the discrepancy between self-ideal and self-concept are indicative of self-esteem, it is clear that John's self-esteem was very poor at that time. He described himself on the test scales as only "slightly good" and "slightly valuable" as well as "quite sad," whereas on the ideal-self scales he said he wanted to be "extremely good" and "extremely valuable" as well as "quite happy."

On the potency dimension he described himself as "quite weak" and "quite soft" whereas his self-ideal would be "extremely strong" and "quite tough" on the same scales. As will be seen, a major part of the therapy was an attempt to increase his self-esteem by reducing the discrepancy between John's self-concept and his self-ideal. Most of this work had to do with decreasing the unrealistic and inflated self-ideal.

The most highly valued person in his semantic space was his son, Billy, who was described as "extremely valuable" and "quite good." On the other hand, his stepdaughter Melanie was described as "slightly valuable" and "slightly good." He claimed to love both of them, and it was evident that he was fond of them on the basis of his interactions with them. Christine's therapist had seen him interact with them in the waiting room at the center when Christine would come in for her therapy sessions, and he appeared to be quite caring and nurturing with them. He claimed to be much more concerned about Billy in terms of the effects of a separation than about Melanie, and he felt he could never give Billy up under any circumstances. For this reason, he felt that he had to find a place to live that would be in easy walking distance for Billy.

John's responses on the semantic-differential scales describing Christine showed his considerable ambivalence about her. He described her as "extremely valuable" and "slightly good" but "extremely sad," "quite unfair," and "extremely weak." He felt she could not make it on her own and that he would want to remain available to her even when they were separated.

John's mother was described as "quite valuable" and "extremely good," although "quite weak" and "quite soft." His father, on the other hand, was described as "quite bad" and "quite unfair" but "extremely strong" and "extremely tough." It was clear that he was very fond of his mother, who he saw as somewhat weak and as victimized by his father. He claimed his father was unfaithful to her. He reported that it was his mother who kept the family together despite their marital problems. He disapproved of his father's adulterous and otherwise insensitive behavior toward his mother, but he was at the same time in awe of the "masculine strength and aggressiveness" of his father. John felt much the same way about his younger brother, Carl, who was two years his junior. Carl was described as "quite bad" but "quite strong" and "quite tough," and also "continuously on the make with women."

The initial work with John toward establishing a separate life went slowly. He kept finding reasons for not looking for or taking an available apartment in the area. At each session he would raise the question of why he had to leave the home instead of Christine and would answer each time that he knew she could not. Then, after about three months, when he finally rented an apartment within walking distance, he spent more time in the house with his wife and children than he did in his apartment. He would claim to go over and "babysit" the children while Christine was away, but it also came out that he would sleep overnight with Christine on those occasions and on weekends. He found it extremely difficult to disengage from her, and she added to the difficulty by calling him and asking him to come over when she felt lonely.

This state of limbo went on for three more months and was a focal point in therapy. John was encouraged to have the children stay over with him in his apartment, to begin to get involved socially so that he might meet other women, and to establish his own life independent of Christine. Much of the difficulty in this stage of treatment had to do with his assumption of the protector role with Christine. Although he described himself as somewhat weak and soft, he saw her as much more so. In fact, much of his highly idealized self was wrapped up in having to be all good and giving under all circumstances.

Karen Horney's (1945) observations about the debilitating effects of idealized self-images in individuals were quite appropriate in John's case. Therefore, much of the work with him was modeled after her therapeutic approach. This approach was to first bring his self-idealizing forces to his awareness; second, to attempt to deflate them; and third, to reinforce and mobilize his real self-forces (Rubins 1980). John's usual demeanor was rather humble, which was consistent with his low self-esteem, but he had to be reminded that the grandiose aspects of his self-ideal were intrinsic parts of *his* self-system, not someone else's.

John was able to mobilize some of his real-self forces in a number of ways. He did begin to spend more time with the children in his own apartment, and he joined a Parents Without Partners branch in his area. He began socializing with and then dating other women. He was pushed somewhat in this regard by the fact that men were calling Christine, making dates with her, and bringing her home. He became fearful that he might lose control of himself if he found Christine in some else's embrace in her home.

He also made some realistic adjustments in his work, which helped him to cope with that aspect of his life. Prior to the trouble with Christine, he had been advanced to a higher, more responsible position in the state insurance system. He had more people under his direction but he was also under considerably more pressure to see to it that they were more productive. He found he had to be more distant and less friendly with those under him, and he found this particularly stressful because he liked to be liked by others. Further, he was not increasing the productivity of those under him and was being criticized from above. Consequently, he asked to be returned to his old position in which he was responsible for fewer people, with whom he had good, even warm working relationships. His request was granted and this reduced the stress in the work component of his life considerably. He even began dating one or two women in the office, which helped him in other aspects of his life.

John's therapy was terminated after nine months. By that time he had firmly established himself in his own apartment. He was spending most of his time with his son, who slept over with him almost every night. There seemed to be a *de facto* arrangement whereby Melanie lived with her mother and Billy stayed with him. He remained active in Parents Without Partners, although he said the women there kept telling him that he was still in love with his wife. However, he had not had sexual relations with her for several months. Further, he had joined a hiking club, and was dating a twenty-five year-old woman who was a member of it. She was the first person he had sexual relations with besides Christine, and he was quite pleased and rather proud about it. However, he worried about the difference in their ages, because he was quite interested in her romantically.

Despite these gains, there were some indications that there were not enough changes in the *self* in relation to the *world,* to use Levinson's formulation. For example, although he and his wife no longer lived together or were sexually intimate, she still called him frequently about problems and concerns—and he continued to encourage this. Also, there were some intimations of unresolved problems about the self in the results of a Repertory Grid Test that John had taken near the end of his therapy. These results suggested that he would have difficulty in building a viable alternative life structure in place of the old one. His responses to the test are shown in Figure 5-2.

The first construct in the Reptest often represents a fundamental dichotomy in the manner in which the respondent construes his or her world. It frequently reflects how the person views the self and significant others in his or her personal life space. This is undoubtedly due to the fact that so much of our personal identifications and later identities are developed within and emerge from that initial, powerful and formative triad of mother-father-child. Sometimes the primary identification is between the child and one of the parents, and sometimes the child is significantly different from both parents.

In John's case the test results were quite dramatic in that they showed that he and his mother were not only alike on that first construct—"quiet"— but they were alike in all but one of the ten constructs on the test. The grid can be used to provide crude measures of association or correlation, and if we look at John and his mother in that manner, we can see they show an almost perfect positive correlation (+ 9) on the ten rows of constructs/contrasts. That is, for each check in a cell for John there was one for his mother, and for each

NAME: John Raymond

Sex: (M)- F   Age: 38

self	mother	father	brother	son (Billy)	step-daughter (Melanie)	wife (Christine)	unhappy person	successful person	person I would like to be		CONSTRUCT	CONTRAST
⊗	⊗	O					X			1	**quiet**	**outgoing**
	O		X		⊗	⊗				2	dependent	independent
O								⊗	⊗	3	content	not self-satisfied
		⊗	X	X		X		O	X	4	friendly	shy
X	X		⊗			⊗	O			5	confused	**straightened-out**
X	⊗				X	O	⊗			6	passive	dominant
⊗		X	⊗	X				⊗		7	males	females
⊗	X						O	⊗		8	responsible	irresponsible
		X	X	⊗			O	X	⊗	9	confident	unsure
		⊗	⊗			O				10	opinionated	open-minded

FIGURE 5-2. John Raymond's Repertory Grid Test

blank in John's column there is a blank in the corresponding row of his mother's column except for seven—"male/female." On the other hand there is something of a negative association or correlation between John and his father (+3) in that only on the male/female construct and the contrasts of "independent" (row two) and "not self- satisfied" (row three) were they alike. A perfect negative correlation would, of course, mean that there would be no similarities in all ten construct/contrast options.

The near-perfect correlation with his mother shocked John. He had expected the negative association with his father and a positive one with his mother, but he did not expect such a powerfully positive association with her. Although he knew he identified with her more than with his father in terms of values and sense of responsibility, his reaction to these Reptest results was revealing. He felt they were true, because the words, the constructs and the contrasts, were of his own choosing. He said he felt "ashamed" of them because they showed he was not a "real man," because he identified completely with his mother and her feminine qualities. In this regard, it is of interest to note that under "person I would like to be" (self-ideal) he did not check "male."

He felt that by being like his mother—"quiet" instead of "outgoing," "shy" instead of "friendly," "passive" instead of "dominant," "responsible" instead of "irresponsible," and "unsure" instead of "confident"—he was an ineffective man and husband, and a bore, much as his wife described him. Clearly, his self-concept and self-ideal were very discrepant on the Reptest.

John admitted to at times secretly feeling that he would like to be an outgoing, aggressive, irresponsible "high-liver" like his father. However, he could not allow himself to be at all like that because it would be wrong to be so irresponsible. These findings were consistent with John's need to be "extremely good" and to denigrate unacceptable emotions like "hate" as shown in his semantic-differential test results (Figure 5-1). Therefore, in our conceptual encounter concerning the implications of all the tests, and his phenomenological description of his own feelings, he accepted that there were aspects of himself (the "bad/masculine" ones) he was shutting off. However, he said that while he could recognize this intellectually, he could not accept it emotionally. In this regard, he said, "Right is right, and wrong is wrong. There's no way I'm going to change that." Therefore, he knew that he was neglecting parts of himself, but he accepted this as a necessity and as something he had to live with.

Indeed, there was later evidence to show that he was not only continuing to live with it, but that it was taking an even greater toll on him and his life. John had come back to the center for psychotherapy one year after our last contact. Although he had made some distinct instrumental gains by the time of our last contact, a basic problem had reemerged in a new guise when he came back to the center the following year. It had come back in the guise of sexual impotence in his new relationship with another woman.

The practitioner who treated John at that time later informed me that John had met and began living with a recently divorced woman he met at Parents Without Partners. Although the divorce from Christine had not yet been finalized, John purchased a trailer home near Christine and began living with this other woman who was thirty-two years old and had two children, aged eight and five. Although he had taken Billy to live with him, he still visited Melanie and responded to Christine's telephone calls when she was distressed about something or if there were repairs to be made on the house.

Thus, he had taken on the role of nurturing rescuer and protector to a new woman and her children, as well as continuing to a lesser extent in the same role with Christine. However, in his attempt to build a new life structure on familiar old ground, the denied (masculine) parts of himself took their toll in his new relationship in the form of impotence and general sexual dysfunction. He had not had this problem in his relationship with Christine, but there were intimations of underlying problems in his role as husband in Christine's complaint that she could not love him "as a man."

It is worth recalling here Parkes's (1971) contention that whenever a major change occurs in a person's life situation, he needs to restructure his ways of looking at it as well as develop new plans for living within it. The crisis provoked by Christine's demand for a separation called for a major restructuring by John of his life situation. However, although he made some changes in the structure of his objective world or life space (his new home, planned change in job status, joining Parents Without Partners, etc.), there was not a commensurate change in his *self.* As Parkes would say, he needed to abandon one set of assumptions and develop a fresh set to enable him to cope in his new life space. Instead, he continued with the underlying assumption that the only "right" way for him to exist in the world was in the somewhat emasculated role of nurturing protector and rescuer of troubled, dependent women and their children. Therefore, this case was identified as a crisis of attachment because there was a unique, yet rigid and typical, way in which John related and attached himself to significant others. He remained somewhat attached to Christine while recapitulating more directly a similar attachment to another woman. To John, the meaning of the loss of this attachment within his life structure was that he could not exist without it or one like it.

SEPARATION CRISIS IN A FIFTY-ONE YEAR-OLD WOMAN

This case represents a clear contrast to John Raymond's, even though the crisis was similarly precipitated by the spouse's desire for a separation and ultimate divorce. However, in this instance the person was able to abandon one set of assumptions and replace them with another when coping with her new life space. As a result, she was able to begin building a viable life structure in her early fifties that was much different from the one she had earlier envisaged for that period of her life.

Joyce Kurland was fifty-one years of age when her husband left her for another woman. Although there were indications in her late forties that the marriage was not sound, the meaning of marriage in her assumptive world was so powerful that she was oblivious to them. She had also been oblivious because she was so intent upon building a new life structure in which the marriage and her career would become the center pieces after their last child graduated from college and left home. Far from dreading the empty nest, she was looking forward to a new and exciting stage in her life.

Consequently, when her husband told her he was in love with another woman and then packed and left the following day, Joyce was emotionally devastated. She was at first unbelieving when he told her, and she then tried desperately to convince him to remain with her and try to work things out. When he left, she was stunned, and literally sat in her kitchen for hours in total numbness. Then the pain started setting in, and she found herself unable to do anything for two whole days. Her husband had left on a Friday afternoon and she had to cope all alone for the whole weekend. She had no appetite, so she did not eat. She was obsessively ruminating about her husband's departure to such an extent that she was unable to sleep. She did not want to call her son in California or her daughter in New York City, because she still hoped that somehow the marriage might be saved and that the children might not have to know about the separation. Although she had begun developing some friendships in her new job, she did to have someone she could really confide in about a matter of this magnitude.

She had hoped that by going to work on Monday, her mind could be taken off of her marital situation to some degree. However, this did not happen. She continued to be unable to sleep for the next few days, until finally she went to her family physician. He prescribed some sleeping pills, but when she went home to her empty house, she had a strong impulse to take the whole bottle of sleeping pills. This frightened her so much that she called her physician and asked if he could refer her for out-patient psychotherapy. He immediately referred her to the center in which I practiced. She was assigned to me and I saw her for the first session on the following afternoon when she finished work.

Joyce was a tall, large-framed woman with iron gray hair who gave the appearance of professional competence. This appearance was reinforced by the well tailored business suit she wore. However, she appeared tired and rather haggard looking as a result of several sleepless nights, and her emotions were highly labile at that first session. She was alternatively angry, sad, resentful, and discouraged. Above all, she was enraged at her husband, Phil, for the way in which he left her—without giving her any forewarning to soften the blow. Furthermore, she was intensely resentful that he had left her for another woman, particularly a much younger woman of thirty-five years of age who had a fourteen-year-old daughter.

Joyce went on to say that she and Phil had often discussed how enjoyable it would be when their children were all grown and settled so that they might enjoy doing things again as a couple. Now, Phil left her to live with and probably marry a woman whose teenage daughter he would have to be a stepparent to for a number of more years. Somehow, this seemed particularly hurtful to Joyce.

After expressing her anger and resentment, the feelings of hurt led into sadness and then discouragement. She said she had just read an article in the newspaper on the "Plight of the Gray Divorcees," women who were being jettisoned by their husbands after three or four decades of marriage. They were badly prepared to cope, psychologically and financially, with the world outside of marriage. Joyce was feeling discouraged about the loss of her husband at this stage of her life and about the difficulties in finding another relationship to replace the lost one. It would be extremely difficult and "strange" to start dating again, and she was well aware of the disproportionate numbers of women to men in her current and older age groups.

Her financial situation was also problematic because she only had a part-time job in a branch of her city's public library. She had recently taken a civil service examination to obtain a full-time position in the city. Fortunately, she had obtained a Master's degree in Library Science the year before, after going back to college on a part-time basis during the last few years of her marriage. Although the market for librarians was not particularly good, she felt almost certain she could get a position in her current library if she passed the examination. This was because they were very pleased with her and her work up to that point.

Joyce was considerably calmer by the end of that first session. It was my impression that there would be no further suicidal impulses, for she had been so frightened by her earlier impulse with the sleeping pills that she immediately flushed them down the toilet after she had spoken to her physician about referring her for psychotherapy. It was clear that she needed the emotional support of therapy in coping with the crisis situation and in working through the loss she had sustained. However, it appeared she had good instrumental coping capacities, which she needed in her current situation.

In subsequent sessions Joyce provided some background information on herself and her family which helped to show the full meaning of the breakup of the marriage in her life; a meaning so disastrous as to make the event a true crisis. Much of this meaning came from the fact that separation or divorce was unheard of in her family of origin. She described that family as "extremely close and loving." She said that her parents were utterly devoted to one another and that they would "turn over in their graves" if they learned that one of their children was going to be divorced.

Joyce had a younger brother and sister, both of whom appeared to be very happily married. They both lived in different parts of the country, but Joyce claimed she would not have felt able to turn to them for emotional support even if they lived in her area. This was because she thought they would not understand, and that she would feel humiliated and be seen as a failure in their eyes. She dreaded the idea of informing them of the separation. She could not even bring herself to believe the breakup occurred, so how could she even begin to tell them or her children?

On the semantic-differential test given in the early sessions of treatment Joyce described herself as "quite tense" and "quite sad." Her self-concept was not very negative, since she described herself as "quite good" and "quite fair," although only "slightly worthwhile." There was, of course, some discrepancy between her self-concept and her self-ideal. She wished to be "extremely happy" rather than "quite sad" and "extremely relaxed" rather than "quite tense." She also wished to be "extremely strong" rather than "quite weak," which was the way she felt. This appeared to be somewhat at odds with her description of herself as "slightly tough." She explained this by saying that she thought she would be tough enough to see this crisis through, but she was feeling weak because she was taking it so hard and above all because she was not strong enough "to really tell Phil off." She said she was never really able to win an argument against him or to fully express her anger toward him. She had been able to stand up to him and to handle some things her own way with respect to the disciplining and care of their two children. She did this in her own quiet manner by steadfastly sticking with her decisions, such as when she went back to college to get her Master's degree. However, when it came to most individual arguments, he always seemed to win them, and she always felt tongue-tied and ineffective in the process.

She pointed out that Phil had a Master's degree in rhetoric and communications and that he was currently teaching public speaking at a local community college. She added that one of the things that attracted her to him was his verbal facility and colorful use of spoken language, an area in which she felt deficient.

In addition to his teaching public speaking, he had also been involved in dramatics and acted in a local repertory theatre company. In fact, this was where he met the woman for whom he had left Joyce. She was acting in the same company and apparently their involvement dated back well over a year. Joyce said she should have suspected something but she was busy finishing work on her degree, and in fact, their own love life and sexual activity had been at a low ebb for a number of years prior to this. She felt this was more due to her husband than to herself, because she had always been responsive to him. She would also make overtures toward him but he had not been very responsive to these in recent years. She described him as "quite cold" on the semantic-differential test.

Joyce claimed that she had been looking forward to the "second honeymoon" that was supposed to happen to middle-aged couples after their children leave home. Her son, Jason, had left home a number of years ago for California. He was now twenty-eight and had a wife and child of his own. Their twenty-five year-old daughter, Gloria, who had been living in New York City, had unexpectedly returned home to live with them two years before.

Gloria had gone to a local college and graduated with an English major when she was twenty-two. She left home for New York City at that time to take a job as a junior copy editor in a large publishing house. The pay was low, but she fell in love with the City and with a young man she met there. Joyce noted that it was ironic that he was an actor "like Gloria's father." He usually acted in off-Broadway plays when employed, which was not regularly. The fact that he did not have a regular income did not help to make Joyce feel any better about the fact that Gloria began living with him. They lived together for a year in an economically marginal and emotionally stormy relationship. Joyce had a very hard time accepting the relationship, given her own high standards concerning marriage and family. She admitted to feeling disappointed in Gloria for this, and because Gloria allowed herself to be exploited by the young man.

When the relationship broke up, largely because of the young man's involvement with other women, Gloria was in great emotional distress and came home to pull herself together. She stayed on for a year working at low paying jobs as a waitress. Joyce admitted to feeling somewhat resentful about Gloria's return home. She was preoccupied with finishing up work on her Master's degree, and she had never really approved of the relationship from which her daughter seemed to have such a hard time recovering. This, plus her usual feelings of inadequacy in expressing herself verbally led her to believe that she had not been very supportive of her daughter and that they had parted on rather poor terms when Gloria went back to New York to work in another publishing house. Joyce was feeling both guilty and regretful about this now that she was going through some of the same pain of separation as Gloria had.

The beginning of therapy was devoted to helping Joyce work through whatever denial of the reality of the separation still remained, and to help her deal with the intense anger she felt toward Phil. This involved having her ventilate and identify the validity of her anger toward him as she expressed this in our sessions. In addition, she was encouraged to divert some of her anger into effective assertiveness statements in her interactions with Phil about the details of a divorce arrangement. She practiced assertiveness skills in our sessions, frequently rehearsing and engaging in role-play in preparation for her meetings with Phil. She obtained a lawyer to represent her in the process, but she also became considerably more effective in her own dealings with Phil on the divorce issue and other matters. In addition, the use of strong "I" statements in the assertiveness training enabled Joyce to begin to establish a stronger identity of her own as distinct from her prior primary identity as wife and mother. The use of statements beginning with "I want" and "I have decided," rather than "I have to," have been found to be effective in helping women to develop distinct identities of their own (Berlin 1976). They certainly helped in Joyce's case.

However, this would not have been sufficient in itself to enhance her identity, because she was experiencing a great deal of disappointment in herself for her perceived failure in her roles of wife and mother. Much of this was tied to her highly idealized image of her parents concerning their marriage and their parenting. She clearly had identified with her mother as a role model in both respects, and she found herself wanting. Fortunately, the therapeutic work on this identification and self-disappointment was aided greatly by some insights she gained in the process of completing the Reptest and discussing its results. She had filled out the Repertory Grid at home, and rather than wait to bring it with her to the following session, she mailed it in the hope that it could be discussed at that session. She sent an explanatory note, which was very revealing in its own right, with the completed Reptest. The note appears verbatim below:

> I thought by mailing this you might have time to do whatever you do with it before our next meeting so that it would be more productive. As you will see by all my erasures I had a hard time with it. I don't seem to want to go to great extremes in opposites. I don't think I want to hit anyone over the head with anything which seems negative to me. This has sort of shown me that words are quite special to me—my private meanings—perhaps it has something to do with my not being (generally speaking) a talker and perhaps a poor communicator. To commit yourself to an expression without qualifying it seems almost impossible to me anymore. I guess I have experienced what I consider enough misunderstanding that I would rather keep my mouth shut—it is too complicated and takes more energy than I have to explain everything. I also think I may be a little hurt and disappointed that the stress on words in our family has overpowered demonstrations and actions which the important people do not seem to read as much. It is too bad to become a victim of words when they can be such lovely and useful tools. Anyway, whatever this test is, I find it interesting and look forward to our next meeting.
>
> P.S. The hardest thing for me was to put down the contrast because the

possibilities are so great Nothing seems to be one thing only to me, and every-thing has to relate to something else. Maybe none of this is important to the test, but somehow it seems important to me. It leads to really defining things—which we discussed my apparent need for.

It is interesting to note her reference to the fact that the test demonstrat-ed that words were quite special to her—"my private meanings"—despite her general reluctance or inability to express herself orally. Also, her refer-ence to feeling "a little hurt and disappointed" that the stress on the spoken word in her family had "overpowered demonstrations and actions," pointed to an issue that had become focal at about the mid-point of her five month course of treatment. It had to do with what she perceived as the attitude of her two children toward the separation and toward her and Phil.

She felt the children had been "hoodwinked" by their father because of his verbosity and greater verbal expression of love, whereas she had demon-strated her love through continuous commitment and actions. Both her son and daughter had urged her not to completely alienate Phil in the divorce process due to her anger, because they wanted to be able to see and interact with him when they would come home for visits on holidays and vacations. She experienced this as something of a betrayal of her and a lack of recogni-tion of how she had ben unjustly injured in the separation process. This showed up in the Reptest results, which are shown in Figure 5-3.

When an individual included in a Reptest is not identified by an "X" in the cell representing a particular construct, it is assumed that the contrast to that construct is more descriptive of the individual. Therefore, when Joyce did not check her son, Jason, as "sympathetic" in row eight she was indicating by omission that he was "unsympathetic." She specifically noted that it meant he was unsympathetic to her with respect to the injury done her by his father. On the other hand, she felt that Jason was a fair person in general and therefore checked off "fair" in row ten. Conversely, she saw her daughter, Gloria, as a sympathetic person in general and as specifically unfair to her in the current situation. Joyce felt that Gloria was unfair in expecting greater verbalization of love and support from her, despite Joyce's demonstration of love and support in taking her back for the year after the breakup of her relationship with the young actor. Joyce also felt that Gloria was unfair in attributing too much value to her father's verbal expressions of love in the absence of demonstrated love in actions. These perceptions about her children changed in the course of therapy, but this was the way she felt at the time of the Reptest.

It has been noted that the first contrast selected in a Reptest is usually a crucial one in the person's life space, and this was certainly true in Joyce Kurland's case. The whole dichotomy of verbal vs non-verbal represented a major way in which she construed her world and the significant others in it.

FIGURE 5-3. Joyce Kurland's Repertory Grid Test

NAME: Joyce Kurland

Sex: M - (F)   Age: 51

CONSTRUCT	CONTRAST	self	mother	father	son (Jason)	daughter (Gloria)	husband (Phil)	disliked person	unhappy person	successful person	person I would like to be
1 verbal	non-verbal	O	⊗	⊗			X	X		X	X
2 loving	non-loving	X	⊗	X		⊗		O		X	X
3 warm	cold	⊗	X	X	X	X	O			⊗	X
4 artistic	not artistic	X	X	O		⊗			⊗		X
5 serious	shallow	X	X	X	⊗	X	O		X	X	⊗
6 pretentious	down-to-earth				O		X	⊗	⊗		
7 male	female		O	⊗	⊗		X			X	
8 sympathetic	unsympathetic	⊗	X	X		⊗			O	X	X
9 selfish	unselfish						⊗	⊗	X	O	
10 fair	unfair	⊗			X			O		X	⊗

The most valuable insight she gained from the test was to recognize that she was significantly different from both her parents on the verbal/non-verbal dimension and that they were like one another in this regard. This led her to a number of other insightful observations about her parents and her relationship to them. She noted that her parents seemed to be so much in love with one another that she often felt shut out by them. She thought this was a "childish" feeling for her to have as an adult, and she felt guilty about it. However, when she was informed that it was a normal kind of feeling to have, even as an older adult, she felt encouraged to go on and identify other ways in which her parents might have been less than perfect parents. She even came to see that she had never excluded her own children through a too intense or exclusive relationship with her husband. These and subsequent observations helped to modify her overly idealized image of her parents and to feel less disappointed with herself in comparison.

She clearly did identify with her mother, as indicated by the fact that she described herself as the same as her mother on eight of the ten construct dimensions of the Reptest. Only on the verbal/non-verbal and fair/unfair dimensions were there differences. The latter difference was explained by Joyce as a reflection of her feeling that her mother was unfair in excluding her from the high degree of love she showed toward the father, and vice versa.

Another crucial insight Joyce gained from the Reptest was that she and her daughter Gloria were even more alike than she and her mother. Joyce and Gloria were alike on every dimension of the test except fair/unfair, which was explained earlier with respect to Gloria. This led Joyce to make even more connections and observations of similarity between herself and Gloria. Not only were they both non-verbal, but they were attracted to men who could express themselves orally. On the other hand, Joyce and Gloria were both avid readers and lovers of the written word, in contrast to the two men with whom they had been involved.

These and other observations of similarity between Joyce and Gloria led to a greater feeling of closeness to Gloria on Joyce's part. She consciously worked at reestablishing connections with Gloria, and also worked at verbally expressing her positive feelings toward her as therapy progressed. By the time therapy was over they were seeing quite a bit of one another. They were making visits to one another in addition to regular phone and written contacts. As therapy progressed, Joyce was also able to assert herself effectively with Phil in their negotiations, so that a divorce arrangement was worked out to her satisfaction by the time therapy ended. She had passed the civil service examination and was given a permanent full-time job in her current library position, so her career was also firmly established. She had also developed some close friendships with other women at the library who had common interests, so her new life structure seemed sound and far superior to the one she had at the time of the separation crisis.

In conclusion, it should be noted that Joyce's case does represent the kind of separation-individuation crisis which Notman (1980) identified as such an important one for women in mid-life. Joyce had indeed tended to define herself in terms of her relationships with others, in terms of her roles of wife and mother. So, much of the identity work involving "I" statements by Joyce in therapy served the process of individuation. This was a necessary process for her, if she was ever to overcome the separation crisis she experienced in mid-life. It was clear by the end of therapy that she was well on her way toward becoming a more individuated person.

A CRISIS OF SEXUAL ORIENTATION AND ATTACHMENT IN A FORTY-YEAR-OLD MAN

This is the case of Gary Robertson, whose carefully constructed life structure, based on a conventional heterosexual relationship with his wife, began to disintegrate from the effect of a homosexual experience and relationship as he entered his Mid-Life Transition.

Levinson (1978) has noted that the Masculine/Feminine polarity is one that becomes salient in the Mid-Life Transition, and it is one that raises questions about masculine identity in many men as they begin to experience the "feminine" aspects of themselves. Thus, it would appear that this case represents a crisis in the resolution of that polarity. However, that would be an error as far as Gary Robertson is concerned. The following explanation should help to clarify this statement:

> Actually, femininity and homosexuality are far from identitcal. Many homosexuals have strong masculine identifications and personal qualities, and many men who are strongly heterosexual in their love lives have intense interests, and feelings deriving from feminine aspects of the self (Levinson et al. 1978, 230).

There was no question about Gary's strong masculine identification. In fact, it was this that made his wife so uncomprehending and doubtful about the nature and extent of his homosexual orientation. She was convinced at first that it was only a passing mid-life aberration and that it would disappear when his "basic masculine," heterosexual nature took over again.

A second, and more important reason for not identifying this as a male-/female identity problem or issue is that Gary himself did not see it as one. There was none of the agonizing and self-questioning about who or what he was, which is so characteristic of identity problems and crises. Like his wife, he had no questions about his masculine identity, but unlike her, he was clear about his basic homosexual preference.

Gary was referred to me by a colleague in the same center for psychotherapy. She had been seeing his wife, Doreen, in treatment for about three weeks, and Mrs. Robertson had asked her if some therapist in the center could see Gary at the same time. Doreen was convinced that Gary would straighten out if he had a chance to work on some of his conflicts in individual treatment. Doreen was also convinced that the two of them seeing one therapist would not work at that time. In fact, the two of them had seen a marriage counselor several months before for a few sessions, and his mediation had led to the current situation which was so distressful to Doreen. The counselor had mediated an arrangement whereby Gary split his time, spending half of it in his home with Doreen and the other half in the apartment of his male lover, Cliff. Although Doreen had reluctantly agreed to that arrangement, for fear of losing Gary completely, she was now finding it intolerable. Since Gary was insistent upon keeping the arrangement, Doreen had gone into counseling to see whether she could somehow come to terms with it or to decide to end the marriage. Gary had nevertheless agreed to see me at her request.

In his first interview with me, Gary made it very clear that he didn't have any real problems about his basically gay orientation or the current living arrangements. He was seeing me for Doreen because of the distress she was feeling, and because he did not want to hurt her any more than he already had. He did say, however, that he was interested in learning more about himself and felt that he could benefit from the self-understanding he could gain through counseling. He was very interested in psychological tests and readily agreed to taking some, if the results could be discussed and shared with him. I indicated that any tests he would take would be based on self-reporting, and that he would be a partner in both the administration of the test and interpretation of the results.

Gary greeted this with enthusiasm and then went on to talk about his background without hesitation. There was a general disarming and youthful enthusiasm about him. He had an easy boyish grin, which together with his physical condition, gave him the appearance of being fully ten years younger than his forty years. He had an athletic appearance. Although not tall, perhaps five feet eight, he was husky and muscular in build, but without any suggestions of the muscle-bound, body-building type. Further, there was nothing even remotely effeminate in his speech or gestures.

He gave the following background information about himself. First, he noted that he was a physical education teacher and tennis coach in a local suburban high school. Secondly, he very quickly added that he was "not one of your stereotyped jocks who has muscles between his ears." He read widely, usually good fiction and current affairs, and he and his wife regularly attended philharmonic, ballet, and operatic performances in their area. However, he believed in physical education and conditioning as important and necessary ingredients for "modern living."

He noted also that he was active in community affairs in his area. A year earlier he had been appointed to the local zoning board in his township, where he was apparently well liked and his opinion was respected. He said that as a result of his involvement on the zoning board, he was finding himself intrigued by the idea of changing careers. He had many dealings with persons in management positions in business and industry, and a mutual admiration and friendship had built up with some of them. In fact, he met his lover, Cliff, in this way.

He described Cliff as not only young (twenty-nine) and handsome ("about six feet two, dark and angular"), but as "brainy and ambitious." He had an MBA, and he was an expert on locating and assessing potential sites for the development of business and industry. He worked for a large national conglomerate that sent him to this region to check out, assess, and report on a number of sites for possible development. He usually stayed in a region or area such as this for four to eight months and then he moved on to another one.

Gary found Cliff's lifestyle and pace to be exciting, and although he did not have the specific kind of expertise Cliff had, he had been told by several people that he could do well in business or industry, given his personality and intelligence. A couple of these people, including Cliff, had offered him some possible jobs with national firms that would have required him to move around, much like Cliff. He admitted this was very tempting, but he had some strong reservations about it.

First, he was not keen on the idea of Cliff helping him get a job with his firm. He felt that the two of them had a relatively equal relationship now, but he feared it might turn into one where he would be dependent on Cliff not only in terms of getting a job but in terms of when and where they would move, how they would live, and so on. He said he saw this possibility of dominance in Cliff, who was a very forceful and determined person.

Another reason for not shifting careers at this time was the fact that he had a lot of seniority in his current teaching position (sixteen years). Also, the security of his salary and the further accumulation of his retirement benefits would be hard to give up. Although he could easily match or quickly surpass his current salary, if he took one of the jobs that had been offered to him, there was no comparable security in business as there was in his current job.

He claimed to be somewhat bored by his current work. Although he still got excited to some extent by finding and developing high school tennis players and teams, as well as by the team competition, these things no longer compensated for the boredom he felt in his regular teaching duties. He noted, paranthetically, that the reason he originally moved to this area from the midwest was the fact that the tennis coaching job was offered in conjunction with the teaching job.

This digression in the interview led him into talking about the area he came from and his family background. He came from a small city of about twenty-five thousand in western Ohio where his father worked as a salesman ("district sales representative," Gary sarcastically added) for a large manufacturer of farm equipment. Gary noted that it was probably lucky for him and his younger brother, Mel, that their father had to travel and be out of town a great deal of the time on his job.

He described his father as "surly, opinionated, selfish, and just miserable." He was not only overbearing toward the two boys but a poor husband to their mother—cold and without affection. Although he did not seem to show their mother much attention or affection, this did not prevent him from having a number of "shabby affairs" with younger women. In fact, one of the affairs involving a local woman became quite serious, and their mother found out about it. She confronted him and threatened to divorce him if he didn't end the affair, which he did. Gary observed, "He didn't even have the guts to make the break for something he wanted, even though he wasn't wanted at home, at least by my brother and me."

He went on to say that his mother had a lot more guts than his father. She pretty much raised the two boys single-handedly, although the father would try to get involved from time to time, particularly in the disciplining of the two boys. Gary noted that the two brothers were good friends throughout childhood, but he only sees Mel about once a year. That is when Gary and Doreen visit his mother in Ohio, where she still resides in the same small house of his childhood. Mel and his family live in a neighboring town about twenty miles away.

Gary said that Doreen and his mother were very fond of one another. His mother would come and stay with them each summer for a stay of three or four weeks. He then observed somewhat wistfully that he did not know what his mother would think about the kind of arrangement he and Doreen now had. He knew she would not approve, but he did not know how badly it would affect her feelings toward him.

Toward the end of the first session, I commented that there appeared to be many questions raised by the current split arrangement between Doreen and Cliff. Although it allowed certain aspects of himself and his life to coalesce for the time being, it left a number of other things unresolved. He quickly replied that one of the things that was not left unresolved was his sexual preference, and anything we would work on in counseling had to take that into account. He said emphatically that he definitely preferred men, so he had no question that he was basically homosexual. Although he was functionally bisexual by virtue of his relationship to his wife, he said he would now be exclusively homosexual if it were not for his marriage to her.

I said that since so much was contingent upon this fact, perhaps it would be helpful if he could tell me how this clear preference or choice came about and what meaning it had for his life in general. He said he was agreeable to exploring these issues at the next session because he had not really had the opportunity to tell the whole story or sort things out with either Doreen or Cliff, since they were too much involved.

Gary did not waste any time at the second session explaining why he was so clear about his preference for homosexuality. He said, "You have to understand this—I'm what's known as the 'down man' in the gay world. Do you know what this is?" Without waiting for a reply from me, he went on to explain that he had become the "down man" for the first time in his life with Cliff. He had never been the recipient of anal intercourse before, and he said he had not been the same ever since.

He was very animated, almost "high," as he described how much that experience had changed his life. He had never experienced such "absolute pleasure," and it continued to be "ecstatic" for him. He went on to explain that he had been aware from early adolescence that he was somewhat attracted sexually to males. However, he had felt his primary orientation was heterosexual, until he became involved with Cliff.

His homosexual experiences from adolescence on were not frequent, and they tended to be furtive and not entirely satisfactory. This, together with the guilt and fear concerning it, made dating and heterosexual involvement with girls and women much easier and less stressful. Given his gregarious personality and "good rapport" with women he had no apparent difficulty in assuming a heterosexual lifestyle. He was always able to perform sexually with women, so the occasional transient sexual encounters with men remained in the recesses of his life. These encounters usually began with another man or youth picking him up in some public place, such as a bar or movie theatre. Most of the time the other man would perform fellatio on him until he reached orgasm. On a few other occasions, the other man assumed the down position and Gary would take the "male" position in anal intercourse. However, given the transient and illicit circumstances, none of this was wholly satisfying and in no serious way suggested itself as an alternative lifestyle.

Then came the experience with Cliff. That reversed his sexual orientation; of that he was sure "beyond a shadow of a doubt." From the beginning of his relationship with Cliff he had assumed the position of "down man," and he noted that the sheer joy of this had radiated out to other areas of homosexual activity.

Now he could enjoy it with others. He went on to describe an evening when he and Cliff went out to a gay bar and met a "very beautiful young man with curly blond hair" who agreed to come back to the apartment with them. Gary made a point of saying that the young man was not at all effeminate, that neither he nor Cliff is effeminate, and that neither of them were at all attracted to such men.

At any rate, Gary described his experience in the down position with this young man as equally ecstatic as his experiences with Cliff. He noted parenthetically, and with some amusement, that Cliff seemed jealous in witnessing this—even though Gary did not feel jealousy in observing Cliff engaged sexually with the young man. He said that even if his relationship with Cliff came to an end, he was sure that his sexual preference would remain unequivocally gay.

At this point I asked him what kind of difference this made in his sex life with Doreen, and he responded by saying that he could no longer achieve orgasm with her. He said he had no difficulty in satisfying her because he could sustain an erection for long periods with her without any difficulty. I informed him that I knew this from Doreen's therapist who provided me with information in making their referral. She had indicated that Doreen was convinced that Gary's performance with her was thoroughly satisfying for both of them—including orgasm as well as intercourse. Gary quickly said, "I fake it—the orgasm—always." He was very clear about this, and the only reason he could think of that would convince Doreen so completely that he was having orgasms was that she so much wanted to believe it. That, plus the fact that she was so consistently achieving orgasm. All of this is consistent with Levy's findings in which he states: "Among those (homosexuals) who can perform with both sexes, many report that, although they function successfully, they do not *feel* the same emotionally or physically with the opposite sex" (1981, 123).

After this I started the process of conceptual encounter (de Rivera 1981) by offering an interpretation of the larger structure of meaning of the initial sexual experience with Cliff. I said that it seemed to me that the so-called "down position" meant a great deal more in his life than just a sexual position. The experience was something that seemed to transform whole areas of his life as well. He not only preferred that form of sex over heterosexual activities, but it had activated his pleasure in other homosexual activities. Thus, these other (formerly unsatisfactory) activities were also preferable to heterosexual activities. This in turn had profoundly changed his sexual relationship with his wife.

I said that it seemed that his experience had transformed his relationship to women as well as men to one that was markedly different in general than before. He agreed this was so, and when I asked him how it felt from that new vantage point—knowing that he was gay—he said, "Great. I feel like a tremendous weight has been lifted from my shoulders. I have a great sense of elation and freedom after all that pretending about being the responsible, macho male. That's the reason I'm so sure about my orientation now."

The following third session was significant in several respects. I began it by recounting his description of the transforming experience of elation and his sense of freedom as a result of the experience. Given this and his clarity about his sexual preference, I asked whether we could explore some of the reasons for the state of limbo in which he was living—"half gay and half hetero."

He appeared to be much less comfortable at this session and had difficulty articulating his reasons for staying with Doreen. For the most part, he emphasized the fact that she still needed him, was rather dependent upon him, loved him, and would be devastated by a sudden and final break. As I suggested additional possible reasons for not making a final break—his home, his standing in the community, the security of his job, the uncertainty and ambiguity about a new career and a new location—he seemed to shrug them off as not terribly significant in comparison to Doreen, but he appeared to become perceptibly more morose as they were brought up.

Gary cancelled two appointments in a row thereafter, and when he came in for his fourth visit he wanted to talk only about the test results. He said he felt "pretty good" about his current life situation with Cliff and Doreen, and that he would like to turn to other matters, to learn more about himself in general. Because of his evident wish to avoid discussion of his current life situation and my concern about his leaving therapy altogether (in view of his missing two previous sessions), I went along with his expressed desire to discuss the test results. We did discuss the results, and he was very interested in them but he seemed increasingly wary about interpreting them. Although we set up another appointment for the following week, his wife reported in the course of seeing her therapist two days later that Gary had decided to discontinue counseling and would therefore not be coming in for our next scheduled session. He told her that he had learned a few things about himself in counseling, but that he did not really have a problem concerning his current situation. Doreen's therapist indicated to me that although this decision on Gary's part caused Doreen some distress, she was also somewhat relieved because she had been fearful that I might influence Gary to make a decision in the direction of a gay life away from her.

Thus, there were only four sessions in all with Gary, and there were many unresolved issues and questions that needed to be handled when he left therapy. However, it should be noted there were compelling reasons for Gary not to continue. Indeed, it was the profound implications of those unresolved issues, of the implications of a basic change in the situation, that probably drove Gary away. There was a great deal at risk for him if he decided to act any more definitively at that time regarding a break from this current life situation.

In a sense, he did not have to act. His wife had not yet reached the point of telling him that she could not tolerate the situation any longer and that he must make a decision.

In order to clarify this interpretation of his motives for leaving treatment, it is important to take a brief look at Gary's carefully constructed individual life structure just before his involvement with Cliff. First, he was married to a woman with whom he was quite compatible, with whom he shared many of the same interests, and whom he claimed to care for and love. It was a relatively late marriage for both of them (he was thirty-two and she twenty-nine when they married), and they both agreed that they did not want children of their own. They were both teachers and felt that they were meeting enough of their parenting needs with the third grade children she taught and the youths he taught and coached. Furthermore they were both very attached to the house they owned, and they spent a lot of time together in gardening and improving the home. Additionally, as a homeowner and an active member in local organizations, Gary was very much immersed in the community where he had a good reputation and some status.

The concept that comes to mind here is "embeddedness," as that was conceived by Schachtel (1950). It should be noted, paranthetically, that Kegan (1982) incorporated Schachtel's concept into his schema, so the following interpretation has relevance and meaning from the perspective of both the authors. Gary was so embedded in his existing life structure that he could not readily bring himself to leave it for the unknown and rather frightening, although exciting, possibilities raised by Cliff, which were a gay lifestyle and an alternative career. Gary was actually experiencing an acute form of anxiety at the prospect of leaving his existing situation. This anxiety has been explained as follows:

> From our viewpoint, anxiety is the embeddedness emotion par excellence. It arises with any separation from the state of embeddedness or the threat of such a separation if the person is or feels helpless to cope with the situation of separation . . . There is a conflict between the person's striving for growth and his clinging to embeddedness. The attempt to emerge from embeddedness sets off anxiety by which that side of the person which is afraid to leave the shelter of embeddedness warns him of the danger of helplessness in encountering the world (Schachtel 1959, 44).

There was an aspect of Gary which made him afraid of leaving the shelter of his life structure and of his possible helplessness in encountering a new world. For despite his professed emphasis on independence and autonomy in life, there were intimations in the third session that he was not so independent and autonomous.

At any rate, it was obvious that there was much at risk in any definitive choice he might make. Schachtel held that it was necessary for the person "to go forward" to leave the embeddedness and to *encounter* the unknown situation: "The determination to go forward to such encounters keeps the doors open to an expanding life, while the seeking of protection in the embeddedness of the familiar makes for stagnation and constriction of life" (Schachtel 1959, 45). This statement or credo of Schachtel's was questioned by Goodman in the course of her study of anxiety when she observed that it ignored "the real limitations on what can be achieved by man in favor of a glorification of the 'creative and productive personality,' the "self-actualizing personality,' or the personality that can surmount 'embeddedness'" (1981, 153).

Goodman's perspective on this issue seems much more descriptive of Gary Robertson in terms of his solution to the dilemma. In effect, he did not make a definitive choice, because he did not have to. He was able to "have his cake and eat it, too" in the sense that he was able to remain in the embeddedness of his relationship and life structure with Doreen. He was able, at least for the time being, to get her to accommodate. Thus, he was able to retain his embeddedness while at the same time engaging in the exciting and preferred alternate lifestyle with Cliff. One would have to say that this was an ideal and understandable state of affairs from Gary's perspective.

There was some additional evidence in the test results to support the above interpretation, which says that Gary was avoiding a definitive choice because of the potential threat of acute anxiety in leaving the embeddedness of his life situation. Not all of the test results had been scored by the last session, when they were discussed with Gary. Those that had been scored earlier were not very informative with respect to this embeddedness issue. The results of the Intolerance of Ambiguity showed that he was very close to the norm, in that he could not be described as very intolerant of ambiguity nor could he be described as very tolerant of it. The same thing could be said about the results of the Locus-of-Control Test. He had neither a marked internal locus of control nor a marked external locus of control. He was very close to the norm on this, as well. The only thing that appeared somewhat discrepant about those results was that his descriptions of himself in interviews tended to show that he felt he had an internal locus (self-determining) and that he was not threatened by ambiguous situations.

The semantic-differential result were also not definitively informative, though perhaps suggestive about the embeddedness issue. However, they were quite descriptive about other aspects of Gary's life at that time. As Figure 5-4 shows, sex was the most highly evaluated item in his semantic space. His ideal self and Cliff were the next most highly evaluated.

The descriptions of his ideal self and Cliff were identical on the following

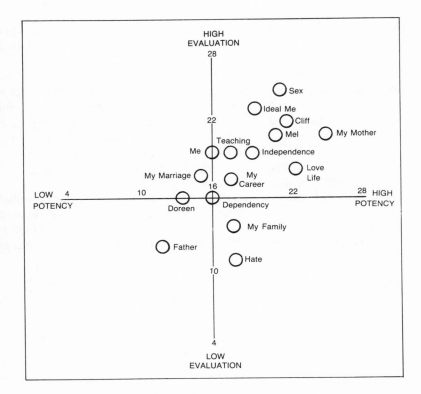

FIGURE 5-4. Gary Robertson's Semantic-Differential Graph

items: "quite valuable," "quite strong," "quite good," and "quite active," among others. Thus, it can be seen that the sexual orientation and the traits and lifestyle associated with Cliff were identified with Gary's ideals and aspirations for himself. On the other hand, his wife, his marriage, his current career (all parts of the prior life structure) were nowhere near as highly evaluated or as potent.

His description of his actual self (self-concept) was "slightly valuable," "slightly good," "neither weak nor strong," and "quite passive." Thus, his self-esteem was not poor since he was mostly on the "slightly" positive side, but his self-concept was not as strong or as active as he might want it to be in terms of his ideal self. This could be suggestive in the embeddedness issue. The self-attributed passivity could be more indicative of a willingness to acquiesce in embeddedness than to "encounter the unknown."

This last point was definitely indicated in the results of the Embedded Figures Test (Witkin et al. 1971), which had been administered at the very last session. It showed Gary to be highly field-dependent, which would argue against the likelihood of a ready willingness on his part to leave his state of embeddedness totally.

Finally, there were intimations of the same sort in Gary's Repertory Grid results. They showed that the most prominent construct was "giving," with its contrast of "taking." The second most prominent was "ill-tempered" with the contrast of "mild-mannered." Furthermore, these two constructs were highly correlated with the "good" vs. "bad" construct. "Mild-mannered" and "giving" were both "good." Thus, when we look at the two main constructs in terms of the diagram shown in Figure 5-5, we see several interesting things with respect to the significant persons in Gary's life space.

Gary is in the upper left quadrant all by himself, since he described himself as "giving" but "ill-tempered." Furthermore, he did not describe himself as "good" as he did his mother, Doreen, his brother, Mel, and Cliff. In the lower let quadrant were his father, a "disliked person," and an "unhappy

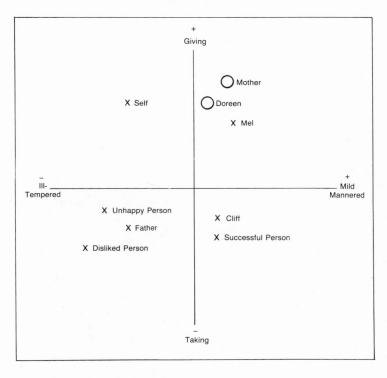

FIGURE 5-5. Gary Robertson's Repertory Analysis Graph
(Gender is indicated by O = female, X = male)

person." None of those three were identified as good, which is interpreted on the grid as meaning "bad." Now the lower right quadrant contains a "successful person" and Cliff, both of whom were described as "mild-mannered" but "taking." What is significant about this is the "taking" idea, for that quadrant looks as though it represents success and achievement. Yet, this is associated with "taking" and not "giving." Now, "taking" is bad in this grid, so achievement and success are bought at the price of being "bad."

The most significant quadrant, however, is the upper right. All four of the people there were described as "mild-mannered," "giving," and "good." Given Gary's interview and Reptest descriptions of these people in terms of their characteristics and their relations with him, it would be fair to say that that quadrant represents both security and nurturance. And, that quadrant is totally positive on the "good/bad" axis.

What I interpret this to mean is that Gary has unknowingly identified the "embeddedness" quadrant (upper right) positively and the "encounter" quadrant (lower right) ambivalently. Overall, then, these test results tended to show that Gary would not be likely to opt for encounter and change, unless forced, in his actual life situation.

What happened was that Doreen was making gains in her own therapy, and she appeared to be coming to a decision to ask Gary to leave. She was becoming progressively more disillusioned with him and dissatisfied with their arrangement, as well as more sure of her ability to live without him. Consequently, it looked as though he would be forced out of his prior life structure and its interim mixed arrangement.

Since Gary was at the beginning of his mid-life transition, according to Levinson's paradigm, it could be expected that he would experience two or three years of some instability and change before entering the ensuing stable period. However, the word "change" seems too mild to describe the kind of dislocation Gary would experience should his wife end their living arrangement and marriage. It would be an unusually stressful and anxious time for him, and there would still be some major decisions and new commitments for him to make before any stability could ensue. How he would live, and who with, would be unsettled. He would also have to make a decision about his job and his career in general.

Let us take a look at the two main components of his individual life structure and see what the likely options and outcomes might be. First, in the affiliative (love, intimacy) component, the last vestiges of a heterosexual or mixed orientation would probably end with the breakup of Gary's marriage. He remained bisexual only because of his relationship with Doreen, and it seems highly likely that he would opt for an exclusively homosexual lifestyle in the immediate future. In this respect he might fit one of the six sociosexual patterns of gay adults identified by Douglas Kimmel (1978): the pattern of a heterosexual marriage "with or without" periodic homosexual relations followed by a gay lifestyle.

The question of what particular gay lifestyle he would choose remains. Bell and Weinberg (1978) have identified four types of gay lifestyles: close-coupled, open-coupled, the functional, and the dysfunctional. The dysfunctionals are the most troubled in all areas of their lives, and do not have the same positive social skills and personal attributes Gary possesses. The functionals are the "swinging singles" who become involved in numerous sexual experiences in the gay world. Gary made it very plain in his brief therapy that he did not want that sort of lifestyle.

However, it is doubtful that he would opt for the close-coupled pattern, which tends to be more exclusively monogamous than the open-coupled. In fact, Gary's relationship with Cliff was taking on the shape of an open-coupled arrangement, in which sexual partners seek outside partners with or without the knowledge of their regular lovers. They tend to focus on sexual techniques rather than on relating, and they often need the presence of a third person in the act. They tend to have somewhat lower self-esteem, are less happy, and somewhat lonelier than those in the close-coupled pattern. Although adjustment in the love/affiliative component of an individual life structure in this pattern would not be as unstable or inadequate as the dysfunctional and functional patterns, it would not be as stable as the close-coupled pattern—a stability he relished in his marriage.

Gary's decision concerning the career component of his life structure will be even more complicated than his choice of sexual lifestyle. In fact it will be complicated *by* his choice of a gay lifestyle. He made it very clear in therapy that he would not want it to be known in his school that he was gay. he scrupulously avoided any sexual involvement with his students or the members of his tennis teams. If he continued on his current job, he would probably try to keep his sexual orientation a secret.

Gary is a very complex person in many ways, and this showed up in his Reptest. With respect to his self-concept, he identified himself as flexible, extroverted, and happy, but "closed" rather than "open," ill-tempered, and not "good." He is somewhat like Lifton's (1968) "protean man" who appears to be a more prevalent psychological type in contemporary life, where the emphasis is on flux and change in personal and public image, if not substance. Gary would try, and indeed had tried, to be all things to all people in his adult life. We could expect that he would try to retain his image in the local community as a "straight," responsible, involved citizen and professional. This would be somewhat more difficult without the "cover" of a conventional marriage, and with involvement in a gay lifestyle—no matter how secret or circumscribed.

On the other hand, of course, he could take on a new career in business and move out of the community with or without Cliff. But given our knowledge of his field dependence and his embeddedness in community and job, it seems unlikely he would opt for a career and job change at this stage of his life.

Although Gary has many personal assets and functional coping capacities, it seems that conditions would certainly be less than optimal for the development of a stable life structure in entering middle-adulthood (ages forty-five to fifty). It is possible that as he ages and matures further, he might opt for a close-coupled gay lifestyle that would offer more stability, but unless and until that happens, there will be a pronounced element of instability in his individual life structure.

In looking back over the three cases included in this chapter, an observation by Roger Gould (1978) comes to mind. He noted the primary gain of successfully negotiating the mid-life decade from thirty-five to forty-five is to achieve "the life of inner directedness," as proclaimed by the statement, "I own myself." He puts it this way:

> Instead of requiring inseparability from a loved one, we can learn to enjoy the benefits of separateness. We discard the old roles, rules, concepts and cliches that we've previously accepted unquestioningly (Gould 1978, 42).

It is clear that John Raymond failed to learn the benefits of separateness, since he seemed unable to discard any of the old roles, rules, and concepts. Thus, he remained locked into an old assumptive world from his past which did not permit him to reconstruct a viable new life structure. He failed to resolve the attachment/separateness polarity of Levinson in the direction of a healthy separateness. Not unrelated to this was the fact that he had even greater trouble with the masculine/feminine polarity as this was posited by Levinson. Although John identified the feminine in him as symbolizing weakness and unassertiveness, he could not accept the masculine part, which symbolized aggressiveness, power, and domination over others. Since these were "bad," he could not synthesize them with the feminine into a more integrated and whole self.

It is ironic that Gary Robertson, who opted for a gay sexual orientation in his mid-life transition, did not have the same trouble with the masculine/-feminine polarity. However, there is no question he had serious problems with issues of attachment and intimacy.

Joyce Kurland emerged as the most fully integrated person of the three, and she also became a more individuated person. So, although Notman (1980) has noted the greater likelihood of a separation-individuation problem in middle-aged women, it is clear that it can be overcome. When compared to the two men, one cannot help but feel that Joyce had greater capacity and flexibility to change her assumptive world and life structure regardless of her gender or stage in life.

Chapter **6**

CRISES OF LOSS AND REATTACHMENT

It was noted in the beginning of Chapter Five that separation and loss are different, although related, phenomena. The management of separation is apt to be difficult but less traumatic than coping with loss. The middle-aged parent has to deal with the separation experience of the empty nest when it is necessary to manage the feelings about being separated from the child or children who leave, as well as finding other objects and/or activities to fill some of the void. However, this is not the experience of out-and-out loss, because a relationship will continue to exist even if it is not as frequent or intense in nature.

In cases of loss, such as death of a spouse, there is an absolute end to the relationship. In divorce, the former spouse might continue to live, but the relationship is lost for all intents and purposes. It might remain at an instrumental level in which the ex-spouses have to work out the logistics of child visitation and care. The person has to cope with the actual loss of the former marital partner in terms of an affective, conjugal love relationship. The divorce represents final loss.

The state of separation prior to divorce is not yet a final state of loss. It is not uncommon for presumably "separated" couples who are involved in the legal process of divorce to continue to maintain a conjugal type of relationship, even while residing in separate residences. Sexual relationships often continue during periods of separation, as in the case of John Raymond in Chapter Five, just as there is often an unconscious collusion and continuance of the affective relationships even though the couple is ostensibly parted.

168   MEANING IN MID-LIFE TRANSITIONS

Weiss (1975) has identified three major stages of divorce that includes the state of separation culminating in divorce. First, there is an erosion of love and persistence of attachment and there is a focus on the ambivalence surrounding the breaking of love bonds. Secondly, feelings of distress, euphoria, and loneliness are brought on by the separation and there is often a need to bring about identity changes. The third stage, "starting over," includes three substages: shock and denial; transition (including disorganization, depression, and unmanageable restlessness); and recovery, or the process of feeling emotionally detached from the ex-spouse, which can take anywhere from two to four years.

In addition to his work in the area of divorce, Weiss (1973) has studied the phenomenon of loneliness, including the type of loneliness that follows divorce or death of a spouse. He makes the useful distinction between *emotional* isolation and *social* isolation as the two major types of loneliness. Emotional isolation results from the lack or loss of an intimate tie such as a spouse, lover, parent, or child, whereas social isolation results from a lack of involvement with peers such as friends, neighbors, coworkers, or kinfolk. In order to overcome social isolation, it is necessary for the person to have access to an engaging social network. In order to overcome emotional isolation, it is necessary for the person to integrate another intimate attachment or to reintegrate the one that has been lost. Weiss is very clear that the kinds of peer networks that serve to remedy social isolation will not work for emotional isolation. He says, "Evidence that the loneliness of emotional isolation cannot be dissolved by entrance into other sorts of relationships, perhaps especially new friendships, is repeatedly discovered by new members of the Parents Without Partners organization" (Weiss 1973, 19).

This observation will become patently clear in the first case studied in this chapter, as will the difficulties and dilemmas of reattachment for the person who has sustained a loss which leads to emotional isolation. Indeed, there are many difficulties and confusions for people who are attempting to establish new relationships after separation, divorce, or death of a spouse. It has been noted that dating feels both awkward and juvenile when one begins to reestablish some form of social life with the opposite sex (Weiss 1975). The painful truth of this is is known by far too many newly single men and women in their middle years. After the initial problems concerned with dating and mating, there are the choices and dilemmas related to commitment in new relationships. These choices and dilemmas include greater involvement or none at all, marriage or no marriage, and so on. For some, these issues involve a basic life decision never to marry again, but for others the choice is never made explicit, and in the long run the choice is sometimes made for them. This is apt to be particularly true of many single women, who significantly outnumber single men in the middle years and in the later years of life.

We have already noted the likelihood that men are more apt to use remarriage as a way of handling the loss and emotional isolation resulting from divorce or death of a spouse. Women do not have the same statistical opportunity in the middle years to use remarriage as a viable form or reattachment. Even among the many women who do have that option, a choice may be made to remain single. Singlehood has increasingly become one of the intentional lifestyle choices in American society (Bernard 1972). This is true for men as well as women. Although they might remarry more readily than women, they too can choose to find and maintain attachments that do not lead to marriage.

These kinds of dilemmas and difficulties will be represented in all three cases included in this chapter. The first two cases illustrate the various stages of both divorce and reattachment. The third case illustrates a crisis of loss through death of a spouse, but with features of sustained distress that have not been depicted in much of the literature on death and dying. A great deal has been written about the experience and process of coping with the death of loved ones. This literature is too extensive to even cite in this brief context. However, very little has been written about the experience of coping with the "death in life" of a loved one who has suffered a massive stroke or other organic condition which has reduced him or her to a bare vegetative existence. The likelihood of this type of experience in late-middle and older adulthood is not negligible from a statistical standpoint. How does one exist and cope with the reality of a spouse who is "as good as dead," is not conscious, and cannot relate on any meaningful level? How does one cope when this condition goes on for months and sometimes years without the likelihood of improvement or even death, given the life-sustaining techniques of modern medicine? How can one make choices or have an influence on decisions of life or death in such situations?

All of these issues will be represented in the last case of this chapter, but in addition to illustrating the experience of loss and distress in such a life situation, the case will also depict the generative experience of growing individuation within the total process. Issues of reattachment are also present, but they are of a markedly different order than those in the first two cases.

DIVORCE AND REATTACHMENT IN A THIRTY-NINE-YEAR-OLD WOMAN

Deborah "Debbie" Rosen was thirty-nine years old at the time she participated in my mid-life study as a member of Parents Without Partners. She retained her married name of Rosen, although she had been divorced for well over a year at the time I interviewed and tested her in the study. She said this was not out of any remaining sense of loyalty or affection for her ex-husband, but because Rosen was far simpler than her maiden name of Drobzhansky.

Debbie was in the throes of making a decision about possible remarriage at the time of our research interviews. The experiences and changes she related to me concerning the psychosocial transition of her marital breakdown and its aftermath include the processes of separation, divorce, and reattachment. She was an exceptionally good informant in terms of her ability to recapture and articulate her thoughts, emotions, and experiences from those transitional events for the purposes of the study. This was undoubtedly due in large part to her professional training and experience as a social worker. This same training and experience also probably enabled her to understand and more effectively cope with the experiences she was undergoing.

Debbie was a short, dark-haired, somewhat plump woman whose overall appearance was on the youthful, girlish side. She was obviously highly intelligent and able to relate quickly and appropriately to my questions and the research instruments. She was not only interested in engaging in the study process but she seemed to gain personal understanding and insight in a purposeful way during the process.

She provided the following background on herself and the events leading up to her divorce and its aftermath. She was born and raised in New York City, the middle child of a family of three children, with an older sister and younger brother. She was of Russian-Jewish extraction, and although both her parents were born in the United States, their parents were born in Russia. Her mother was a grade school teacher, and her father was a physician with a large family practice in a stable working class neighborhood in New York City. All three children received college educations, and she attended a prestigious women's college within commuting distance of New York City. After receiving her Bachelor's degree she worked for two years as a caseworker in the New York City Department of Social Services, and that experience convinced her that she wanted to go on to graduate study in social work.

The myriad experiences she had in attempting to help people with serious personal maladjustment and the disorganized families she worked with led her to desire further professional education, either in psychiatric or family social work practice. She attended a graduate school of social work in New York City, and that was where she met her former husband, Jeff. He was studying for a career in community organization while she was pursuing studies in the area of clinical social work practice, but they met on an ad hoc school committee organized to get the student body to participate in an upcoming peace march protesting American involvement in Vietnam. Like so many of their fellow students at that time, they continued to be active in various demonstrations and marches against the war and in favor of civil and welfare rights.

Debbie explained that although her father was a physician, and therefore a high-status professional, he identified with his working class patients in terms of their political and pro-union beliefs. She therefore admired Jeff's active engagement in the peace and welfare movements during their graduate study years. Yet, he seemed so young and vulnerable, as well as idealistic, to her at the time. Although he was just a year younger than she, physically he was on the small, frail side, which made him look younger. In addition, he had an asthmatic condition that would have kept him out of the service. The fact that he could generate so much energy and commitment to a cause in "such a frail body" was inexplicably appealing to her.

Jeff's father was also a high-status professional, a successful lawyer who volunteered a good deal of his time to the Legal Aid Society. He also identified with the poor, as did Debbie's father, so this was another thing Debbie and Jeff had in common from their backgrounds. Therefore, they felt they had a great deal going for them when they got married shortly after receiving their Master's degrees.

Jeff had a promising job offer from a community organization in another city in upstate New York, so the two of them moved there, where Debbie readily found a job in a family service agency. She stayed at that job for almost two years, until their daughter was born. Laurie was a rather small, colicky baby who required a lot of care and attention. Debbie stayed home with her for three years, and then went back to work only part time in order to be more available for her. When Laurie entered the first grade, Debbie took a full-time job as a psychiatric social worker in a mental health center in the city.

Their lives continued like this for three more years with only occasional and passing indications from Jeff that he was somewhat dissatisfied with his job and some aspects of their lifestyle. Professionally, he had done quite well by rising to the second highest job in the health and welfare planning council in the city. He was highly regarded for his intelligence and hard work, and it would only be a question of time before he would be offered the directorship of that council, or one in some other city. However, he was restive and felt that he had to deal too much with "the establishment"; the kinds of political and business leaders of the community who tended to be on the boards of most health and welfare agencies and his council. He also complained from time to time about their own "bourgeois" lifestyle. Since they were both earning full-time salaries, they were able to invest in a new suburban house at Debbie's urging. He felt this was taking them further away from the people they were both supposed to be serving in center city. Debbie's widowed mother was highly influential in the decision to buy the house, contributing generously to the cost of the moving and the furnishings. Jeff acquiesced sullenly in this, after offering some initial opposition. Because of his asthmatic condition, he was able to have an air-conditioned work room to himself where he could prepare the written reports and plans which overflowed from his office, as well as have the opportunity for the reading and privacy he seemed so jealously to guard of late.

Despite these occasional complaints, Debbie was not at all prepared for his announcement that he was so dissatisfied with their marriage and their life that he wanted a separation. She was in a state of shock and utter disbelief at first. There just had not been that much evidence of dissatisfaction, as far as she was concerned. When she pressed him about this, he said he had a chance to work for a community action group that was helping tenants in public and private housing to change their living conditions through rent strikes and various other forms of social action. However, it would pay less money than his job on the council, and he would not be able to afford, nor would he want to keep up payments on their suburban house.

In her desperation she even said that they could give up the house if "worse comes to worse" and he could change his job, if he was so unhappy with it. At this point he admitted that there was another woman in the picture. She was a worker in the same community action project he wanted to join, and she represented everything he wanted in a woman—she was "progressive, committed to social action" and she would be a true partner and compatriot in the kind of life he wanted to live.

He would not consider marital counseling to see if their marriage could be saved, and in a matter of a few days he had moved out of the house and into an apartment in center city with the other woman. In describing all this Debbie said that it was only in retrospect that she realized "how sullen, secretive, and perverse a person he really was." She was amazed that she could have been so oblivious to all this and so much into her own "little domestic world." At any rate, it did not help for Debbie to learn that the woman with whom Jeff had gone to live would be bringing her two children to live with them. She, too, was separated from her spouse and preparing for a divorce.

Debbie's own experience of the divorce process did indeed follow the three stages identified by Weiss (1975) which were formerly outlined. There was an erosion of love beginning almost immediately following the brutal suddenness of his announcement of his desire to break up. The fact that he kept his relationship with the other woman a secret and that it was not a new or unencumbered relationship added to her negative feelings and the erosion of love. She was aware of some persistence of attachment in some of her behavior, usually her contacting him on the pretext of child care or some other concerns with respect to Laurie. She still had certain tender feelings toward Jeff based on what she felt to be his physical and emotional vulnerability. However, he turned out to be as demanding and litigious toward her in the divorce process with respect to money and possessions as he could be with a slum landlord in his community action project. She had never seen this "selfish" side to him before, and it tipped her ambivalent feelings for him in a more clearly negative direction.

The separation certainly did bring very distressful feelings along with euphoria and loneliness. These feelings persisted in a particularly acute form for almost two months after which she began to work on some identity changes. Unlike Linda Craft in Chapter Five, she felt that she had been a failure as a wife. Despite Jeff's heavy contribution to the breakup, she held herself responsible. She also felt it necessary to assert and strengthen her identity as a professional. Therefore, when she was offered the opportunity of running a special program involving a family treatment approach with certain inpatients in her mental health center, she accepted the job. She did this despite the lethargy and regressive pull of her reactive depression. She felt that she could do a good job, especially when she would begin feeling better, and she knew this would give her depleted sense of self-esteem a boost.

The third, or starting-over stage of her divorce process did, of course, include the initial shock and denial substage. Not only was this experienced at the time of the initial breakup but it was also experienced to a lesser degree, though acutely, when she received her divorce papers. She recognized that much of her reaction was associated with the fact that so much of her prior identity had been wrapped up in wifehood and that, in effect, she was mourning the loss of a former self.

The transition substage was characterized by depression and unmanageable restlessness. She lost her appetite and over twenty pounds in the process. She also experienced an "ache" and a "void" in her life, which is so descriptive of the kind of emotional isolation that follows the loss of a love object. She turned to her daughter Laurie to a greater extent but this was problematic, too. Laurie was very hurt and angry as a result of the separation, and she would in turn be hurtful toward Debbie when Debbie was feeling most needy. Laurie, not knowing any better, tended to blame her mother for the separation to a large extent. Jeff's relationship to Laurie was more tentative than Debbie's, for he had never been a warm, demonstrative father, although he made a point of spending time with his daughter on various projects and games, usually of an educational nature. Consequently, Laurie felt more secure about expressing her anger and resentment toward Debbie than toward Jeff. This was not particularly helpful to Debbie in her time of difficulty.

Debbie first turned to two of her close girlfriends, then her mother and her sister, for emotional support during this time. Her mother and sister lived too far away to be of very much face-to-face support. Her two friends were of more help, but since they were both married and had their own families, Debbie felt she could not impose on them too much. She also came to feel somewhat more estranged from them because their marriages were intact and she was now feeling "different."

She felt very far removed from the image of a "swinging single," and she waited months before she got involved in dating. She did join Parents Without Partners and, consistent with Weiss' findings, she did not find the support there sufficient to fill the void she was feeling. She therefore tried to organize a women's support group from among some of the women she met at PWP, as well as some other separated and divorced women she knew. Although the group did not survive as a formal group, three or four of those women became close friends over the ensuing months.

Debbie began dating in the fourth month of her separation, at first with men introduced to her by her friends. Her brief encounters with singles bars and singles groups, including a Jewish singles group, completely turned her off that avenue. She found herself feeling inept and "juvenile" in her dating behavior. In short, she felt like an awkward teenager again. So, the whole process and arena of reattachment felt strange and somewhat unmanageable to her. However, the facilitator for her PWP group, a divorced man of forty-two, became very interested in her and began dating her.

Ken was an electrical engineer for a large industrial firm in the area, and he had joined PWP after his marriage broke up. He found it very helpful and wanted to learn more about human relations skills, which were so far removed from his training and work as an engineer. He took workshops in communications and group skills and got great satisfaction out of his work as a group facilitator for PWP. He became attracted to Debbie because of her excellent relationship and support skills in the group.

Ken had changed his lifestyle a great deal since his divorce. He changed from a workaholic to a person who valued a more leisurely and pleasurable type of life. He owned a small sailboat, which he enjoyed very much, and he enjoyed such physically active pastimes as water skiing, downhill skiing, and tennis. He soon got Debbie involved in these activities, and he became the first man with whom she had sexual relations since her marriage broke up. They became lovers, sleeping over at one or the other's home.

This relationship went on for months, and Debbie began to feel that they might be able to build a life together as a couple. He did not seem to have the same feelings, although it appeared that theirs was an exclusive relationship. When Debbie pressed him for some kind of commitment, he indicated he was not prepared for one at this time. In fact, he had wanted to talk with her about his going out with another woman with whom he had come in contact on a professional basis. Since the relationship was no longer exclusive, Debbie began to detach herself somewhat from Ken and began to date other men.

She found out later that Ken had rather regularly become involved with new female members of his PWP group for varying periods of time. Nevertheless, she and Ken remained friends, though not lovers, after she finally detached from him and began dating other men.

As her intimate relationship with Ken wound down, she began dating another engineer from a different division in Ken's company. However, this man, Carl, had moved out of engineering into upper management in the firm. He too was divorced, but he had his two teenage children living at home with him. He was an excellent cook and host, and actually gave sumptuous dinner parties at his large home, which was in an area where most of the upper executives from his firm lived. One of her friends had teasingly referred to him as the "Pearl Mesta of the executive set." This introduced Debbie to a lifestyle she had not really experienced before, but it was more casual and less ostentatious than she anticipated. Carl, too, had been impressed with Debbie's social skills and grace, so he would often invite her to one of his dinner parties or take her to a nice restaurant to be by themselves. His approach to her was gentle and low keyed, with no pressure for sexual relations or further commitment. He seemed to enjoy her company very much and was prepared to leave it at that.

This arrangement pleased Debbie, for she did not want to get sexually or romantically involved with another man as her relationship with Ken ended. She also had some reservations about the depth and substance of his lifestyle. Before long, she did become involved with another man as her romantic life took an unexpectedly more active turn. This man, Bruce, was a surgeon who had been introduced to her by one of her new close women friends. He had strong interests in art, music, and antiques, so they often went to galleries, symphonies, and operas. As a life-long bachelor and a successful surgeon, Bruce could afford to be a serious collector of art work and antiques. Debbie's love of antiques was something she had gotten from her mother, so this became one of several areas of common interest she and Bruce had.

They became lovers after the intimate relationship with Ken had ended. However, there were certain things about Bruce that prevented them from getting really close. He was quite fastidious and a bit snobbish, which led to considerable selectivity in their social lives beyond their immediate relationship. He was also rather fastidious and disconnected as a lover, and she suspected he was perhaps even less warm than Jeff had been.

Through all this, Carl had called and dated her from time to time, still without pressure for sexual relations. He did, however, finally tell her that he had come to love her and asked if she would consider the possibility of marrying him at some time of her choosing in the future. She told him that she would think about it very seriously, because she had drastically changed her initial impression of him as the "Pearl Mesta of the executive set." She had come to see him as a devoted father and a steady, warm human being. He was solid and supportive, and he seemed to cherish many of the same family and lifestyle values she had. When I interviewed and tested her for the study, she was leaning strongly in the direction of marrying Carl.

Up to this point I have presented much of Debbie's own personal experiencing of the divorce and reattachment process. It would be informative now to look at this process from the individual life structure perspective. First of all, her Settling Down period (age thirty-three to forty) seemed to be moving in a direction she wanted. She and Jeff had a child, she had her career, and they had bought the house she so much wanted. Then a major part of her life structure came apart. During the breakup, she enhanced the career aspect of her life structure, but the rest was in disarray. She also developed a very effective support network, and it looked as though the marital and family aspect of the structure might begin to take shape.

It is crucial to note at this point that Debbie never tried to shed her identification with wifehood, as Linda Craft had done. She said that throughout the whole divorce process, although she felt she had failed in her first effort, she never gave up her "inner conviction" about marriage as the only way of life for her at her age. She said she was her mother's daughter in this regard, and although she entertained the idea of singlehood it would only be out of necessity—that is, if she did not find a suitable man.

It would be helpful to take a look at some of the test results from her participation in the research project, for they shed some light on Debbie's perceptual attitudes, her assumptive world, and her cognitive structuring or construing of her situation. She turned out to have a high tolerance for ambiguity in terms of Budner's (1962) test. Her perceptual attitude was one of openness to new experiences and not prejudging. This allowed her to use and develop her support network in her own way and at her own pace, and it enabled her to interact with several different men with their own particular characteristics and lifestyles.

She had neither an external nor an internal locus of control. Her test results showed that on the one hand she saw it was her own efforts that got her into her current respected and effective professional position. On the other hand, she strongly agreed with the statement, "Most people don't realize the extent to which their lives are controlled by accidental happenings." She recognized the external locus of this statement and said she was not sure she would have felt the same way before Jeff dropped him bomb shell on her life. Before that, she did believe that her efforts and her social skills would enable her to have the kind of life she wanted. She was no longer certain of this but she still believed in it to some extent, which was why her locus of control measure was somewhat mixed.

She was not surprised to hear that she turned out to be distinctly field dependent on the Embedded Figures Test. She said, "I'm a people person, and I always have been." This was one reason why she picked the profession she picked, and it was why she had a hard time projecting herself into a life of singlehood.

Overall then, these test results showed that Debbie was able to revamp her assumptive world and even some of her values in response to the changes in her life. She said she learned a great deal about herself in the divorce and reattachment process, and there was not much doubt about that. Her assumptive world during her marriage was not really congruent with the reality of their relationship. To her, Jeff was a vulnerable idealist in need of nurturance and protection in his domestic life, while also being able to slay the dragons of social oppression in the outer world. It is clear that she did not really know Jeff, and that she probably did not really hear him when he expressed his opposition to buying the house. She thought she knew the house was something he needed, a solid base to come back to after grappling with social and economic dragons all day.

Even with his presumed secretiveness, Debbie should have had more of a sense of Jeff's basic dissatisfaction. She undoubtedly would have been sensitive to this in her clients or patients in her professional practice. In retrospect, she was able to see some aspects of Jeff more clearly, but as often happens, there was some distortion in her new conception of him. She had gone from an essentially positive conception of him to an essentially negative one. Her Reptest results showed this quite clearly. Her construing of Jeff's social idealism was that it was a way of making people abstractions so as to sympathize with them but to keep them at a distance, whereas he was actually unable to relate to the real people in his family. She now associated him with selfishness, whereas she associated Carl with the opposite of this, "warmth and givingness." Interestingly, Carl's love of good food, his large home, and other material things would, in the past, have been associated with selfishness in her mind. It was now associated on her Reperatory Grid with the positive values of warmth and givingness.

This is what I alluded to earlier in noting her change of values, and this was reflected in a written comment she made at the end of one of the research instruments she filled out. She wrote:

> Joy and pleasure should be sought out and given priority over many "responsibil-ities." People cannot be rescuers toward others; it provides little health, little growth for either in the relationship. Risk taking is important.

She said that this meant she had tried to be a rescuer or protector of Jeff in their marriage, and this did not serve either of them well. Also, she saw the need to take risks, and to change her lifestyle, if need be. She had been introduced to three somewhat different lifestyles in the three men she became involved with during her reattachment period. Ken represented pleasure and leisure rather than "responsibilities." Bruce represented "things"— antiques, artwork, collectors items. Carl turned out to represent both of these lifestyles in one person. Although a hard worker and responsible man (her old values), he liked leisure, pleasure, and material things. He loved good food, good wine, a fine home with durable but good quality furnishings.

These material values were certainly not alien to her background. She acknowledged that her mother was very impressed with Carl because of this, even though he was not Jewish. However, these values were now more explicit and accepted by Debbie in her new lifestyle, and she was putting her former idealism into a perspective that reduced the guilt she might have felt in the past. Jeff was no longer there to remind her of it, and he demonstrated by his actions that idealistic people can be quite selfish.

Debbie did decide to marry Carl while I was still interviewing and testing other participants from her PWP group during following weeks. I have since heard that she and Carl and their respective children seem to be doing well in reconstituting their families as Debbie enters the final phase of her Settling Down period.

CRISES OF DETACHMENT AND REATTACHMENT IN A FORTY-TWO YEAR-OLD MAN

This case, like the preceding one, involves a divorce, but the term "detachment" is used here in preference to divorce. This is because the type of loss represented in this case has a meaning that goes well beyond, although it includes, events like divorce and separation. In this sense, detachment refers phenomenologically to the type of loss in which the severing of a relationship is experienced as a severing of the self. This will become more clear as this case unfolds, but for the moment it is important to make the distinction between the subjective experience of detachment and the objective event of divorce.

Warren Cates was a most helpful and articulate informant in my mid-life study. He was a member of a Parents Without Partners group I contacted in the course of the study. It was my good fortune that he was a highly articulate and expressive person, with an excellent command of the English language by virtue of his occupation as a professor of English in a local college. He was also a writer of fiction, primarily short stories, which enabled him to express his feelings, insights, and life circumstances exceptionally well. This was important for the purposes of his case study because, as in the case of Steve Gornecky in Chapter Four, it was necessary to retrospectively recapture his first crisis of detachment in his broken marriage four years earlier, and more recently, the crisis of reattachment with another woman. He was able to recapture these events with direct and intense feeling in the interviews, so much so that his experiencing rating would generally be in the six to seven range on the EXP scale. He claimed that he would never have been able to achieve those ratings before, during, or immediately after the breakup of his marriage. He said that his feelings were "too close, too overwhelming," especially his pervasive anxiety, for him to be able to get in touch with them, explore them, and then express them effectively.

Warren was a tall, angular man of about six feet three inches, with light brown hair and blue eyes. The small amount of gray in his beard and on his full head of hair was scarcely noticeable, so he appeared younger than his forty-two years. He had a highly intelligent and sensitive appearance and gave the impression of someone who was both earnest and eager to please. He was a very easy informant to relate to during the study interviews and when going over the research instruments he readily filled out.

He explained that he probably gained his ability to experience and relate his feelings from psychotherapy, which he went into when his marriage was in jeopardy and he was "in the midst of other intense emotional problems." Although he had been highly motivated for treatment, he had nevertheless been doubtful and mistrustful of the therapist and the treatment relationship when he went into it. Therapy represented a need/fear dilemma for him, just as all of the really close relationships in his life did. He had gone to a psychiatrist who had to work very hard to gain his trust. The psychiatrist accomplished this in large part by helping Warren deal with specific anxiety-provoking events and phobias he was experiencing. Rather than prescribe Valium or some other medication, the psychiatrist taught him tension reduction techniques, including deep breathing and muscle relaxation, even though his orientation to therapy was Freudian and psychodynamic. This aided the treatment relationship, because Warren was quite fearful of medication and the techniques helped.

Despite his misgivings, there was no doubt in his mind that he wanted and needed psychotherapy. He acknowledged that his marriage was in trouble, but he was also bothered by his low self-image and his lack of confidence in both his personal and creative life. His professorship was secure, since he had tenure at the college, and it was not his teaching abilities he was concerned about. It was his writing, or lack of it, that caused him great concern and feelings of self-doubt and ineffectiveness. He was working on a novel, which was going very slowly. Most of the time he could not write, and when he tried he would become unduly meticulous and obsess over every word and line. Yet, as he looked back on that painful time, there was one problem that overrode and yet pervaded all the others. That was anxiety. He was exceptionally anxious, not only about his marriage, but about everything of any significance to him. In describing his experience of the events which caused him anxiety at that time he used words very similar to those of one prominent phenomenologist: "They enshroud me like night and rob me of my individuality and freedom. I can literally no longer breathe; I am possessed" (Merleau-Ponty 1945/1962, 286).

Warren Cates was indeed often possessed by his anxiety; he *was* his anxiety. There was no play, no distance between himself and the events that obsessed him. He recognized and often discussed this kind of emotional nearsightedness in which he could not see any solutions to or respite from the things which obsessed him in his immediate life space. Much of his therapy involved efforts to help him to gain some distance from them.

How did Warren get this way? How did he develop this anxious world view or being-in-the-world? He was aware of some factors in his family background which served to provide such a view. In general, it could be said that when he began therapy he saw his parents as almost entirely responsible for both his intrapersonal and interpersonal problems.

He described his mother as a needy, self-preoccupied woman, addicted to soap operas, permanents, and new clothes. He felt that in her own fantasized world, she romanticized or vaguely eroticized her relationship with him. She taught him how to dance, took him on shopping trips for her dresses and discussed her selections, as well as other things that would make her happy. If he was "nice" and made her happy she made it clear he was a "good boy." If he behaved badly, but not toward her, she would chastize him in a teasing semi-serious way about his "bad" or "devilish" behavior. She let it be known that he was indeed devilish but that this was not entirely unattractive. Consequently, he would feel vaguely good or rewarded for being "bad."

Despite this almost playful relationship, he did not experience his mother as a loving or a giving person. She was not capable of that because she was "too self-centered and childish." He felt his father kept her that way because "he idolized her and spoiled her." The one who did offer him real warmth and nurturance was his paternal grandmother. She was the only one he felt good and secure with, but he would "make her life a misery" by misbehaving, doing risky things, and otherwise frightening and upsetting her. Although he could not remember any specific incidents, he felt that he often did these things to his grandmother at his mother's connivance, or at least with her silent appreciation. He said he did not trust his mother, and he never had.

He felt his father was "more of a real person" than his mother, but he was a very worried, insecure man who was always very concerned about keeping up appearances. His father was a salesman in a rather exclusive men's store in Chicago. He made a decent living at his job, but he never felt any real job security during his working years. However, it was a white collar job and it allowed him to associate with men of some education and importance. That meant a great deal to him, because he felt he came from a well educated and "well established" background. His father had been a lawyer and his mother a music teacher in the small midwestern town in which he was raised. He had started college but never finished, because of the depression and his father's loss of savings and paying clientele. He had to raise his own family in a "tough" ethnic (mostly Polish-American) blue collar neighborhood. He felt like a beleaguered "WASP" in a sea of "ethnics."

Indeed, Warren was warned repeatedly about the dangers in the outside world, such as the neighborhood with the tough ethnic kids. He was admonished not to "start up with them," but he recalled that when he actually got involved in a fight with one of them his father looked on from inside the house and did not intervene. When Warren ran away from his tormentor, his father made it clear that he was ashamed of him for running away from a fight. Paradoxically, despite his generalized fearfulness, his father was an enthusiastic sports fan and he wanted Warren to excel in sports, particularly baseball. However, Warren felt that he was inept at sports, although interested in them, and this was another area in which he experienced his father's disapproval. His father felt that it was important to keep up the appearance of strength and athletic ability, because you would appear vulnerable and an easy victim otherwise.

Given all of these warnings, these conflicting do's and don'ts, Warren never felt sure of when he was safe and when he wasn't. The rather capricious relationship with his mother did not give him a very firm basis of trust to begin with. He always felt somehow manipulated into doing "nice things" for her, against which he would often rebel and try to assert his autonomy. This was seen as bad or "devilish" behavior and, though it was rewarded with a perverse kind of approval from time to time. it was never accepted in a forthright way as a natural expression of autonomy and self-assertion at that stage of his development. Consequently, when he reached his teens, and the same needs for self-assertion and identity became so great, Warren was in a state of unbridled negativism toward the constraints of his parents and their concerns with appearance. Anything he could do to shock them, to appear unconventional, gave him a gleeful, perverse satisfaction. On the other hand, he was sensitive to their disapproval, which made him feel bad about himself. Soon, though, he would feel hurt, then angry, and finally resentful about their disapproval, which would start another round of shocking talk or opinions by him to upset them.

He remembered feeling terribly unhappy and out of step in his teens. If he had not discovered his interest in and then passion for modern literature, he does not know what would have happened to him. Interestingly, it began with his reading of Henry Miller "with the dirty-mindedness of a teenager." In the process, however, he gained a taste for unconventional but good modern American writing. Before this, he had vague thoughts of becoming a lawyer "or something like that," but this did not seem to have any internal or personal meaning in terms of his feelings or interests. Now, he knew he wanted to pursue a career in modern literature, either as a writer or a teacher. Fortunately, he had a charismatic English teacher in high school who recognized his passion and writing talent and encouraged his pursuit of this career line.

Thus, at the age of seventeen he experienced a vivid identity crisis and resolution. He had been doing reasonably well in academic subjects, despite some difficulty with mathematics, but when he turned to literature he became totally absorbed in it to the exclusion of everything else. He began failing his academic subjects, but he had "found himself." He turned to his bedroom and spent almost every waking hour there, reading, writing, and reading again, when he was not in school. His parents thought this was strange behavior and warned him that other people would think he was strange. This did not bother him very much because he always thought of himself as something of an alienated "beatnik" during his teens. He liked jazz, arty people, and representatives of the "beat generation," such as James Dean, in the pop culture, and Jack Kerouac and Allan Ginsberg in the creative culture of the late fifties and early sixties. Therefore, his new-found passion fit his lifestyle and image of himself, much to the chagrin of his parents.

He managed to pull up his other academic grades and to graduate from high school. He went to a public university downstate for his B.A. in English. His academic performance there had been good enough to get him into a graduate program at the University of Chicago. He received his M.A. and was given a teaching assistantship while pursuing his Ph.D. at Chicago. It was there that he met his wife, Sally, who was an undergraduate student in one of the classes he taught.

They became romantically involved and began a Pygmalian type of relationship in which Sally learned and incorporated almost everything he taught her about literature, culture, and ideas about life in general. In the process she became something of an alter ego for him; the person he could turn to for appraisal of his writing, his impressions of the work of others, his ideas, and so on. She could be trusted to reflect back to him in pristine form his own standards, norms, and ideas about the good or bad and the beautiful or ugly. Needless to say, this was immensely reassuring to him, not simply because she was almost always positive about his work and ideas, but because of his many self-doubts and compulsive questioning of his own motives, thoughts, feelings, and actions. She became indispensible to him, particularly in terms of more personal and interpersonal matters. He came to trust her abilities to appraise and deal with other people, and he deferred to her judgments in these areas. She did, after all, share his own low opinion of his parents.

His parents did not share the same opinion of her, however. They thought she was a very nice young woman and that she would be very good for Warren. Warren's father knew her father, who was one of his customers, and approved of her family. Ironically, then, Warren and Sally were secret fellow despisers of his parents, while at the same time his parents approved of them as partners, and hopefully partners for life. They were married in a traditional ceremony with a large conventional wedding celebration paid for by their parents. Sally was twenty-one years old and had not yet graduated, and Warren was twenty-six and just preparing to take a new teaching job on the faculty at a college in the east.

Warren had been frightened at the very prospect of marriage, but he felt pressured by circumstances and their families into marrying Sally. He was also fearful that if he did not marry Sally, he would never find a woman who could understand him and take care of his needs as well as she. However, he still felt trapped and almost immediately after the wedding he accused her of trapping him. This led to a bitter fight and extremely hurt feelings on Sally's part. They had no sexual relations during the week of their honeymoon before going to their new home in the east.

Warren informed me that he had been "a virgin" before he met Sally. He had, after all, been something of a social isolate in his teens, both in his ethnic neighborhood and in high school when his passion for modern fiction kept him locked in his room. Sally, on the other hand, had been a sociable young woman who had a number of close girlfriends. She was also reasonably popular with boys, for she was attractive and personable. She claimed that the only prior sexual experience she had was "a few times" with the young man she dated exclusively for a year before she met Warren. Still, this was more experience than he had, and he felt she was more knowledgable than he in sex and felt at a disadvantage as a result. He always had the feeling that she could control him through sex, which he very much wanted to engage in when they first started dating. It took him quite a while to convince her to engage in sex, and it did not happen until they were formally engaged, but he remembered feeling very grateful to her for doing so. He always felt vaguely grateful, as though she were doing him a favor by having intercourse. Therefore, when she refused to have sex with him because he hurt her feelings on their honeymoon, he experienced this as a clear indication of her willingness to use sex to control or punish him.

This was hardly an auspicious start for their marriage, but Sally idolized Warren and was devoted to him. She also recognized that he was frightened by the full import and magnitude of the relationship and responsibility in marriage, but she felt she had the emotional strength and ability to see them both through this difficult time.

She occupied herself by taking a course at the college, but most of her time was spent taking care of their apartment, cooking, cleaning, shopping, and so on, while working at part-time clerical jobs in various offices in the college to add to their income. She did this for a year until their daughter, Naomi, was born, and then she devoted herself entirely to the child and to Warren. The birth of Naomi added to Warren's ambivalent feelings about the marriage; he was proud and fond of the baby, but it represented even more attachment and responsibility. He began feeling more trapped and manipulated, and he would take it out on Sally in various ways, such as criticizing her for her clothing, her physical appearance, her handling of household finances, and so on. He also had an affair with an attractive married woman in her late thirties, who attended one of his evening courses at the college.

Sally found out about the affair and there was a confrontation between them, after which Warren ended the affair for fear of losing Sally. He then settled down and began working very hard to firm up his academic career. He finished his dissertation, received his Ph.D., and published a number of articles in scholarly journals on the work of certain contemporary American fiction writers. He had to put his own creative impulses to write fiction "pretty much in cold storage" during that period of time.

When he was thirty, Warren took a more promising position of associate professor at another college in the east. By that time he had a one-year-old son, Peter, as well as three year-old Naomi. This added responsibility made him feel more anxious but he was somehow able to harness some of that anxiety with a great deal of support and help from Sally, and work harder on his academic career so as to obtain the security of tenure. He finally was reviewed for tenure as he was approaching age thirty-seven.

The whole tenure process was terribly stressful for him. He admitted to feeling "extremely scared and paranoid" at the time. This was exacerbated by some opposition in his department to his receiving tenure by at least two women faculty members, and one man who sided with them. This opposition came about as the result of a short story he had managed to write and to have published while he was working so diligently toward tenure. The story concerned a married man who murdered his mistress because of his obsession with her and his jealousy of her life apart from him. One woman colleague in his department took particular offense to it, claiming it represented "the kind of violence against women that is rampant in this country." She convinced another female and a male colleague that this was evidence of Warren's basic sexism, which she claimed also showed up in his teaching activities and departmental relationships.

Warren was appalled at these charges for he felt they were grossly distorted and unfair. He countered by claiming that the story actually represented a pro-feminist position, and he laid out his reasons for his claim. He was not able to convince his opposition, but they only numbered three, and the remainder of his department voted in favor of him. He received tenure, but at a terrible cost—the alienation of Sally.

She had been very supportive of him during the tenure process, but he admitted to being "more paranoid and more difficult to live with." He seemed to take most of his tension out on her, and to a lesser extent on Naomi, whose behaviors tended to irritate him more than Peter's. However, Sally got the brunt of it. He had always gotten her caught up in his anxieties and obsessive concerns and "worry them to death" in tense extended dialogue with her. Then, with these much more momentous concerns and anxieties in the tenure process he became "utterly impossible." They had terrible verbal fights and, almost as a matter of self-protection, Sally became involved in the political campaign of a reform candidate in their district. This took her away from Warren for extended periods of time during each week. It also got her involved with several other women in the campaign who were active feminists and who openly decried Warren's treatment of her. She became more and more angry at Warren, and when he received official word that his tenure had been approved she told him she wanted a divorce. He was horrified by this prospect of divorce, and "practically begged" her to reconsider. He suggested they go into marital counseling together to try to work it out. She refused and advised him instead to find a psychotherapist for himself because he was the one who needed the help, especially now that he would have to learn to live on his own. As his anxiety built up to near panic proportions, he did begin therapy with the psychiatrist mentioned earlier.

Let us take a look at the meaning of these developments to Warren at that time. He was supposed to be in Levinson's Settling Down period (ages thirty-three to forty) at that time. He had achieved tenure and security at age thirty-seven, so the work and career part of his individual life structure was solidly in place. He had worked hard to build that part of his life structure, but now the love (marriage and family) aspect had come apart. He had envisaged having the job security of tenure in order to support and be with his wife and two children, but now that he had that security he could not have them.

It was possible to get some sense of the meaning of these events from the perspective of his cognitive structure by going over some of the instruments he filled out in my research contacts with him. He was able to go back in time mentally to indicate how he would have responded to the instrument items during the period when his marriage was breaking up and he had begun therapy. Of course, the instruments also provided some understanding of his cognitions and constructions of his current reality at the time of the actual testing. For the most part, the following analysis tries to recapitulate Warren's perceptual attitudes and assumptive world before and during his marital breakup by noting the responses he would have given on the instruments at that time, while briefly mentioning the changes that occurred.

The results of his Intolerance of Ambiguity Test showed that he saw the world as a complex, uncertain, and ambiguous place in which it was difficult to find right or wrong answers or even adequate information for solving problems. This was particularly so at the time or marital breakup but less so at the time of testing. Interestingly, his Internal/External Locus Test results showed that he did not have a pronounced internal or external locus of control, and he felt that this had not changed. On the one hand, he agreed with the statement, "Most people don't realize the extent to which their lives are controlled by accidental happenings" (external locus). On the other hand, he agreed that "Getting people to do the right thing depends upon ability, luck has little or nothing to do with it" (internal locus). This last statement or perception, when put together with the high field dependence score on the Embedded Figures Test, indicated a unique kind of compulsive dynamic in critical interpersonal relationships in his life. In the past, the ambiguity he tended to see all around him exacerbated his anxiety, which in turn, drove him compulsively to gain control over the doubts and fears generated by threatening ambiguous situation. Phenomenologically, this combination of perceptual attitudes would be experienced as an intense need to control the ambiguity and chaos he saw in the world by getting others (field dependence) to control it and ward it off for him. His attempt to get the other person to do this would usually be in the form of obsessive-compulsive concern with the minutiae and details of the ambiguous and threatening situation. His wife, of course, played this role in his life through all the years of their marriage.

He gave an example of a typical type of interaction with this wife in which this type of dynamic was epitomized. This involved their taking an automobile trip in which they would have to plan their routes ahead of time. Warren admitted to being very fearful of such road trips all his life, and yet he did not want to be the one to work out the travel plans or to use a map. Therefore, Sally would figure out the route ahead of time while Warren would worry that she might have made a mistake. He would then insist that she check and double check her plans in minute detail before they started. During the trip he would not be able to relax and would be hypervigilant about any possible change in route or plans, however small or insignificant. If she did take a short cut or alternate route from the prepared plan, he would fly into a panic and rage, accusing her of having gotten them lost. This scenario repeated itself quite a number of times throughout their marriage.

The dynamic is very clear in this example. Sally would have to take control and assume responsibility for the fearsome trip, and Warren would attempt to contain his growing anxiety by making her plan the trip down to its most minute detail, while vigilantly checking on her throughout the trip. This dynamic extended into many other areas of their life, in which she would have to deal with landlords, salespeople, bill collectors, and all the other threatening people and organizations in the world outside their little home and family—a recapitulation of the conflicted forebodings and warnings of the world outside the family provided by his father during his childhood.

There were some other features of this dynamic which should be noted. One was the essentially symbiotic nature of the interaction. Warren had to get Sally to undertake the necessary but feared activities with him. He would not do them alone, and this had been pointed out to him as a pattern by his psychiatrist who was a Freudian with an object-relations orientation. He felt Warren had basic separation-individuation problems dating back to early childhood. His interpretation was that Warren's mother's needy and capricious relationship with him prevented him from satisfactorily going through the separation-individuation process in his first three years of life. This fear of separating and moving out into the world was reinforced by his father's warnings about the world. Therefore, Warren recapitulated an earlier symbiosis and got Sally to go out into the world with and for him.

In discussing his fear of road trips, Warren told me that he was "deathly afraid" of getting lost, and his most vivid association or image with that fear was of the story and plight of Hansel and Gretel. He could feel the utter panic they must have felt in being lost in the woods and of having their carefully laid markings for the way out of the woods eaten by the birds. It is worth noting that the story of Hansel and Gretel has traditionally symbolized the theme of abandonment. It is also worth noting that Hansel and Gretel are symbiotic as well; they are lost, as one, together. In the story, it is significant that being lost represents the ultimate fear of abandonment, of being left as small and defenseless children to the wiles and devices of the wicked witch (world). This expressed the way Warren felt about those travel situations, and when Sally missed a turnoff or took a different route, she was no longer the strong protector but rather the helpless Gretel to his Hansel—and therefore they were both lost. The important point to emphasize here is the symbiotic nature of the relationship Warren had with Sally, and his underlying abandonment anxiety, when considering the meaning of his separation from her.

Elliott Jaques's (1965, 1980) theory of the mid-life crisis seems to account for a number of key features in Warren's case, including the psychiatrist's interpretation. It should be recalled that Jaques developed his theory based on his study of creative men in their middle and late thirties. He noticed "a marked tendency toward crisis" in the creative work of these men. There was often a sharp quantitative reduction or total drying up of their work, as well as a change in quality and content. Warren's controversial short story represented a change in the content as well as the rate of his creativity. It depicted violence between the sexes, whereas his earlier fiction tended toward the erotic. Secondly, the writing of his novel was painfully slow as he became more methodological and obsessive with every new line he wrote.

It is possible to view this change in the content and method of Warren's writing as the type of creative crisis Jaques depicted. This crisis is supposed to have its roots in a death anxiety, and it occurs when the fact of his own mortality begins to impress itself on the creative artist in his middle thirties. It is not death *per se* that Jaques is writing about, but rather an unconscious, infantile conception of death that is more fearsome. He says, "It is not in fact death in the sense which we think about it, but an unconscious fantasy of immobilization and helplessness, in which the self is subject to violent fragmentation, while yet retaining the capacity to experience the persecution and torment to which it is being subjected" (Jaques 1965, 507). This conception of death actually describes the experience and phenomenology of abandonment anxiety, for "the infant's relation with life and death occurs in the setting of his survival being dependent on his external objects . . . and the chaotic internal situation is thus experienced as the infantile equivalent of the notion of death" (Jaques 1965, 507).

This experience of infantile abandonment gets us closer to Warren's basic anxiety at that stage of his life. As the marital relationship between Warren and Sally deteriorated in the period preceding the actual separation, Sally became more and more the "persecuting and annihilating bad object," in Jaques's paradigm, and less and less the good, protecting, and nurturing object. This shift from erotic to violent content in his writing could represent the internal object-shift, and the greater the feelings of rage and persecution toward the bad object, the greater the impulse toward violence, as depicted in the short story. This same theme was being carried out in the novel he was trying to write. In contrast to the short story, it was the protagonist's wife who was the object of his murderous impulses. Warren recognized how close this was to Norman Mailer's plot in *An American Dream,* in which the novel's central act is the protagonist's murder of his wife. However, Warren felt there was a basic difference between Mailer's vision or theme and his. Mailer's protagonist, Rojack, committed the murder as an existential act—that is, in the sense of acting out "an American (male) dream." Warren's protagonist, on the other hand, was driven, was *compelled,* to kill his wife. Furthermore, in killing her, he recognized he was killing himself. Thus, there seemed to be an inevitable homicide/suicide motif in Warren's vision of the novel.

This was discussed in Warren's therapy, and his psychiatrist came up with the following interpretation, which, in retrospect, Warren felt was true. Furthermore, it was also consistent with Jaques's paradigm. The interpretation ran as follows: As Sally became the "persecuting bad object" in the process of marital deterioration, the more enraged Warren became and the more compelled he was to (physically) kill the "annihilating bad object." However, in the symbiotic sense, the object, whether good or bad, is necessary for survival of the self. Therefore, to kill the object is to kill the self, and that was why Warren felt the novel's inexorable motif was both homicidal and suicidal.

Several months after Warren began therapy, Sally demanded a divorce. She wanted an immediate separation and was clearly becoming increasingly enraged at what she felt to be years of emotional exploitation and humiliation by Warren. She announced she would remain in their house where she would take primary responsibility for the care of Naomi and Peter.

Warren mounted most of the same arguments that many husbands raise when they are asked or told to leave their own homes in the case of marital separation. Since he had worked and paid for the house, why should he be the one to leave? He used this and many other arguments to say that he had every right to remain in the house. In his case, of course, it was more the fact that he was the one being asked to physically move out and separate himself when he did not want the separation. The justice of his leaving his house was very much secondary or incidental to his basic resistance to separation. However, over the following weeks, Sally became increasingly more insistent about his leaving and even hired a lawyer to pursue a legal basis for having him removed, if he continued to refuse to leave. She had been promised a job as a legislative aide for the reform candidate who had won the election, and she would be employed as soon as he took office in the forthcoming legislative session. Also, her new friends and colleagues on the political scene encouraged her to insist upon an immediate separation. Therefore, Sally demanded that Warren leave within a matter of two weeks or she would obtain a warrant to have him removed. She said she was assured by her lawyer that this could be done without any delay.

The relationship had deteriorated so badly those last few months that living together was intolerable for Sally and becoming so for Warren. She was livid, incensed over the years of "oppression and humiliation" he had subjected her to, and now her pent up hatred and resentment knew no bounds. She could not speak to him without anger, and simply could not stand the sight of him. This was finally so demoralizing to Warren that he prepared to move despite his fears and misgivings.

Warren had some help in dealing with the process of moving out. In addition to his therapy, Warren had a support network of good friends and colleagues at work and in the community. He turned to them for emotional support and physical help in moving to a furnished apartment. He strengthened these relationships, and he especially cultivated the friendship of an old childhood friend who now lived in the area. This was a recently divorced man who was very helpful to him during the separation and in the reattachment process, when they began going on dates together. Warren also joined a support group of recently divorced or separated men and women at a local family service agency.

Warren was able to engage in effective expressive coping through the emotional support of friends and others. His instrumental coping was also much more effective than he had anticipated. He obtained a furnished apartment on an interim basis of two or three months until he could find a larger apartment with room for a studio to work in and with a location which was easily accessible to his children. He did find such an apartment, which was only two blocks away from his old home and which took only five minutes to reach on foot. He also worked particularly hard to strengthen his relationship with Peter, since he now saw this as the most important relationship in his life. He always felt much closer emotionally to Peter than to Naomi, who he thought he had alienated further with his highly irritable and "paranoid" behavior during his tenure struggle. It was clear that she sided with her mother in the separation crisis, and she pretty much restricted her visits to Warren after the separation to obligatory ones.

He also tried to firm up his relations with his parents. He made a special trip to Chicago to visit them with Peter, and he found his parents to be very supportive of him at that troubled time. Before the trip he had strong misgivings about their reactions because he was not sure they would understand the separation, given their imperatives about maintaining the family as protection against the many threats of the outside world. He could not recall ever having had such positive feelings toward his parents, and he began to feel that Sally had denigrated his parents to serve her own purposes, in order to keep him more dependent on her. At any rate, he now saw his parents as an emotional resource in his life as he never had seen them before, and when his father survived a heart attack some months later, their relationship became even closer.

Consequently, when his divorce became final at age forty, Warren's new life structure had taken shape and had stabilized to some extent. He had tenure and good collegial relationships in his teaching position, and he was becoming much more productive in his writing for literary and scholarly journals, if not for his novel. His friendship and support network was solidly in place, and he now had a woman in his life who he found intellectually compatible and exceptionally exciting sexually. So, the love or affiliative aspect of his life structure appeared to be getting better along with the work aspect.

Warren discontinued therapy as a result of this apparent stabilization in his life structure. He was experiencing growing individuation and autonomy after the dependent and symbiotic tie he had with Sally. He had learned to prepare his own meals and manage his personal affairs effectively by himself. However, a potential new crisis, this time related to reattachment, began to loom. This involved the new woman in his life, Norma, who was working toward a Master's degree in his program. She was in one of his classes, and the first time they got together outside the classroom was at a faculty-student party at a colleague's home. She was somewhat older (twenty-seven years old) than most of the students in his class, and it seemed to him that she was personally interested in him on the basis of a few interactions he had had with her in class. She was indeed interested in him, and they became intimately involved almost immediately after getting together at that party.

Not only did Norma provide Warren with the most exciting and satisfying sexual relationship of his life, but she was intelligent, very knowledgable about literature, and an excellent companion when they were in company with others. It seemed as though all of his friends took an immediate liking to her, and before long even his faculty colleagues accepted and actually favored her as his companion at dinner parties and other social affairs. His son, Peter, also took an almost immediate liking to her. So, after only a few weeks, Warren's relationship with Norma became, imperceptibly, an exclusive one. There seemed to be no need to date another woman, even though he might have a passing interest in doing so from time to time.

Norma had given indications that she would like their relationship to become more serious when she received her degree, but he had not given these too much thought at the time. However, he was somewhat fearful about dating another woman in the event Norma might find out and break off their relationship. His primary concern seemed to be that it would be very difficult to find another woman with whom he could be so compatible in so many ways. He was quite comfortable with her and did not want to risk that relationship for an unknown one. However, as her graduation date approached she began pressing him for a commitment to live together. She would be giving up her shared apartment with another female graduate student, and she wanted him to join her in looking for a new place so they could live together.

Norma was an ardent horsewoman who had gone to exclusive women's schools all the way through college and then married a graduate of Yale Law School. Their childless marriage ended after three years as they found themselves to be more and more incompatible, both intellectually and socially. She was intensely interested in literature and the arts while he was interested in the social life and concerns of the corporate world of New York City, where he was employed. However, they both did share a preference for the "exurban" Connecticut lifestyle, including horseback riding. Therefore, she wanted the same type of home with Warren in an exurban or rural area, whereas he very much preferred city life and was almost phobic about nature and the outdoors.

He was getting quite anxious under this pressure from Norma, because it contained the implied threat that she would break off the relationship if he did not move together with her. At first he tried to placate her into keeping their present arrangement, but when this did not work, he attempted to convince her to move in with him on a trial basis. She would have none of that; she wanted them to start on "a whole new relationship." His current apartment was too close to his former home, and she felt the apartment was more Peter's home than hers. This reflected the fact that her attitude toward Peter had changed. She felt that he was impolite in the way he conducted himself with adults and that he was too demanding of Warren's time and attention. She felt Warren was too indulgent with him, and she has some strong opinions about how he should be handled.

The increasingly stressful relationship between Warren and Norma became the overriding concern of his life at that time. A clue to the evolution of their relationship and its repetitive theme was provided when Warren told about an auto trip he and Norma took in which she planned the route and made a wrong, unplanned, turn while driving the car. Warren had flown in to the same kind of panic and rage he formerly did with Sally. Indeed, Norma had made a specific point on several occasions of saying that she knew things like auto trips made Warren anxious, but that she was good at handling them and that he could rely on her in those circumstances. It seemed that some of the old symbiotic collusions were appearing in this relationship that had existed in his marriage.

Norma had also begun talking about the possibility of marriage and children in their future, and this upset Warren even more. He could not imagine having any more children, and he had absolutely no desire to get married. On the other hand, he was frightened at the prospect of Norma walking out of their relationship. This prompted him to contact his former therapist for help in this new stressful situation. He began his new round of therapy by expressing many concerns about losing Norma. First, they had so much in common—art, friends, good conversation, and a good sexual relationship. Secondly, all his friends thought she was wonderful, so wouldn't he be missing out on the one person in his life he could make it with if he let her go? Wouldn't he be considered strange for not wanting her? When asked if he loved her he said, "I really don't know—but, if I *did* love her wouldn't I know it for certain?" Even if he did not love her, how could all his friends be wrong: they all said she was so right for him.

Over the next few weeks Norma increased her pressure for them to find a place to move to. She was also becoming more critical of Peter, his table manners and other behaviors, and she wanted more of a direct hand in changing his behavior. After a few clashes over this issue, Warren began avoiding having Peter and Norma together in the same social situations. He began to find her behavior toward Peter to be jealous; the behavior of a sibling rather than an adult. This impression was reinforced when she accused him on several occasions of loving Peter more than he loved her.

In one therapy session shortly thereafter, he told his therapist he did love Peter more, and that he did not even know whether he loved her. So, if it had to be a choice between the two of them it would have to be Peter. However, he continued to be fearful of losing her. It became evident to him that so much of his motivation for not losing her was based on fear—fear that he would be terribly lonely without her, fear that his friends were right and that he would never find another woman like her, and fear that he could not make it alone without her. When reminded by his therapist that he was able to make it without Sally, he dismissed this by saying he had simply set up a similar relationship with Norma. The therapist focused on Warren's healthy recognition that he seemed to be acting almost completely out of fear in regard to Norma, and that this was not a satisfactory basis on which to make a decision concerning the relationship.

The therapist spoke directly of Warren's abandonment anxiety, and how it was important for him to recognize and acknowledge his real, adult feelings concerning the threat of loss but to also recognize the debilitating infantile feelings of helplessness and distinegration for what they were, relics of an early childhood consciousness that had no useful place in his present adult reality. Warren had to prepare himself for future separations, which are an inevitable part of life. It was emphasized that he had survived one major loss (Sally), and that he could survive others—even Norma, if necessary.

As a result of that therapy session he told Norma he did not wish to go with her to look at an available house she wanted them to see together. He told her he was content to stay where he was, and if she wanted to live with him it would have to be in his current apartment near Peter. She said this was not possible; it would be Peter's home and not hers. She was very angry and refused to see him or answer his calls for almost two weeks afterward. He had tried to see if he could make it without calling her, but decided he had nothing to lose by calling her. She finally did respond to one of his calls. Thereafter, their relationship assumed an on-and-off quality in which they would get together for a few days, have an argument, and then not talk to one another for several more days. She finally became so exasperated at this situation that she went out and invested in a house of her own, thereby allowing him the option of moving in with her and sharing the mortgage and other expenses. He was vastly relieved by this, because now he was no longer faced with the ultimatum of having to rent or buy a place with her, which would have committed him to living with her. The extent of his relief convinced him that he did not really want to live with Norma, if only he had the strength to hold out and not give into the fear of losing her. However, he did not want to break with her entirely.

He acknowledged to his therapist that he could not bring himself to break off the relationship, but if she chose to break it out of frustration with him he would try to accept it, even though he would have powerful feelings of abandonment along with intense loneliness and probably depression. Therefore, his strategy for coping with the situation was to continue with the status quo, which was what he actually wanted, but with less conflict and demands from her. This was totally unacceptable to Norma, and after a few more weeks of fighting, getting together, and fighting again, she demanded that he move in with her and he refused. He first argued that she had taken a place in a rural area, and that he could not tolerate. However, the argument became more heated, with accusations of insincerity and lying and finally with name calling. In the heat of this, Warren retorted to one of her accusations that he would not live with her even if she moved into the city or any other place he might prefer. At this, she said their relationship was ended once and for all, unless he committed himself to the relationship and moved in with her.

With much trepidation, Warren decided that he had to stick to his retort and all it implied. It was the only honest and adult thing he could do. Therefore, he was determined not to call her, but he was not sure what he would do if she called him to ask to get together. If she promised there would be no strings attached, no further demands to live together, he would probably get together gladly. He acknowledged to his therapist that he did not think it was either fair or realistic for Norma to accept the ongoing exclusive but noncommitted form of relationship he wanted. He therefore had to prepare himself for the almost certain reality of complete separation from her. He speculated that perhaps he was simply not suited to conjugal life. He somehow seemed too fearful of its closeness, yet he wanted its security. If only he could make it on his own without one exclusive relationship, at least for a significant period of time, he might find that out for himself. He did not like the idea that he would desperately need someone for the rest of his life. He had to get over that idea and that feeling.

His therapist supported him in this position and encouraged him to join Parents Without Partners or some other reputable singles group in order to meet some of his normal needs for female companionship. However, it was understood he would not quickly attach himself to one woman and form an exclusive relationship. Warren did join PWP, and he did not call Norma, even though he was sorely tempted to do so. She, true to her word, did not call him. After several weeks he began dating other women, primarily from PWP. He purposely did not date any one woman on a regular basis for fear of repeating his pattern, as delineated by his therapist. He also heard from mutual friends that Norma was now dating other men, and this gave him more impetus to date other women out of what he called a "childish kind of retaliatory jealousy." Nevertheless, it served his purpose for he learned, to his immense relief and satisfaction, that he could relate to women without immediately engaging in a needy, exclusive relationship.

Warren ended his second round of the therapy after about three months, when it was clear that he had adequately dealt with the separation from Norma. At first, he was feeling intensely lonely and needy. He said he literally "ached" with loneliness at first, and he compulsively sought others—friends, Peter, and his parents. When he asked for his first date with a woman in PWP, he felt intensely anxious and inept, but he soon realized how easy and natural it could be. He did have to admit that some of the women were every bit as needy as he, but this made it easier to get together. However, this sometimes made it more difficult to keep the relationships short term and nonexclusive. He managed that, however, as well as occasional sexual relationships which were enough for him to retain a modicum of satisfaction in that area of his life.

When I interviewed and tested Warren, he had just turned forty-two years old. He had completed his second round of therapy about four months earlier, and he was planning on leaving Parents Without Partners. He said that it had been a "true safety net" for him as he was going through the stressful experience of separation from Norma. However, he no longer needed the safety net, and the group held no inherent interest for him. He had not met any men in the group who had become close friends. He already had a good network of male friends outside PWP with intellectual and social interests akin to his. He did meet and would continue to get together with several women from PWP with whom he had "good" relationships. At the same time, he had met several other women outside the organization he felt the same way about.

He went on to explain that he considered these women to be "friends." That is, they liked him and he liked them and they enjoyed one another's company. He might have sex with some of them but not each of them. Some were simply good social and intellectual companions, "someone you could go out with and enjoy without the expectation of sex on either side." To be able to relate to a woman without viewing her as a potential sex object was something he never thought would happen to him.

He no longer had the problem of pervasive anxiety. I did administer the State-Trait Anxiety Inventory to him, because of the nature of his earlier difficulties and lifelong pattern. He was somewhat high on the "anxiety-proneness" (trait anxiety) part of the Inventory, but not abnormally so. He said that he would probably always be a bit on the anxious side, which his therapist had assured him was not unusual or a problem in its own right, but he was much less anxiety-prone than he used to be. This did indeed seem to be so on the basis of how he would have answered some of the STAI items in the past as compared to responses at the time of my testing. His current level of tension and apprehension (state anxiety) was in the normal range.

He told me that he was feeling much better about his life than at any time in the past, even though there were a number of unanswered questions about it. The primary question was whether or not he could or would ever again enter into an ongoing conjugal relationship with a woman. In raising this question he made the following observations:

> I'm not sure whether I'm acting out of fear or courage by not getting involved in a sustained relationship at this time, but I feel that it's right for me. The longer I make it on my own as a single person, the more whole I feel. Sometimes, I wonder whether I'm becoming too complete or self-contained—that I might never need or want anyone. Then I wonder whether that is right or healthy. I don't know whether I can ever have a full, mature relationship with another person, but I *do* know it would be wrong to go back to what I had in my marriage. I also know that I appreciate and relate to women in a new and different way. I enjoy them and I'm less fearful of being controlled by them, so maybe there's a chance that I might be able at sometime in the future to find and sustain a mature relationship.

Warren was quite pleased with the way the other aspects of his life were going. He was enjoying his teaching in a way he had not before. He enjoyed encouraging and cultivating the interests and aptitudes of his students and was getting great satisfaction out of his mentor role with new faculty members. His interests in writing had turned to literary analysis and criticism, which fit more with his academic career than did his fiction writing. He was not pursuing these interests for the purposes of academic advancement but because he was more proficient in analysis and criticism and he relished this activity and proficiency.

He had been asked to be a regular reviewer of contemporary fiction for a monthly publication with wide national distribution. He had put off a decision about the offer while he was in the throes of his troubles with Norma. He did accept the offer at first as a forced way of keeping himself busy and his mind off Norma during the initial stages of their separation. Then he began to get an inherent satisfaction from it. He came to feel that literary criticism and analysis was his creative forte in the same way that he once thought his fiction writing was. In fact, after having worked through the breakup of his marriage and the relationship with Norma, he had lost his old compulsion to work on the novel he had started. He felt that the novel reflected the real life situation he had been going through, and now that it was resolved the old compulsion was gone. There was no need for the novel now.

Warren Cates was in the midst of Levinson's mid-life transition (ages forty to forty-five) when he participated in the mid-life study. At age forty-two, according to Levinson, he was still in the process of dismantling his former life structure and replacing it with the foundations of a new one for the next period of "Entering Middle Adulthood" (ages forty-five to fifty). He had made a decision to go with his inclination and talent for literary criticism and analysis, which was also congruent with his academic career. He was enjoying his teaching as well, so the foundation of the work dimension of his future life structure was securely in place.

The love dimension, of course, was not yet in place, and it would be in this area that decisions would have to be made and issues resolved. Regardless of how that dimension would evolve, there was clear indication that Warren's mid-life decade was one in which generativity was gaining the ascendency in its dynamic balance with stagnation. He was feeling creative in his literary activities, and he was experiencing true generativity in relationship to his students and in his mentoring role with certain new faculty members.

Furthermore, his relationships with women were significantly different. He seemed to be socializing rather than sexualizing these relationships, which Peck (1968) has identified as one of the important developmental tasks of mid-life. In the past, he had had the tendency to sexualize relationships even with his female students, at least in fantasy. He had also sexualized his Pygmalion-type relationships with Sally and Norma. Now, he was finding it much easier to relate to his female students and to other women in a manner free of sexual overtones. At the same time, he was capable of participating in the sexual aspect of a relationship when this was an appropriate and normal part of the relationship.

Levinson (1978) contends that individuation is an area of focal concern in the mid-life of men. Certainly it was for Warren Cates. In his case, this was compounded by his previous problems with the issues of individuation and separation. It should be clear that Warren had made some substantial gains with respect to those earlier issues. He found out that he could survive without a symbiotic relationship with another adult figure. This, of course, represented "unfinished business" from the past rather than the individuation "business" of mid-life as Levinson formulated it. However, Warren was on his way in the right direction, and he still had time in his mid-life decade to work on and possibly resolve some of the remaining issues of individuation for that period.

The case of Warren Cates raises some significant questions concerning issues of exploitation and ethics. These questions arise from Warren's behavior toward the women with whom he was most intimate in his adult life, most notably his wife, Sally, and then Norma. Viewed purely objectively from outside observation, Warren's behavior could be considered exploitative and unethical. From this perspective he could be seen as using his socially sanctioned position as teacher to draw these women into a more intimate relationship which went beyond the normative limits of the teacher-student relationship. Once the women were in this intimate and binding relationship, they would be used to meet and be responsible for an inordinate number of his needs. They were responsible not only for his sexual needs, but also for coping with and fending off the many demands and stresses of the outer world for him.

What complicates the picture is the fact that Sally and Norma were both adults when they were his students. There is no question that if they were children or minors, his behavior would be patently exploitative and unethical. Although the implicit influence and potential power of his status as teacher put the women at a disadvantage, as adults they still had the option of not becoming intimately involved with him. There is no evidence that he engaged in any manifest coercion or harrassment, which would be undoubtedly unethical and exploitative.

There is a more subtle form of influence which emanates from the respected and admired status of teacher. There is also the strong pull of identification with the teacher as role model, particularly if he is seen as successful and creative in his field. There is no question that Warren was a mentor to these women, and this extended beyond his role of teacher into his roles of husband and lover. Yet, the women got something out of his mentoring, especially his wife who gained in terms of her intellectual and esthetic development. In this respect the relationship was not totally one sided. It also has to be recognized that there was some implicit collusion by both women in the otherwise exploitative relationship.

Warren had given both women responsibility for large areas of his life, and their overt acceptance of that responsibility gave them a good deal of control over his life. This was why he felt controlled by them, despite the fact that he had abdicated his self-responsibility and thereby instigated their actual control. Still, within these relationships there is no question that the two women behaved in more mature and responsible ways than he. Therefore, in this sense they "gave" more than he and the resulting relationships were not truly equal in their reciprocity. These inequalities could be seen objectively by an outsider.

Subjectively, however, Warren Cates did not feel he was exploitative. In fact, he felt both women had undue control over him. While he might not accuse them of being exploitative, he certainly experienced them as being manipulative and controlling. At times he would get a fleeting recognition that he was not behaving fairly, that he was being exploitative, but he would quickly switch into the mock-guilty frame of mind he learned at his mother's side. That is, he would briefly sense his wrongdoing but would grin at his "devilish" behavior, as this had been labelled and learned in collusion with his mother early in his childhood. He was actually incapable of feeling guilt about these behaviors because he was caught in the bind posited by Erik

Erikson as "autonomy vs. shame and doubt." He was often ashamed and doubtful but rarely guilty about his relationships with women. Developmentally, his dilemma of autonomy vs. shame and doubt indicates that he was largely fixated at a stage prior to Erikson's next stage of initiative vs. guilt.

Clinically, Warren shows a serious impairment in his object relations based upon these dynamics from early childhood. From a psychoanalytic perspective, his repetitive dysfunctional and symbiotic relationships with women would be seen as compulsive and beyond his conscious control. From this perspective it would have to be asked whether he could be considered personally responsible for his exploitative behavior. On the other hand, the two women also seemed to have their own problems with object relations and separation/individuation issues by virtue of their involvement and collusion in the symbiotic relationships with Warren. However, this has to be tempered in the light of Gilligan's (1982) findings that women tend to define their identity in a context of relationship and judge it by a standard of responsibility and care. From a sociomoral point of view, Sally and Norma were more developed, mature and responsible than Warren. Furthermore, Sally's development in terms of the psychological dimension of separation/individuation was considerably ahead of Warren's, as evidenced by her strong initiative in the separation and divorce process. Ironically, much of this growth came from her relationship with Warren.

The existentialist position on these matters is that people are "free" to make or not make choices and are therefore responsible for their acts. Since modern existentialist thinking is derived from the same phenomenological base as this book, it needs to be considered here. It would say that by not choosing or claiming not to be able to choose, the person has made a choice. Therefore, Warren has to be considered responsible for his acts. From an existentialist perspective, he had a choice not to enter or not to remain in those symbiotic relationships, regardless of how emotionally painful and depriving these choices might seem to him. The clinical deterministic argument would counter this by saying that he is not a truly autonomous adult capable of such choice, because he is fixated at an early childhood level of development with respect to such relationships. In response to this it can be said that he did have psychotherapy and showed some gains as a result of it. In fact, he learned through his psychotherapy that he had a strong tendency to enter into symbiotic and exploitative relationships. Therefore, he was forewarned that it would be wiser to live within the normative boundary of teacher-student relationship when faced with female students to whom he was attracted. In this sense, he truly had a choice and the knowledge to go with it. Given this foreknowledge, his behavior toward Norma could be considered more exploitative and irresponsible. This latter, existentialist position represents this author's point of view on the exploitation and ethics issues in Warren's case. However, the author also recognizes that this is a complex matter which cannot be sorted into a simple dichotomy of good and bad, virtuous or evil.

LOSS AND INDIVIDUATION IN A FIFTY-FIVE YEAR-OLD WOMAN

Alice Decker, an English teacher in a junior high school, was referred to me for psychotherapy by a friend of hers who was a guidance counselor employed in the same school system. This friend described Mrs. Decker's current situation as "emotionally unbearable," because it seemed impossible that Alice would not crack under the strain of seeing her husband exist "without consciousness or hope," after suffering a massive stroke five months earlier. He was still in the hospital that he had been taken to when he suffered the stroke and where it had been believed he would shortly die. However, he continued to exist in a vegitative state by virtue of life-sustaining medical efforts. The strain of all these months, of his hovering between life and death while she carried on with her work as a teacher, was simply too much for Alice to sustain without some kind of professional help. This was all I knew of the situation before I met Alice Decker in the first therapy session, two days after the referral.

Alice was a graying, dark-haired woman who appeared small and fragile in stature. She also appeared thin and gaunt, which made her look almost ten years older than fifty-five. She was obviously depressed, and it was clearly an effort for her to talk about her plight since it was so depleting. Although she possessed an excellent vocabulary, she had great difficulty expressing the overwhelming feelings she was experiencing.

When she was able to find words for these feelings, they came slowly and it was necessary to continually encourage her to follow through on more of the depth and range of feelings and thoughts her few words were meant to convey. This was indicative of the slow, hard, and painful work involved in the whole therapeutic process from beginning to end, which lasted a total of one and a half years.

In the first session she told me how painful it was to see her husband, Harold, in his current condition. She knew him as a highly intelligent and literate man, a lawyer by profession, but he devoted all his years "to the life of the mind rather than litigation." The real tragedy was that his mind had been demolished by the stroke, and he was now in a state he had feared much more than death. He had often said that he did not believe in "heroic" medical measures to keep people alive against their own will and without a certain quality of life. He was quite emphatic that in his case the quality of life had to do with his mind rather than his body. His body could deteriorate as long as his mind remained intact, but he did not want to live if his mind ceased to function and had no chance of recovery.

The horror and unreality of her current situation was further compounded by the fact that Harold had been kept alive despite his explicit wishes to the contrary. It was a tragic irony that when he suffered his stroke, the hospital to which he was taken just happened to be a Catholic one. Consequently, when his condition had stabilized and it became evident that he had suffered massive and irreversible brain damage, a number of medical actions had been taken to sustain his life without either full or satisfactory consultation with Alice. For example, he had to be fed intravenously because he could no longer masticate or swallow whole foods. His brain could no longer initiate or regulate even those primitive survival functions. After many weeks, when it was apparent this would not change, the hospital doctors strongly recommended that she give written permission for an operation to enable him to be fed directly into his stomach by tube. At first the medical staff explained that a number of complications could arise from the current intravenous feedings—his veins could collapse, there was greater risk of infection, and so on. When they became aware that Alice was not in favor of sustaining his life through surgery or other exceptional medical interventions now that she knew he would probably never regain consciousness, they seemed to change their tactics.

Some of the doctors claimed that although it was unlikely he would ever gain consciousness again, "stranger things had happened" and there was always an "outside chance" he could. Furthermore, they stressed the discomfort if not pain he was suffering from the needles and other procedures of intravenous feeding. She was skeptical but could not allow Harold to suffer unnecessary pain because of her refusal to sign, even if it might mean sustaining his life longer in a condition contrary to his wishes. She feared that he might still acutely feel pain and discomfort, because his body would be wracked from time to time with spasms. These occasional spastic activities in his limbs, torso, and eyes distressed her greatly, and she sometimes thought they might be brought on by pain or discomfort. However, they were the result of the neurological damage from the stroke, for they continued after he had the operation and was fed directly into his stomach.

It should be noted at this point that Alice and Harold were both Jewish, but nonpracticing in any religious sense. Harold was described by her as a student of the Old Testament, but this was in the same sense that he was also a student of American Transcendental writers. Both of them, therefore, would be somewhat at odds with the combined medical and Catholic ethos that guided most of the medical staff in the hospital. In fact, one doctor did say to her that he would not be responsible for the omission of any life-saving medical intervention regardless of her or her husband's own wishes. She recognized these as genuine and not malicious differences of opinion. However, when she found that Harold had been given antibiotics for a respiratory condition when they knew there was virtually no chance for recovery of conscious brain functions, and she had not been consulted, she became irate. In addition to all the horrendous conflicted emotions she experienced in seeing Harold in his distress, she was now feeling intense emotions of betrayal, anger, and resentment.

This, then, was the emotional turmoil she was going through when I first saw her in therapy. After some sessions devoted to having her express and cope with some of these emotions, she began to talk about her own life—her early family background, her youth and young adulthood, and her adult life with and without Harold. Quite briefly, she was born into a family consisting of two older sisters, her parents and herself. One sister was eleven years older than she and the other nine years older, but it was the younger one who had always seemed like "a second mother figure" to her. This sister had been particularly helpful and supportive to Alice since Harold's stroke. She and her husband, as well as the other sister and her husband, lived in the same geographic area as Alice. However, both of Alice's parents were dead, her mother for four years and her father for seven years.

She said her father was a very hardworking man who owned a furniture store and spent many hours there in the evenings and on weekends, so she saw little of him during her childhood. Her mother was much more involved in her upbringing and was the head of the household. She felt her parents both loved her but that they were overprotective of her because she was the youngest and because it was suspected she might have rheumatic heart disease after she contracted scarlet fever. Although it turned out that she had no problems with her heart, her parents seemed to remain overprotective.

When she graduated from high school she lived with her parents while she did secretarial work. However, she really wanted to go to college to study English literature, because she was an avid reader and was particularly fond of nineteenth century English writers. She saved her earnings to pay for college tuition, because neither her mother nor father believed that girls needed a college education in those days. After a few years she had saved up enough money to pay tuition and go to college in New York City. This distressed her parents who worried about her being alone in the City, and she remembered with affection that her father came down to the City to tell her he was proud of her but worried about her. He asked that she return to her hometown and go to a college there, and told Alice that he and her mother would be willing to help in any way they could.

Alice finished her first year of college in New York City and returned home in response to her father's plea. She continued to work at part-time jobs to pay for her tuition and for incidental expenses, while she was provided with room and board in her parents' home. When she graduated from college she took a teaching job in the local school system and went to live in an apartment of her own. She remained in close and frequent touch with her parents and sisters thereafter. She continued to take courses at the local university. This allowed her to increase her salary and finally to obtain a Master's degree in English literature, which in turn enabled her to teach English at a high school level.

Teaching was something she felt she was good at and something that gave her great personal satisfaction. Teaching students who were interested in the literature and language she so much enjoyed and valued held many rewards for her, so many that she claimed to be quite prepared to end up "an old-maid schoolteacher"—a quite desirable end state as far as she was concerned at that time. However, that was before she met Harold.

She met him at a poetry reading by a well known poet at a local college. She had gone with a woman friend who knew Harold and his wife before the wife had died. The three of them chatted after the reading long enough for Alice and Harold to find out they had many literary and other interests in common. He began asking her out, and they soon began spending almost all their leisure time together. She was forty-one and he was fifty-four at the time, and they married one year later. He had been a widower for two years. His first wife had died of a cancer that was diagnosed late and had progressed rapidly.

Alice was to learn later that Harold probably did not handle his wife's death too well, at least as far as his children were concerned. He had kept her diagnosis from the children—a son, Dennis, who was then twenty-one, and a daughter, Karen, who was then twelve. By the time he did let them know, their mother was already unconscious and on the verge of death. Consequently, none of them had the chance to prepare for or work through the fact of her death in any complete sense. In the case of Dennis, this did not seem to have any lasting effects, but it did seem to have a profound effect on Karen. This became a factor in the subsequent relationship between Alice and Karen.

Alice met Karen and Dennis two years after their mother's death, so that when she and Harold were married, Karen was fifteen years old and living at home, and Dennis was twenty-four and had left home to live and work in the Southwest. He was already engaged to be married, so Alice never really got to know him well. He would visit about once a year, and Alice and Harold did go to visit him, his wife, and family of two children a year before Harold's stroke.

Alice said that she almost immediately identified with Karen, who did not seem to have gotten over her mother's sudden death, since she seemed rather sad most of the time. She was small in stature and active, with a nervous kind of energy. She was also an avid reader and wished to major in literature in college, so she was similar to Alice in her youth in a number of significant ways. Alice reached out to her in a nonintrusive way, for Karen was rather distant and wary of her at first. Over time, however, they formed a very close relationship in which Alice became something of a mother figure, an older sister, and a friend all in one.

The relationship with Harold was more than she could have hoped for. He was not only kind and considerate, but also intelligent and informative in a relaxed and unassuming way. She found these qualities to be highly compatible with her emotional and intellectual needs. She began to look up to him in matters philosophical, literary, and political because he had an easy and nondominating command of them. He, on the other hand, began to look to her for her reasonableness and strength in practical matters of finance, household matters, and so on. Although he was a lawyer by profession, he did not practice in the courts. He was a state employee in a department which dealt with estates and wills, and he was much more dedicated to his avocation of literature than to law. In fact, he had published a few critical essays on some lesser known nineteenth century American authors and schools of writing in a literary journal.

His and Alice's interests were so close that they truly became partners in every sense of the word. Harold was very appreciative of the special attention and affection Alice showed toward Karen, for he was feeling somewhat remiss and at a loss in dealing with a daughter who had to go through the loss of her mother at such a difficult age. Although Karen went away to college and then took a copy editor's job in a publishing house in New York City, she remained in close touch with Harold and Alice. They would talk by phone once or twice a week as well as visit one another at least once a month, since they were only a three hour drive apart.

Harold retired five years before his stroke but Alice continued teaching. She enjoyed her teaching very much, and her schedule allowed them to go on extended trips during her long summer vacations and to attend concerts, films, and plays in the early evenings. It was at the end of an extended summer vacation in late August that Harold suffered the stroke. Therefore, Alice had less than two weeks between the trauma of his stroke and hospitalization and the beginning of classes. She felt utterly unprepared emotionally or intellectually to begin teaching that fall, and it turned out to be the most stressful and unsatisfying year of teaching she ever experienced.

She would go to the hospital every day after school to be with Harold, even though he could not recognize or respond to her. She would spend hours there, looking for any small sign of recognition or response from him, while her mind and emotions raced wildly around the issue of his condition and her feelings that he would rather be dead. Consequently, she could not even force herself to prepare adequately for school. She relied on old lesson plans she was dissatisfied with, and she was invariable exhausted physically, emotionally, and intellectually, after spending hours each night at the hospital in addition to suffering from insomnia. She seemed to be living in an unreal, nightmarish world, and it had been going on for months before she began psychotherapy.

After the first few sessions, which were largely devoted to emotional support and ventilation of Alice's pent up feelings, there was a need to break into the internal cycle of turmoil Alice was experiencing every day. Her emotional and physical exhaustion, together with her insular life of classroom to hospital room and back had magnified a number of morbid thoughts and fantasies which added to her feelings of unreality and oppression. Somehow, this cycle of oppressive reality and cognitive-emotional distortion had to be broken. My approach was to have her engage in cognitive monitoring and review using Beck's (1979) Daily Record of Dysfunctional Thoughts, and to have her change her daily pattern of activities. It was my hope that the monitoring of distorted thoughts and fantasies would reduce their morbidity and that the changes in activities and behaviors would allow for some relaxation and reduction of stress.

Therefore, she was encouraged to go to the hospital four instead of seven times per week. She was also taught deep-muscle relaxation (Jacobson, 1938) and given a cassette tape of relaxation instructions for home use. She was also encouraged to accept the invitations for dinner she had been getting from her sisters and friends, anything to take her away from her empty apartment and the hospital for a change. She had to force herself to make these changes, but they seemed to help with the problems of physical tensions and insomnia.

An example of the system for monitoring and review of her cognitions is provided below. It includes a few selected entries she made in her daily record forms over the course of several weeks of therapy. They were selected to represent some of the salient issues, feelings, and cognitions she was experiencing in that stressful period. These entries therefore serve to telescope much of the therapeutic activity over that range of time. (Parentheses have been placed around pseudonyms used in otherwise actual quotes.)

Alice Decker's own words in the above entries speak eloquently of the kind of mental and emotional torment she went through during the beginning weeks and months of therapy, and what she had gone through for five months before that. It is important to note that between the entries of 10 March and 16 March Harold was transferred from the hospital to a Jewish nursing home which Alice had tried to get him into earlier but which had a waiting list. Therefore, the entry dated 6 April related to a situation in the nursing home. She was appalled to find him dressed in suit and carnation in recognition of the religious ceremony of Seder, when he had no recognition of place, time, and self, much less a religious holiday. Although she wanted this nursing home because it was supposed to give the best quality of care in

Alice Decker's recorded entries.

DATE	SITUATION (events, thoughts, or recollections leading to unpleasant emotion)	EMOTION(S) (specify)	THOUGHT(S) (automatic thoughts that preceeded unpleasant emotion)	RATIONAL RESPONSE (rational response to automatic thoughts)
14 February	"At home. Stream of thoughts while reading some poetry (Harold) loved."	"Sadness"	"Realizing that he can no longer enjoy the words he savored so much."	"He can no longer enjoy anything. (I stop reading to encourage better mood.)"
22 February	"Visiting (Harold) at hospital"	"Anxiety"	"Should I limit these visits when they are comforting to me? (Or, at least part of the visit is of comfort.)"	"Most of the time they are not beneficial."
25 February	"Visiting (Harold at hospital"	"Confusion"	"Helping to groom (Harold's hair, nails, clothes, etc., one minute and then closing the door on him and returning to an existence without him."	"I can't rationalize this at all!"
10 March	"Seeing Harold look so gaunt, haggard, lying in that state for so many months."	"Regret/ Guilt"	"He should have had the right to decide to live or die, and I should have the right to speak for him or perhaps to have done it myself."	"I think of (Karen) & (Dennis) and what it might have done to them—also the effect on myself."

Alice Decker's recorded entries.

DATE	SITUATION (events, thoughts, or recollections leading to unpleasant emotion)	EMOTION(S) (specify)	THOUGHT(S) (automatic thoughts that preceeded unpleasant emotion)	RATIONAL RESPONSE (rational response to automatic thoughts)
16 March	"Seeing newspaper article, re: allowing life-sustaining device to be removed when no life can be seen for future."	"Anxiety"	"Recurring thought: Should I go to the court to ask that artificial feedings be stopped?"	"Could I take it emotionally?"
25 March	"Reading a book on woman's experiences as a widow."	"Anxiety"	"After reading of different stages of grief and realizing I am already going through them, I ask: Will they reoccur after (Harold's) funeral?"	"Perhaps they might not or if they do, the length of time for each would be shortened."
25 March	"Re same book (Stream of thought)."	"Anger"	"It's not fair that I've had to bear all this pain and agony in reverse and still have the funeral to face."	"No one said life is fair—other people suffer in other ways."
6 April	"Visit to (Harold)—Deterioration since last visit, plus assorted clothes in room belonging to others."	"Sadness and mixture of emotions—confused—anger at doctor and nursing home."	"Paler than death, soundly sleeping, arms bent under, he looked unreal. Then found out he was dressed in pants, jacket, tie, plus a carnation for Seder. What a mockery!"	"Arriving home, I realized he'd be better off dead. How long are they going to try to dress him for a role he obviously can't play? Why can't they leave him alone?"

the region, she was upset to find other people's clothing deposited in his room as if for temporary storage.

The reader has probably recognized that the entry column entitled "Rational Response" calls for the person to replace the irrational thoughts or distorted cognitions that usually occur in the form of automatic thoughts when experiencing upsetting emotions. Sometimes, of course, the situation is actually so intolerable that it is impossible to give a "rational" response—as in her entry of 25 February. However, there was a perceptible change in the quality of these coping responses. They moved toward a broader, more philosophical and almost stoical, perspective and replaced the more panicky and obsessive thoughts of the earlier entries. As time went on, it became even clearer that she was developing a perceptual attitude and was changing her assumptive world to accommodate, accept, and deal with the reality of Harold's condition and her life situation.

It is important to note, however, that she never verbalized a growing sense of mastery to me in the therapeutic sessions. This increased mastery tended to show up in her written entries and in actual decisions made and actions taken on her own. It was also true during these early months of therapy that she gave no hint of feeling any pleasure, however minute, in her life and no indication of hope for any future pleasure. This is not surprising under the circumstances, but it is indicative of her clinically depressed, not simply sad, condition. Beck (1979) and his colleagues have documented the inability of depressed persons to feel a sense of mastery or pleasure, even when there is behavioral and empirical evidence they experience both. It was certainly true of Alice that in her affect and her verbalizations to me, she appeared depressed throughout the whole first year of therapy. There were good reasons for this, given her husband's condition and then his death within that same year. It was a true reactive depression. Nevertheless, it meant that she did not verbalize any sense of mastery or of progress in therapy during that whole time, even though there was evidence she was coping with remarkable effectiveness.

This was particularly true of her instrumental coping. She would make decisions as well as plans and carry out actions without ever specifically asking me to help her make a decision or even to go over her options. She would talk about her confusion, about all the disturbing thoughts and discouraging options that would go through her mind, but she would give no hint that she was engaging in a decision-making or planning process as she discussed these things with me. Yet, she would make decisions and take actions very effectively, as she did in the case of Harold's transfer to the nursing home. When an opening became available she never hesitated, either to consult me or anyone else, before accepting it and having him transferred.

This was her style of problem solving and of relating to me throughout therapy. In her therapeutic sessions she would ventilate, often crying and expressing feelings of hopelessness and helplessness, and then go out and take effective action in the "real world." Just how effective and extensive these actions were will now be recapitulated. First, she decided to retire from teaching at the end of the school year, and she did indeed retire at the end of June—five months after she entered therapy. This decision and action was taken in the light of many reasonable considerations on her part, but these have to be pieced together after the fact, because they did not come out in any cohesive sense in the course of therapy.

She was most certainly depleted emotionally and physically by her current situation, and she knew that she would drain herself even further between her work and her regular stressful visits to Harold. She felt she was short changing her work and her students since she was not developing any new or challenging materials and assignments. She also claimed to have become disenchanted with the school system and the changing student body she was teaching. There were more and more behavior problems and fewer and fewer motivated students in the classes assigned to her. She had been discouraged about continuing with her chosen and cherished profession even before Harold's stroke. In fact, she had been tempted to retire before this, but she did want to reach at least the early retirement age of fifty-five. Now that she was old enough, she chose to retire under the earlier option in her retirement plan.

During that summer, in order to keep her mind occupied and to "try something new" she went into a training program to obtain a real estate license. She worked hard at this but with more determination than enthusiasm. When I asked her if this was something she really wanted, she said she did not know but that she needed to keep active at something and to obtain some sense of accomplishment. However, before the summer was over something occurred which changed all this and led to perhaps the most momentous decision of her life.

One day when she visited Harold at the nursing home, she found a nurse frantically trying to reinsert the feeding tube that had fallen out of the surgical opening in Harold's stomach. When she questioned the nurse about why she was doing this without her permission, the nurse replied that the charge doctor had told her to reinsert it. One reason Alice was initially so favorably inclined toward this nursing home was that the doctors assured her they would not make any major decisions concerning life-sustaining medication or procedures without consulting with her. She was assured that they would not unilaterally give Harold antibiotics in the case of infection or flu, as had been done in the hospital. She therefore became quite upset by this incident, and although she let the nurse reinsert the tube, she complained to the charge doctor about not being consulted. He said that he did not consider feeding to be the same as medication and that he felt he had to intervene unilaterally. Neither he nor the home would allow the tube to be removed or to be left unconnected if it fell out.

Alice was not satisfied with this interchange with the doctor, so she sought the advice of a doctor she had been referred to by a friend. He was considered to be sympathetic to patients who expressed, through "living wills" or other such means, the desire to be allowed to die and to be spared further medical interventions when they were in hopeless vegetative states. Harold did not have a doctor of his own when he suffered the stroke, and Alice's former doctor had moved away. Therefore, this was the first attempt she had made to obtain medical advice independent of the institutions Harold had been placed in since his stroke.

The doctor was away at his summer camp, so he could not visit Harold but he did agree to talk to Alice. When she visited him at his camp, she asked him about her rights and the advisability to have the feeding tube removed from his stomach. He informed her that the nursing home doctors were within their rights in refusing to allow it to be removed as long as he was in their care. The one option she had was to take him out of their care and into her own home. He also discussed the effects of removal of food and fluids from Harold in terms of life expectancy and possible physical distress or discomfort. This conversation plus the personal encouragement of a particularly empathic nurse at the nursing home helped her decide to take Harold home with her. This nurse had given very good and sensitive care to Harold and had been quite comforting to Alice from the beginning of his placement in the nursing home. She, like Alice, had seen Harold deteriorate and become more gaunt and spastic as time went on. As Alice put it, even his eyes seemed to be looking more "haunted and pleading." Therefore, she took him home without opposition from the nursing home or its medical staff.

During the few weeks Harold was home with her in their apartment, she told me in her therapy sessions that she was sure she had made the right decision. She said that from the moment Harold was put in his own bed at home "he seemed to look relieved and at peace—he even seemed to give me a thankful look." She said she was probably imagining it, but he did seem to know where he was. He was much more calm and much less spastic than he had ever been since his stroke. She continued giving him only water so he would not dehydrate, but he showed no signs of physical discomfort or distress from lack of nourishment. He died quietly of cardiac arrest in the early dawn, with Alice at his side, within four weeks of being discharged from the nursing home.

This marked a new stage in her therapy, for although she was no longer in the awful limbo between Harold's life and death, she did experience a profound and final sense of loss and grief as a result of his death. Her lot was not made any easier by the fact that she had to make all the arrangements for Harold's funeral and burial. His son, Dennis, was out of state, and his daughter, Karen, was having difficulty facing his death. The difficulty over her mother's death, when she did not even get to view her mother's body, had come back during her father's funeral when she first refused to view his body. Alice had to convince her it was the right thing to do for her own emotional well-being, and she had to help Karen through the full process of grief and mourning over her father as well as work on the previously unresolved loss of her mother. Again, I found Alice's capacity to cope with all these things to be exemplary, but in therapy she continued to give the impression that it was all too overwhelming and that she was not doing them well.

In an attempt to handle her own grieving process, Alice joined a local widowed-persons support group. She found that it did not help very much with her emotional isolation, as Weiss (1973) had earlier observed in his research. She was also astonished to find that some of the widows (there were very few men) had been members of the group for as long as three, four, or even five years. She said she could not see how the group experience could have been effective if they remained in it that long. She wondered whether "they enjoyed continuing to share their misery together over such a long period." At any rate, she was apparently quickly perceived and highly valued as an empathic and helpful person in the group. The professional social worker who coordinated the support groups and trained the group facilitators from among the members encouraged her to go through the training and to lead a group. She did this for a number of months thereafter, and then decided to take some graduate courses in counseling at the university. She said she thought she might like to work with troubled adolescent girls, even if only as a volunteer. She remembered some of the positive experiences she had with a number of girls as a junior high school teacher, and she recalled the satisfaction of helping Karen during her difficult adolescent years.

Why was it that a person who demonstrated such good coping capacities and relationship skills, and who received positive feedback and validation from others about these strengths, should present herself as rather hopeless and helpless in therapy? There seemed to be a number of related reasons from the past and present for all this, all of which lent a structure of meaning to her life with Harold and in her therapy after his death. In a chapter on the psychotherapy of depression, Silvano Arieti (Arieti & Bemporad 1978) delineated a dynamic in the depression of many women which has to do with the presence of a "dominant other" in their lives, and it seemed to me that this dynamic helped to explain much of Alice's behavior in this period. In a still largely patriarchal society and culture, women have been trained overtly or in subtle ways to depend on others for approval, appreciation, and support, and they often allow a dominant other (usually a husband) to assume this specific position in their lives. When this dominant other dies or is otherwise lost, the person not only becomes depressed but also broods over what she or he did not have and realizes that many of the gratifications he or she once desired in life were given up. There is also "a feeling of hopelessness about remedying or retrieving what he has lost," and this last observation by Arieti goes far in explaining much of the hopelessness Alice was expressing in her therapy sessions—even while she was coping so effectively on an instrumental level.

As far as the feelings of helplessness go, my interpretation is that Alice had allowed Harold to assume the role of a dominant other in her assumptive world. Not that he was in any way a dominant or domineering person. As Arieti noted: "Many husbands, certainly helped by the prevailing patriarchal character of society, are not even aware of playing the role of a dominant other." Although she was factually able to conduct most of her own life in an effective and autonomous manner before she even met Harold, she did indeed tend to look up to him, to admire, and perhaps even to idealize him because of many of his admirable qualities but also because of the subtle ways in which she was trained as a woman to find a dominant other. Some of this attitude was probably reinforced by her overprotective parents who gave her an additional message that she needed someone else to look out for her, because she was fragile, if not totally helpless.

Now when the dominant other is lost and the person is in therapy, there are certain stages which follow:

> When the therapist succeeds in establishing rapport and proves his genuine desire to reach, nourish, and offer hope, he will often be accepted by the patient, but only as a dominant third—a third entity or person in addition to the patient and the dominant other (or goal). Immediate relief may be obtained because the patient sees in the therapist a new and reliable love object (Arieti & Bemporad 1978, 215).

In the normal course of therapy in depressions such as these, the relationship moves onto another stage. Arieti puts it this way: "After the first stage of treatment, however, the therapeutic approach must be characterized by a therapeutic relation in which the therapist is no longer a dominant third, but a *significant third,* a third person with a firm, sincere, and unambiguous type of personality who wants to help the patient without making threatening demands or requesting a continuation of the patient's usual patterns of living."

In addition to the dominant other dynamic in the therapeutic relationship, I think there was a continuous but not necessarily explicit effort on her part to clarify her most deeply held values and even her own identity so as to survive through that trying and ambiguous time before Harold died. At any rate, after his death and after I was beginning to be perceived by her as a significant third rather than a dominant third, I made a specific point in therapy of countering any remaining expression of helplessness on her part by giving clear evidence of her effective decision making, problem solving, and especially her autonomy. I was particularly concerned that she recognize her effective coping as hers and hers alone, for the purposes of her own identity and individuation, which would otherwise be undermined by the mental or actual device of a dominant other.

The results of a Reptest Alice took about two months before the termination of therapy lent some credence to the above interpretation of the meaning of these critical events in Alice's life. Figure 6-1 gives her responses to the Reperatory Grid Test.

Her self concept by this time was quite good, as noted by the close correspondence (seven out of ten) of her responses to "Self" as compared to "The Person I Would Like To Be" (Ideal Self). It is worth noting, however, that she still did not see herself as "decisive" despite the momentous decisions she had already so effectively made. This was the period of therapy in which heavy emphasis was being placed on having her recognize her own effectiveness.

Some other points worth noting in Figure 6-1 is the close correspondence between "Self" and the following significant others: therapist (8), Harold (7), father (7), and Karen (7). These correlations or correspondences were somewhat changed from those she gave on a Reptest ten months earlier in therapy. In that test "Self" showed the following correspondences: Harold (9), therapist (9), father (6), and Karen (5). Therefore, it seems to me that this reflects a reduction in her perception of or reliance on Harold and me, the therapist, as dominant others. I suspect that the therapist at this point was more of an identification figure because of her growing interest in becoming a helping person, as she went on into graduate study in counseling. This also represented a shift toward more generativity in her life at that time. Her closer relationship to Karen was also evident in the second testing. Finally, she was cognizant of her parents earlier overprotectiveness, as evident in the first row of Figure 6-1, and its subtle effect on her beliefs about herself in later life.

The psychiatrist, Theodore J. Rubin, made the following observation, "The stifling effects of overprotection provide ample seed and root for future illusions of helplessness, incompetence, and dependency," but then he went on to say "there is still a vast difference between *being dependent* and having *illusions of dependency* . . . I have met many seemingly dependent people who turned out to be extraordinarily competent . . ." (Rubin 1975, 94).

I certainly found Alice Decker to be extraordinarily competent. However, I was never sure whether my comments to her about her autonomous effectiveness and competence were falling on deaf ears. I was also uncertain as to whether any of my clinical efforts were contributing anything more than window dressing for her fundamental underlying competence and effective-

NAME: Alice Decker

Sex: M - (F) Age: 56

self	mother	father	Harold	Karen	Dennis	Therapist	Disliked Person	Unhappy Person	Person I would like to be		CONSTRUCT	CONTRAST
O	⊗	⊗					X	X		1	over protective	ability to grow
X	⊗	X	X	⊗		X	X	O	X	2	self-respect	deflated ego
⊗	X	X			X	⊗	X	X	O	3	cautious	free spirit
X	X	⊗	X	X		X	O	X	⊗	4	compassionate	insensitive
X			⊗	⊗	O		X		X	5	creative	not creative
				O	⊗		⊗			6	self-centered	good natured
		X	⊗	X	O			⊗	X	7	sense of humor	serious
⊗		X	X	X		X		O	⊗	8	flexible	rigid
	X	O	⊗	X		⊗	X		X	9	decisive	indecisive
⊗		X	X	X	X	X	O		⊗	10	gentle	demanding

FIGURE 6-1. Alice Decker's Repertory Grid Test

ness. This uncertainty was due to her characteristically unexpressive and "down" manner in therapy sessions. However, I was somewhat reassured by a letter she sent to me shortly after therapy. She always did express herself better in writing than in spoken words, and this letter showed it. The body of the actual letter is quoted below, not as a positive testimonial to the therapy I provided, but for the questions it answers and for the light it sheds on a number of important points in her case:

> I really don't believe I expressed my true appreciation for all you've done for me during the past months.
> Your living through my unearthly situation, supporting me among the living, gave my existence some semblance of life although I hovered in oblivion. Your "assignments" helped to assuage my fears and often changed my irrational thinking. The personal constructs and values showed me more clearly where my worldview was and is focused. Most of all your being there every week to listen, empathize, and interpret a myriad of emotions was truly a catharsis for me. Before, I didn't think that one person in the entire world could help me. Leaving after my first visit I remember feeling years lighter, as though tons had been lifted from my shoulders. I'll not forget that.
> Despite my frequent crying spells and anxiety attacks resulting from the simplest situations, I feel, in general, enveloped in a calmness generated by my own energy. Also internalizing many qualities and attitudes that (Harold) possessed has added new dimensions to my life. All of these have given me a strength for the future, and I go forward with confidence to living, to "becoming." As Camus said "The fall is brutal, but we set out again."
> Thank you!

Not only was I reassured by this that empathic listening was helpful to her, as it should have been, but also that she found the cognitive monitoring and review forms (the "assignments") helpful to her in her highly conflicted state at the start of therapy. Also, although she said she internalized many values and attitudes that Harold possessed, I would say that this was a reflection of many of her own deeply held values which she saw personified in Harold, rather than simply a reflection of him as a dominant other. In this regard, her comment that she was "enveloped in a calmness generated by *my own energy*" was especially heartening. I take this to be evidence of her increased sense of individuation.

It is interesting to see that she quotes Camus, an existentialist thinker who expressed the nature of individuation in its fullest dimensions. Just before finishing therapy, Alice had filled out an instrument containing Yalom's (1980) existential values questionnaire, and she came out with the highest possible existentialist score on it. As an example, she strongly agreed with the following statements: "No matter how much or how little support and guidance people get from others, they must take ultimate responsibility for the way they live their lives," and "I have to recognize that no matter how close I get to other people, I must still face life alone." I would take these responses to be indicative of much greater individuation on her part in the face of the severe loss she had suffered. The fact that she retained the illusion of dependence on a dominant other throughout most of her therapy clearly indicates how much more individuation is a state of mind than it is a set of behaviors. It seems to me this last statement was equally true in the case of Warren Cates, regardless of the marked differences in circumstances and gender in the two cases. The subject of individuation and the related issues of this chapter will be explored in greater detail in the next, concluding chapter.

Chapter 7

CONCLUSIONS AND IMPLICATIONS

The purpose of this book was to contribute to an understanding of the nature of mid-life transitions by taking an approach that focuses on the unique personal meaning of the transitional events and experiences for the individuals undergoing them. This approach was based on the assumption that there is an implicit structure to the way in which an individual mid-life transition is experienced. The approach incorporated certain procedures, techniques, and methods for making that structure explicit in order to better understand the experience. The question at this point is to what extent has this approach, as applied in the case studies presented here, provided further understanding about the experience and about the phenomenon called a "mid-life crisis." Does this approach allow for any new insights or perspectives on the phenomenon, and can any conclusions be drawn from these kinds of studies about the vagaries and outcomes of mid-life transitions? If so, what implications do these methods and conclusions have for clinical practice and intervention in actual crises? What are the implications, if any, for current adult development theory and our current state of knowledge about the transitions and crises of middle adulthood? Finally, what are the implications for *living* in the middle years that might be drawn from these studies?

This chapter will attempt to address these questions after first recapitulating the crucial place *meaning* has in determining the nature, course, and outcome of mid-life transitions. Then, the factors of gender, types of crises, and coping patterns identified in the first chapter from adult development theory and research will be reassessed in the light of the case studies in this book.

217

MEANING AND MID-LIFE CRISES: A RECAPITULATION

Hill's (1965) formula for determination of a crisis, which was presented in Chapter One, was enacted in each of the crisis situations presented in the case studies. Let us recapitulate that formula here: A (the event) → interacting with B (person's or family's crisis-meeting resources) → *interacting* with C (the person's definition—i.e., the *meaning* of the event) → *produces* X (the crisis). Now, it should be apparent that "C," the meaning element of the sequence, was highly instrumental in each of the crises depicted in the case studies. Thus, although there might be a crude consensus about the kinds of events and developments (the "A" element in the formula) that seem to lead to mid-life crises in the adult development literature, there is no guarantee that these events are going to be defined as crises by the middle-aged person who encounters them. As noted before, some of these events may be defined by some as challenges or opportunities rather than crises or catastrophes. The variability in definitions or personal meanings of these events is probably very great among middle-aged persons. Even the "B" element (crisis-meeting resources) is subject to the meaning element in a significant way. One of the major crisis-meeting resources is the person's coping capacity, and this is very much affected by the person's own perception of that capacity. For example, in the case of Allan Kahn in Chapter Three, Allan overestimated his coping capacities, which contributed to the crisis dimensions of his problem. Conversely, in the case of Alice Decker in Chapter Six, Alice underestimated her coping capacities, which contributed somewhat to prolongation of the resolution of certain crisis issues.

Looking back on these and the other cases, it is clear that meaning is phenomenologically inseparable from the self. This is true with respect to the various structures of meaning covered here. The meaning of the *world* component in the individual life structure is provided by the *self* component. That is, the person's assumptive world is crucial in determining the meaning of events in the real world. With respect to the cognitive structure, the meaning of events is most profoundly and pervasively affected by the core cognitive structures related to the self (Guidano & Liotti 1983; Raimy 1975). Finally, phenomenology and its concept of the structure of experience certainly identifies the self as the center of meaning. One phenomenological psychologist put it this way: "We may say that we can understand what something means to someone only if we can see *his* implicit sense of who he is, which is a critical horizon against which events appear to that person and gain their meanings" (Keen 1975, 22).

Given the uniqueness of meaning to the self, and the variability of people and the meanings they attach to events, the strategy selected here was to organize the material around themes related to problematic events of mid-life rather than around the specific events (e.g., "empty nest," "divorce," etc.) themselves. Indeed, meaning tends to be thematic by its very nature.

Just how well this strategy worked the reader will have to judge. It is important to keep in mind that I selected the themes and then organized the case material around them. This does not mean that the persons depicted in the case would have necessarily identified these themes. The meaning of crisis-laden events are experienced, structured, and expressed differently by different persons. Therefore, the meaning of the events, and even more, the themes, might not be apparent to the person. For example, in Chapter Three the theme of mortality and finiteness was experienced differently by the persons in the case studies. Doris Pierson experienced it overtly in the form of death anxiety. Allan Kahn, on the other hand, did not experience it overtly, but it was expressed symptomatically in the form of a panic attack which was not directly (consciously) related to death anxiety. Yet, the meaning of the particular traumatic and threatening events in their respective lives triggered an emotional crisis impelled by an implicit recognition of their finiteness and limited time left in life.

Sometimes, social scientists—social gerontologists among them—will impute meaning to certain life events based on their normative views of aging and adult development from a societal perspective. These meanings are seen as related to social roles which are supposed to provide normative standards, expectations, and guidelines for social conduct and living in broad areas of life. Obviously, one of the most important of these roles is occupation, which provides both purpose and direction to one's life. It has been said that we do not have a recognized and cohesive social role or status as "retired persons," which puts the older person in a weakened position characterized by "norm-lessness" or anomie (Rosow 1973). Fortunately, not all social gerontologists have focused on the negative implications of the increasing lack of normative restraints on individual action in the later years of life. An influential and compelling alternative interpretation has been offered by the social psychologist Vern L. Bengtson of the Andrus Gerontology Center at the University of Southern California:

> Decrease in specific social requirements and expectations can also be interpreted as a gain in *freedom*. I would argue, that the loss of norms (and roles with which they are associated) represents a potential *opportunity* to pick and choose among alternative behaviors—a degree of freedom from societal restraints that is perhaps greater than at any other period of the life cycle (Bengtson 1973, 25).

This speaks again to the importance of the meaning of an event. Retirement for one person is experienced as a disaster, for other persons, sometimes even in the case of forced retirement, it is experienced as a challenge and an opportunity. Gail Sheehy (1981) wrote an entire book about people who were either stagnating in or forced out of occupations, and who in the process became "pathfinders" who found new and generative paths for themselves in later life. The case of Steve Gornecky in Chapter Five depicted a situation in which the loss of an occupational role and status was initially experienced as a personal catastrophe, but in the course of coping with that loss and crisis he developed his own alternative nonlethal, life-sustaining and generative standards and activities. He thereby demonstrated the validity of Parkes's (1971) position that psychosocial transitions can lead to higher levels of functioning, and he lived out the theme of Sheehy's "pathfinders."

Although the social role construct has a great deal of explanatory value, it has sometimes been overextended in its application to aging and adult development. The above argument about the negative effects of occupational role loss in later life compares to Robert Peck's (1968) delineation of the need for "ego differentiation vs. work-role preoccupation" in order to effectively resolve the crisis of ego integrity vs. despair in Erikson's eighth and last stage of life.

Furthermore, the social role construct has been extended and tied to personal identity in the middle and later adult years. This was done here in classifying Steve Gornecky's case as a crisis in identity in Chapter Four. This was done for the purposes of placement of case materials on the basis of the most salient or evident themes and issues involved in mid-life transitions. It was not done in the same all-embracing and over-determined sense that the social role construct has often been used in sociological interpretations, or in what Wrong (1961) has referred to as "sociology's over-socialized view of man." Certainly, social identity is an extremely important dimension of personal identity, but it is not all of personal identity. For example, as depicted in Chapter Five, much of Linda Craft's behavior in early adulthood, before her disillusionment in marriage, was determined by her socialization as a girl and woman into the social role of "wife" with its set of normative expectations, and was reinforced by parental precept and example. Thus, she did not question her identity in that role until she discovered her husband's infidelity, which ran counter to her sense of justice (role-reciprocity) in marriage and thereby undermined a major portion of her assumptive world. However, as a result of coping with that crisis she developed a much more differentiated and richer sense of self or personal identity. Helen Merrell Lynd summed up this whole issue very well:

> Others tend to confine the self-image as well as the self to an internalization of roles, or system of role expectations. Too great fluency in the use of the terms role and status marks many discussion of the relations of social role to the image of the ideal self. Finding oneself is different from finding one's role or roles, and, if this

distinction is lost, we have blocked off an essential road to the understanding of identity (Lynd 1958, 170).

Most of the above discussion of the importance of meaning in mid-life has focused on its place in the crisis paradigm, assuming that the personal meaning of a crisis-laden event will be pivotal in determining whether the event becomes a crisis and what its outcome might be. There is another sense in which meaning is an important developmental issue in mid-life. Some gerontologists have identified the years from fifty until death as a period in which meaning is a central concern: "The primary integrating theme of this life stage, no matter how long it lasts, is a search for personal meaning" (Newman & Newman 1979, 126).

The ages of fifty through sixty can be said to cover just the latter part of middle age, and there is little doubt that the search for meaning becomes a more explicit and purposeful activity after fifty. However, it should be clear from the case studies that meaning and the various structures of meaning are by no means always explicit and purposeful in any self-evident sense. Indeed, the meaning element was more often implicit and couched in feelings and behaviors of the middle-aged persons studied, rather than in explicit or stated intentions to search for meaning. In this implicit sense, even the youngest persons in the case studies, beginning with thirty-five year-old Doris Pierson in Chapter three, were engaged in a form of "meaning seeking." In this regard, we are in agreement with the newly emerging school of "interpretative anthropology" in which human beings are viewed as "symbolizing, conceptualizing, meaning-seeking" creatures who wish to "make sense out of experience, to give it form and order" (Geertz 1983). Kegan's (1982) concept "meaning-making" in the course of human development is essentially of the same order. This has certainly been an underlying assumption about the people depicted in this book, and we will return to it later in the chapter in order to explore its implications for both theory and practice.

THE GENDER FACTOR

Since the questions which prompted my preliminary research and then the writing of this book had to do with apparent differences between men and women who were coping with mid-life transitions and crises, there is a need to come back and address those questions in the light of the case studies and other relevant research and literature.

It will be recalled that in my clinical practice, women seemed to cope better with the stress of marital breakup than did the men. In order to see if my perception of this could have been skewed by the kinds of cases that were being referred to me and other practitioners in our particular practice setting, I looked carefully at the relationship of the marital factor to the comparative morale or life satisfaction of men and women in the available National Opinion Research Corporation (NORC) data. Indeed, the data seemed to show that separated and divorced men had significantly lower life satisfaction measures than women who were separated or divorced in the forty to sixty year age cohort. Furthermore, the women who were separated, divorced, or widowed did not have lower morale than the married women in the forty to sixty range. In fact, they seemed to have somewhat higher morale as a group than the marrieds. Married men, on the other hand, showed a significantly higher level of life satisfaction than the separated, divorced, and widowed men in the same age section of the sample.

How do these findings compare to the to recent empirical findings on marital breakup concerning men and women in the mid-life period? One of the most comprehensive studies of adaptation to marital separation in later and earlier life has been carried out at the University of California in San Francisco. Some of the more recent findings from that study were reported by David Chiriboga (1982), based on an evaluation of the psychosocial functioning of recently separated men and women (N=310) ranging in age from twenty to the late seventies. He found that, regardless of gender, "those in their forties were significantly lower in overall happiness than those in their twenties and thirties" (Chiriboga 1982, 111). So, age seemed to be a more important variable than gender in explaining variation in happiness. In fact, those aged fifty years and over of both genders were the least happy of all in the study. We can say that marital separation is a highly stressful situation for people in mid-life, particularly for those in their forties and fifties.

This should not be taken to mean, however, that there is no difference between men and women with respect to psychosocial functioning during marital separation. Some clinical reports reflecting the same kinds of impressions I was receiving in my clinical practice tended to suggest that men may be more vulnerable than women during the transitional period of divorce (Wallerstein & Kelly 1980; Weiss 1975). Chiriboga (1982) actually did find that men were significantly less happy than women from the relative numbers reporting themselves as "not too happy." The percentages reported as "not too happy" by gender and age were as follows: men in their thirties—21%, vs. women in their thirties—15%; men in their forties—35%, vs. women in their forties—25%; and men in their fifties and over—60%, vs. women in their fifties and over—50% (Chiriboga 1982, 111). It can be seen that men were lower in self-reported happiness than women in all the age categories that were covered in that study. At the same time, these figure show that the differences in happiness were greater between the age categories than they were between men and women.

Another point has to be quickly added to this, and it is that "although recently separated men may experience a lower sense of overall well-being, the women experience greater emotional turmoil" (Chiriboga 1982, 112). That is, women reported significantly more psychological symptoms as well as more of the agitated emotions, such as "feeling angry," "unable to get going," "too much to do," and "uneasy." These findings might seem somewhat contradictory, but in fact they reflect the complexity of the emotional effects of marital breakup with respect to gender. Chiriboga summed up his findings concerning gender in the following manner:

> ... There may be differential areas of vulnerability between the sexes. For example, men were found to be less happy, tended to report being more troubled by the separation, and exhibited less improvement in perceived health status from before to after separation. On the other hand, women manifested greater emotional tension and were more disorganized on the personal level and more dissatisfied on the life evaluation chart for both the past five years and the present year. Both sexes were equally optimistic about the future (Chiriboga 1982, 113).

Given these findings from this more complex empirical analysis of the gender factor, let us take a look at the case studies in the light of these findings. John Raymond (age thirty-seven) in Chapter Five and Warren Cates (age forty-two) in Chapter Six were certainly very unhappy and troubled by their marital separations on the basis of their verbal reports of the experience. On the other hand, Linda Craft (age thirty-six) in Chapter Four was much more unhappy within her marriage, after she found out about her husband's infidelity, than she was during the separation itself. In fact, she was impatient for the separation to take place.

Despite the congruence between these cases and Chiriboga's findings, it should be noted that the emotional experience of separation is very much determined by who initiates the separation. Linda Craft initiated hers, as did Sally Cates, while Warren Cates and John Raymond were the unwilling recipients of those initiatives. Joyce Kurland (age fifty-one) in Chapter Five and Debbie Rosen (age thirty-nine) in Chapter Six were also the recipients of an unexpected and unwelcome separation experience. They certainly did experience real unhappiness as well as much emotional distress during the separation, regardless of how well they managed to cope in the long run.

There is another aspect of the gender factor which needs to be looked at in terms of marital stress and breakdown. Prior research has shown that men are apt to be relatively more unaware of marital problems that precede separation and divorce than are women (Chiriboga & Cutler 1977-78; Weiss 1975). Chiriboga (1982) noted that "women tend to see life before separation as a particularly excruciating time," and his findings in the 1982 report did indeed show that women were aware of serious marital problems well in advance of their husbands.

This was certainly true in the cases of Warren Cates and John Raymond. It was perhaps even more dramatically clear in the case of Allan Kahn in Chapter Three, who was quite unaware of the severity of the problems in his marriage and the depth of his wife's dissatisfaction. Nevertheless, there has to be some qualification to this generalization, just as there were qualifications to other generalizations. Joyce Kurland in Chapter Five was not prepared for her husband's leaving her for another woman. Although she was aware of some possible problems in the marriage, some growing apart between herself and her husband, she had planned on a closer relationship after all the children had grown and left home. Even more than Joyce, Debbie Rosen in Chapter Six seemed oblivious to the underlying problems in her marriage until her husband announced his intention to separate. Perhaps the presence of "the other woman" in such situations is a confounding factor. In other words, when marriages are inherently going bad within the relationship and without an outside love object, women are generally much more aware much sooner of the problems than are the men.

Certainly, if a person, man or woman, leaves a marriage for another love object, that person is probably much better prepared and much less vulnerable than the one who has been dropped. However, separation might be more difficult for men who do not have an alternative love object than for women, because men do not seem to have the same kinds of social supports, especially confidantes, that women have. This did seem to be true in the interview survey I conducted, in which the women turned more quickly to more sources of emotional support than did the men. As far as these case studies were concerned, Linda Craft and Debbie Rosen certainly quickly moved to other support persons in coping with their marital breakdowns. Joyce Kurland did not have a confidante to turn to immediately, but she did rapidly move toward establishing new friendships and a support network.

In one sense, it can be said that Warren Cates was an exception because he moved quickly to establish a support network. On the other hand, he became almost immediately attached to an alternative love object at the point of separation. Both he and John Raymond had only their wives as confidantes right up to the time of separation. Perhaps the most dramatic example of men using their wives as confidantes was Linda Craft's husband, who asked his aggrieved and appalled wife to help him determine what to do about remaining in his marriage to her or going to live with the other woman.

The use of confidantes and other sources of support brings us to the whole issue of coping, and whether there are distinct and consistent differences between men and women in dealing with mid-life crises. It seems safe to say that in general women seem to more readily make use of sources of support in coping with the crises, but what about other forms of coping? What about the presumed differences between the sexes in instrumental and expressive forms of coping? The prevailing but untested assumption has been that women tend to be more effective at expressive coping and the handling of emotions than men, who are supposed to be more effective at instrumental coping and problem solving. Chiriboga's (1982) findings that, at least as far as marital separation is concerned, women reported more trouble with agitated emotions, such as "feeling angry." This should give us cause to reflect on this conventional or prevailing "wisdom." If we look back on the case of Doris Pierson in Chapter Three, it was indeed her ineffective expressive coping that was central to her problem. Her inability to manage her feelings of anger, along with her inability to express warmth and affection proved to be her undoing in the marital relationship and then the cause for the depression she fell into as a result of her crisis.

Although Doris's case ran counter to the conventional wisdom, Allan Kahn's case seemed to confirm it. He seemed to represent the type of male who was not at all in touch with his feelings, and much less able to express or manage them. In fact, he was so poor at expressive coping that he fainted in a panic attack; the emotional roots of which he had practically no awareness. Instead, he tried to cope instrumentally by changing jobs and becoming self-employed rather than continuing in his former stressful employment situation. While this might have relieved one source of immediate stress it would do little to handle the emotional origins of his mid-life crisis.

If we look back over the cases presented in this volume, it is difficult to discern a pattern with respect to gender, or to type or effectiveness of coping. Linda Craft, Joyce Kurland, Debbie Rosen, and Alice Decker, all women, showed effective expressive and instrumental coping, but so did Steve Gornecky. Of course, the number of cases in this volume are too small in number to reflect any systematic pattern, especially since they were so selective to begin with. However, they are sufficiently variable to forewarn us against any hard and fast generalizations about gender and type or effectiveness of coping with mid-life crises. It would seem that Folkman and Lazarus's (1980) findings of relatively little difference between the sexes in terms of type of coping is probably closer to the truth than the conventional wisdom.

It is hard not to come to a similar conclusion about some of the generalizations that have been made about the differences between men and women with respect to issues of separation-individuation and attachment-intimacy. Chapter Five began with the observation by one clinical expert that women were particularly vulnerable when confronted with crises of separation (Notman 1980). Men, on the other hand, were apt to have more difficulty with issues of attachment and intimacy in mid-life. Perhaps part of the problem is that these "issues" are actually different aspects of the same fundamental issue rather than entirely different issues. For example, a person's development along the separation/individuation continuum would seem to be inextricably related to the person's capacity for attachment and intimacy, as well as for dealing with detachment and reattachment. This is essentially what Kegan (1982) means when he proposes that there is a lifelong dialectic between the poles of separation (independence) and integration (inclusion) rather than a preferred linear development toward separation/individuation.

At any rate, of the three cases in Chapter Five, the two men, John Raymond and Gary Robertson, had more trouble with the issue of attachment and intimacy than the woman, Joyce Kurland. On the other hand, the two men also had more difficulty with separation in the long run in the sense that they did not satisfactorily deal with or resolve it. Joyce Kurland, although she initially had difficulty with separation from her husband, did finally deal with it effectively. Furthermore, it was clear that she was the most individuated person, in Jung's (1971) maturational sense, in the three cases.

Then, again, in Chapter Six it was the man, Warren Cates, who had the greatest difficulty with separation rather than Debbie Rosen with her marital separation. or Alice Decker with the loss of her husband through sickness and death. It is also true that Warren had more trouble with reattachment, which is an intimacy/attachment issue, than did Debbie Rosen. This was consistent with the earlier observation about men's greater difficulty with this issue. Alice Decker had some difficulty with individuation, but by the time she left therapy she was a much more individuated person than Warren Cates was after two rounds of therapy. There is some question remaining as to whether Debbie Rosen developed any further along the separation/individuation continuum as a result of her separation and reattachment experiences. She had purposefully gone from one marital relationship to another without any serious consideration of living outside such a relationship for a major portion of her life.

After reviewing the inconsistencies concerning separation/individuation in the above cases, it becomes clear that Kegan's (1982) distinction between "embeddedness in" and "relationship to" is a crucial one. "Embeddedness in" indicates a fused, dependent type of relationship to others because of an incompleteness of self-as-object and other-as-object. "Relationship to" infers a mature adult relationship of a more complete, whole self-as-object to an other who is whole and distinct as an object from self.

In this sense, the more extreme field dependent position on Witkin's (1965) measure would be indicative of an "embeddedness in" orientation in a person. If we look back at the cases from this perspective, we can see even more clearly that gender by itself is not the determining factor. Although Doris Pierson had a very high field dependent score on Witkin's measure, three men, Allan Kahn, Gary Robertson, and John Raymond, also had very high field dependent scores. In fact, we could say that there was a failure of adequate separation from object (mother) and inadequate gender identification in John Raymond. This showed up in his Reptest results, and it led to a major problem in his relationship to women. He became embedded in relationships with them, rather than relating as a complete and distinct self to them as complete objects. Thus, although Lillian Rubin (1983) notes the unfortunate results in men's lives of denying their early identifications with their mothers, John Raymond illustrates the costs of not being able to develop an alternative identification with the father and an adequate gender identity. While Rubin (1979) has identified certain problems women have in mid-life in finding "a clear sense of self," they could not have the same kind of embeddedness problem men such as John Raymond might have.

Indeed, Rubin would undoubtedly be in essential agreement with Gilligan's (1982) position that women are generally more developed in the "relatedness to" dimension than are men. In fact, Robert Kegan (1982) has acknowledged that Gilligan is probably correct in her contention that men find it harder to evolve to the most mature "interindividual" stage in sociomoral development.

On the basis of all this, it would have to be said that the most important differences we find in mid-life crises are between different persons, not between sexes. This might seem self-evident; simply a truism, but it needs to be said for a number of reasons. For one, there has been a great deal of recent societal change with respect to sex role norms, and much of the conventional wisdom about differences in the psychosocial functioning of men and women are based on stereotypes derived from earlier sex role expectations and experiences. These changes have had an impact on middle-aged persons, as well as younger ones. Giele (1980) has pointed to an ever increasing transcendence of traditionally limiting age norms as well as sex role norms in our population. Nancy Datan (1976) has suggested that much of this transcendence might be a synthesis based upon an inherent dialectical process. She writes: "While the dominant male and the submissive female are easily called to mind as sex role stereotypes, the nurturant female and the male seeking sanctuary with her are also readily recognized. Sex role differentiation, then, is not defined as any fixed set of behaviors which are invariably male or female, but rather expressed by a polarity in behavior, one sex defining the other and defined by it" (Datan 1976, 44). Thus, mid-life issue involving separation/individuation and identity go much deeper than the gender differences based on the normative expectations of social role functioning. At these more fundamental levels of adult development, it would seem that the issues are far more personal and the differences much more between persons than they are social or between groups of people.

If there is one central conclusion that one can come to on the basis of these individual case studies and related literature, it is that generalizations from social and behavioral science theory and research about phenomena like mid-life crises have to be tempered by a recognition of the considerable and important exceptions to them. By their very nature, these generalizations have to be simplifications of the complex reality upon which they are based.

TOWARD A PHENOMENOLOGY OF AGING

The preceding statement about the problems of generalizing from the usual type of (nomothetic) behavioral science research might seem to call into question the efficacy of that approach for the study of adult transitions an crises. That was not the intent of the statement, for such studies are highly informative and indeed essential, if we are to advance knowledge in human development and the processes of aging. This author has done such studies and continues to do them. However, he recognizes that drawing representative samples of individuals and then generalizing to whole populations from those samples not only runs the usual risks of sampling error and generalizing from a biased or atypical sample. There is also a reduction of the data of observation and study to very discrete measurable variables, which are fine for mathematical and essentially statistical manipulation and analysis. Nevertheless, by reducing the data in this way, we are necessarily reducing much of its richness and detail; what phenomenologists call "dense data," to predetermined, directly observable categories of data which will be amenable to measurement. The word "predetermined" is crucial in this regard, because the empirical scientist predetermines the kinds and aspects of data to be observed on the basis of the theory or hunches on which the research hypotheses are based, as well as the operational needs (i.e., necessary but limiting "operational definitions") of the research and researcher. In this respect the researcher is putting "methodological blinders" on for the purposes of controlled observation. This predetermination of observational categories is necessarily exclusive rather than inclusive, and therefore not open to the full range of phenomena. More important is that the exclusiveness is predetermined by the scientist's own categories of thought.

It is this fact which led Whitehead (1969) to say, "Science has remained predominantly an anti-rationalist movement based upon a naive faith ... it has never cared to justify its faith or to explain its meanings." I assume the faith Whitehead alluded to is the faith that the scientist's categories of thought and observation are indeed the most objective, unbiased, and reflective of the true nature of things. He might also be referring to the "naive faith" that scientific method is the sole or preemptive means of truly "knowing" in our time.

These are rather far reacting epistemological issues, and are far beyond the domain that is my primary interest here, which is knowledge about human development and aging in the adult years. The important point here is *human* development, for this criticism of modern science is largely a criticism of the methods and assumptions of natural science and how these methods and assumptions have been applied to human affairs. These methods and assumptions have been taken over in a literal sense by the social and behavioral scientists of the second half of the Twentieth century. While this has added a great deal to our knowledge about humans, particularly about the behavior of the "human animal," it has left out a whole dimension of understanding human behavior. It has left out the experiential dimension; the human being's subjective experience of the forces and events in his or her environment and world. This dimension or realm has to do with the meaning rather than the measurement of forces and events in human life space. It is the domain of what Dilthey (1947/1976) called the "human sciences," which are directed toward understanding of the meaning of things. This in contrast to natural sciences' direction toward the explanation of the forces and events in life.

This whole book is directed toward a study of meaning, but meaning as it applies to the circumscribed arena of mid-life transitions and crises. Much of the methodology described in Chapter Two and applied to the case materials has been phenomenological. The reasons for choosing this approach and methodology for this subject matter have already been set forth and need no further explanation at this point. However, it would be useful to explore the possibilities of expanding the parameters of the application of a phenomenological approach to the field of gerontology, as proposed by Carol Ryff (1985). If we talk about a "phenomenology of aging" we have to mean the study of aging as it is experienced by the aging person. It is hoped that the case materials in this book have served to show that aging is both experienced and understood in the context of transitional events, events that are often of crisis proportions and laden with emotion and meaning that move the person to another stage of adult development. Such events become the focal points not only of the transitions but should also be the points of intervention to prevent a crisis or a breakdown. At these points, the transitional process can be deflected in the direction of growth and maturing rather than regression or stagnation. Regardless of whether such formal or professional intervention takes place, the important feature is that the person has moved to a new point in adult development as a result of the experience of the transitional event. Thus, "aging" in this phenomenological perspective is much more evolutionary (process oriented) than temporal (stage oriented) in nature. The sheer passage of time is not the central ingredient in this conception of aging, but rather it is the experiencing and living of the transitional events. This idea agrees with the process view of aging, which Marjorie Fiske (1980) claims is much more able to accommodate the myriad facts and features of aging than does the more prevalent stage theory.

Such a phenomenology of aging should serve to complement the more objectivistic and quantitative approach to aging of most social gerontologists. It can do this by providing the subjective, experiential, and meaning perspective on understanding the aging process, and it can serve to prevent the reification of some of the statistical findings from the nomothetic natural science type of gerontological research. Ideally, these two forms of research might serve as counterpoint for one another in the development of knowledge about human aging which would allow for a more comprehensive view—both objective and subjective.

Before going further with the idea of a phenomenology of aging, it is important to recognize that phenomenology does not represent a single, monolithic view in the realm of human science. There are different kinds of emphases in phenomenological study just as there are different types of phenomenologists. I have already indicated that the structural phenomenology of Merleau-Ponty, which has been the preferred phenomenological approach of this book, does not represent a pure, Husserlian phenomenology or approach to the study of phenomena. There is perhaps no one "right" way to "do" phenomenology, any more than there is any one "right" way to age. Therefore, I would like to state my reasons for selecting or favoring certain positions and figures for a phenomenology of aging.

There are two predominant concerns that have guided the selection of the particular approaches and emphases that will be proposed here. The first concern is with finding those approaches that seem most promising for providing new insights and perspectives regarding the experience of aging, for the purposes of understanding rather than explanation or prediction. This means finding approaches that highlight areas of understanding that are not really accessible to nomothetic research. The second predominant concern is to find approaches that will serve to inform clinical practice and intervention of the problems of aging. The selection of approaches will not only be guided by the need for new insights and perspectives on problems, but also by the ethical and ontological implications of the methods used for assessment and intervention.

This last statement concerning ontological implications needs to be clarified. The concern about ethical methods should be self-explanatory when we are talking about intervening in human lives. The ontological issue, on the other hand, is one that underlies the twin concerns noted above, but is not explicit or self-explanatory. In phenomenology, there is a fundamental, nondeterministic assumption about the nature of being as far as humans are concerned. This is derived in large part from phenomenology's proactive view of human intentionality. Phenomenology sees all behavior as intentional, even in animals, but when it moves into the human realm and the realm of meaning this intentionality has a distinctly nondeterministic ring to it. Most certainly, it is not the reactive view of human behavior which is implicit in most modern behavioral research and practice.

By taking a nondeterministic stance, one has to rule out the use of controlled, predictive, and deterministic methods in both research and practice. This is perhaps most obvious with respect to research, where it is no great obstacle since phenomenological method by its very nature eschews control or prestructuring of phenomena for study. This nondeterministic stance is probably less obvious when it comes to issues and methods of clinical practice and intervention. This will be spelled out in more detail later in this chapter, but the reader needs to be alerted to it as a consideration at this point.

The preference for Merleau-Ponty's structural phenomenology in the structural approach of this book has already been noted. It was preferred over the approach of Levi-Strauss, which focuses on "deep structures." this selection was made for several reasons, not the least of which are the clearly deterministic and nonphenomenological features of Levi-Strauss's approach. Phillip Pettis (1977) has gone so far as to identify Levi-Strauss as distinctly "*anti*phenomenological" because he rejects the standpoint of subjective consciousness taken by phenomenology. This rejection of subjective consciousness and the tendency to negate the individual person as a reality has led some writers to put Levi-Strauss in the "antihumanist" tradition (Blasi 1976; Eagleton 1983).

In addition to Levi-Strauss's antihumanistic position, there is the fact that Merleau-Ponty's form of structuralism is much more compatible with the view of modern adult development theory, particularly the Eriksonian ego-psychological view:

> Erikson has little affinity with ... that brand of determinism represented by his arch-opponent, Claude Levi-Strauss. He had greater affinity with those moderating figures such as Paul Ricoeour or Maurice Merleau-Ponty who tend to see life as a subtle interplay between man's involuntary bodily tendencies and his higher capacities for self-awareness, reflection, and freedom (Browning 1973, 180).

This quote by Browning helps to clarify my preference for Merleau-Ponty's structuralism over Levi-Strauss, but it does not explain why Erikson prefers it. Browning explained this by noting that Erikson saw man in the same way as did phenomenologists like Husserl, Heidegger, Merleau-Ponty and Binswanger in that all of them study man from the perspective of his "being-in-the world." Erikson's modes or modalities of action are really patterns or styles of being-in-the-world, so "... Erikson's contribution is that of demonstrating developmental order to man's being-in-the-world as well as suggesting how the basic patterns of the ego's hierarchy of states and action possibilities make up the ground plan" (Browning 1973, 159). The underlying ontological or being assumptions of structural phenomenology about humans is quite compatible with the perspective of adult development theory and complements that theory in its subjective and experiential dimensions.

Chapter Two contained a discussion of the strong hermeneutical trend in phenomenology and noted that the approach of this book is very much in line with that trend. The importance of everyday language to provide clues to the "structure of meaning" was noted and utilized in such devices as the Reptest and the semantic-differential. However, these tests are necessarily prestructured to some extent, and there is a need to develop hermeneutical methods that will tap the experience and meaning of aging in the natural, contextual use of language by the person in reminiscence, life review, and life histories. Howard (1982) says that hermeneutics can be a theory of "... the understanding of life experiences as they are given in linguistic expression" and that "the method of empathic understanding" is a fair though truncated description of the essential approach of hermeneutics. At least it is the essential approach of the type of hermeneutics I would propose as appropriate for the phenomenological study of aging.

This method of empathic understanding is of course quite consistent with the approach that was outlined under "Structural Case Study Methods" in Chapter Two. This empathic method is particularly characteristic of what Howard (1982) calls "ontological hermeneutics," whose foremost figure is Hans-Georg Gadamer (1976). Gadamer was not only a student of Heidegger, but he further developed Heidegger's conception of the central role of language in human existence. He was a pivotal figure in phenomenology's turn toward language as the key manifestation of the way in which a person constructs his or her world. In fact, his phrase, "being that can be understood is language," became emblematic of this essential position.

Gadamer rejects any transcendent language or grammar and any efforts to interpret and impute meaning from language independent of the experience of the person using it. He is in disagreement with de Saussure (1966) who would hold that language can be understood only in its universal aspects and, further, that these are above the individual users and determine the individual use. This represents the same antiphenomenological and antihumanist position as Levi-Strauss. This further recommends Gadamer's approach to hermeneutics for a phenomenology of aging, with its emphasis on the person's own expression of self and meaning in language.

If we read the letter of Joyce Kurland in Chapter Five and Alice Decker in Chapter Six, it is hard to believe that there was not an expression of some new understanding and of their being-in-the-world in their written language. The expression was in their own words and in their own preferred (written) form of self-expression and self-understanding. These would be given thorough credence in Gadamer's "ontological hermeneutics." Of course, some of the methods (empathic and phenomenological) used in the therapy of these two women enabled them to tap the subjective realities of their lives and crises. Then, these new understandings were articulated and thereby realized in language, notably in those meaningful letters. Of course, Gadamer does not restrict his approach to written language. He is particularly cognizant of the importance of spoken language, particularly language we use when we are freely expressing ourselves on topics we feel deeply about. According to Gadamer, it is when we get away from a conscious choosing of terms and instead let our unshaped thoughts find their own expression that we are apt to gain the greatest understanding. This is very close to Gendlin's (1961) conception of "experiencing and the creation of meaning." Here, again, Gadamer's hermeneutics are quite consistent with and are a valuable addition to the phenomenological study of aging being proposed here.

In ending these few preliminary thoughts about the need for an approach to a phenomenology of aging, I would like to call on Herbert Speigelberg, who has written clearly and informatively about the application of phenomenology to a range of concerns and disciplines. He seems to be clear about the limitations as well as the value and promise of phenomenology as a method:

> By aiming at insights into essential structures and relationships, phenomenology has supplied new patterns of understanding for relating phenomena, which are otherwise merely juxtaposed in time and space except for functional relations of "explanatory" covering laws. By putting the phenomena into the context of lived experience in a "life-world," by exploring the meaningful connections experienced in motivation, by using methods of interpretation sometimes called "hermeneutic," phenomenology has added new dimensions to empirical exploration (Speigelberg 1972, 362).

This is what is being proposed here for further extension into the broad field of aging. This book used phenomenological methods to gain insights into structures of meaning in the experience of mid-life crises, but it still used some of the findings and even some of the tools from quantitative behavioral science research in the process. This is as it should be, for the phenomenological approach proposed here is meant to complement rather than supplant behavioral science research. Speigelberg says that the phenomenological approach must not be considered a rival of "scientific" research, because ". . . its main *raison d'etre* is to serve as an ally to the scientific enterprise" (Speigelberg 1972, 361).

CLINICAL IMPLICATIONS

There are several implications for clinical practice which can be drawn from the case materials and methods of this book. In fact, we can actually begin with the first two cases in the book, Doris Pierson and Allan Kahn in Chapter Three. In both instances certain cognitive-behavioral approaches were attempted, and with mixed results. Both persons tended to favor the behavioral aspects of the approaches and eschew the more cognitive elements. Allan Kahn preferred the behavioral techniques of relaxation training, deep breathing, and so on, which tended to relieve the most distressful physiological symptoms of his anxiety. Doris Pierson liked being trained in assertiveness skills, being told how to conduct herself behaviorally under certain circumstances. However, she had difficulty with the cognitive monitoring of her thoughts associated with specific emotions, because she claimed the emotions overwhelmed her. She could not bring herself to think about what was behind or associated with the distressing emotions. Allan Kahn had a similar problem with the cognitive monitoring techniques; they just "didn't work" for him. In his case there was much to indicate that he was engaging in massive denial about the seriousness of his marital and family situation, as well as the underlying developmental issues. In Doris Pierson's case the problem with cognitive monitoring was probably avoidance rather than true denial, because the thoughts behind the emotions were simply too painful for her to handle.

In both cases the element that was missing and was needed was insight. Aaron Beck (1876) has been quite emphatic in stating that cognitive therapy is insight-oriented. Unlike psychoanalytic and some other psychodynamic therapies, cognitive therapy deals with conscious meanings rather than unconscious impulses to help the person gain insight. Therefore, the person has to be capable of monitoring conscious thoughts and meanings. If not, then the cognitive-behavioral techniques are not going to be totally effective. Perhaps the behavioral techniques will alleviate some of the symptoms of distress, but the person will not grasp the meaning of his or her situation.

This is extremely important for psychosocial transitions of the type involved in mid-life crises. In these situations there is a disjuncture between the person's assumptive world and the changed real world (Parkes 1971). It is not enough to cope behaviorally with the distress, either through relaxation techniques or even changed behaviors based on skills training. What is needed, obviously, is to make the necessary changes in the assumptive world, and this takes insight. So, insight and cognitive change in the person's assumptive world are necessary to even know how to behave differently and appropriately in the changed real world. Simply training people in "coping skills" is not enough for solution of psychosocial problems of the dimensions of mid-life crises. Therefore, one would have to raise serious questions about the efficacy of cognitive-behavioral techniques such as coping skills and stress innocula-tion, as proposed by Meichenbaum (1977), Novaco (1978) and others for such crises.

Before this line of argument is carried too far, it is important to point out that the cognitive monitoring and disputation technique helped Alice Decker cope with the awful distress over her husband's condition for those many months before his death. That was a most important finding based on clinical experience, as far as I was concerned, and it has clear implications for further work in such distressful situations. In her case most of the work was cognitive. Although she did use deep muscle relaxation and attempted some systematic desensitization, the greatest help came from the cognitive monitoring and disputation of the morbid thoughts which she was obsessed with. The other thing that distinguished her case from those of Doris Pierson and Allan Kahn was that there was no need for her to gain insight into her situation which was very obvious and oppressive.

It is very possible that some of the reasons which led David Chiriboga (see Chapter One) and some others to question the efficacy of self-conscious coping in such crises are similar to mine regarding coping skills and stress innoculation techniques. It seems that in order for such cognitive-behavioral techniques to be fully effective, it is necessary for the person to be able to cope both cognitively and behaviorally. Doris Pierson and Allan Kahn were not able to cope cognitively, and the techniques only met limited and short term success. Also, it seems that the cognitive and the behavioral components of the techniques have to be used differentially, depending on the nature of the problem, as in the case of Alice Decker, where the cognitive component was appropriately dominant.

Another point needs to be made about the cognitive component, and that is that the type of cognitive monitoring and review that operates only at the self-talk or automatic-thoughts level might be too superficial for some of the more deep and pervasive issues concerning the self and the assumptive world that occur in mid-life crises. It is apt to be the deeper cognitive structures and meanings that are affected and need to be worked on. At best, the more superficial cognitive review techniques in cognitive-behavioral approaches will only serve to cope with some of the more immediate symptoms of stress, as in the initial work on anxiety in the case of Warren Cates. Ultimately, his therapist had to get at those deeper levels where the faulty and distorted object-relations issues were at work, before Warren could make any gains on those issues in his contemporary adult world.

Assessment instruments like the Repertory Grid Test and the semantic-differential can help to graphically portray some of these structural issues and thereby help the person gain insight into the issues, or at least into how he or she is construing current reality on the basis of those issues. However, to bring about change, insight is not enough any more than is abreaction, which is a highly emotional reexperiencing of the original issue. As Allen Wheelis (1969) has pointed out, it takes the *will* and the courage to change once the insight has been gained. It also often takes hard and repeated work and risk taking in order to bring about significant change in psychosocial problems like mid-life crises. This is the kind of work and risk taking that Ralph Kane in Chapter Four would have had to undertake in order to break out of his mid-life stagnation. Even if he was able to engage in the kind of emotive ventilation and encounter he wanted, and even if he achieved an emotional abreaction, he would have had to engage in risk taking and further work.

It should be evident by now that cognitive therapy is not a uniform approach. It is one that allows for individual differences on the part of practitioners and considerable freedom in the way they apply it. Yet, I am convinced that it is the most promising of the existing crop of therapies for adult transitional crises, precisely because of its flexible and adaptive potentialities (Arnkoff 1981). However, it is important to recognize that there are marked differences in the practice of cognitive therapy and to make note of the effect these differences have on the focus, techniques, and goals in different practice situations.

Howard Goldstein (1982) has identified two models of cognitive practice based on different orientations to human thought and to different conceptions of the role of cognition in human behavior. One orientation he calls "mediational" and the second is "phenomenological." The mediational model takes the objective-reactive position in which "cognition is defined as an intervening variable that processes the input of outer stimuli and, in turn, affects the output of emotional or behavioral expression" (Goldstein 1982, 544). This model emphasizes the person's reactive nature and sees cognitive processes as responsive to external inputs in a linear form: (a) an external condition or event excites cognitive operations that produce a particular response and then (b) these cognitive operations are causally linked to the interpretation of past learning and experiences. It is easy to see why former behaviorists, who had little or no use for cognitive processes in the past, would choose this mediational model in order to add some of the new cognitive techniques to their repertoires. It is much closer to their former conception of human behavior and it is less far reaching in its implications for their rethinking of the role of cognition in behavior. This mediational model is basic to the rapidly expanding field of cognitive-behavior therapy (Foreyt & Rathjen 1978; Mahoney 1974; Meichenbaum 1977).

The phenomenological view of cognition takes a proactive-subjective position in which "cognition itself is seen as a determinant—its intentional, selective, and interpretive qualities are not only able to ascertain what is outside but also to process what that outside means" (Goldstein 1982, 549-50). In this view, the mind is able to create its own reality of phenomena in accord with its own constructs and interpretations, sometimes quite apart from the influence of outer stimuli. We have just seen in some of the case studies how the assumptive world of personal constructs and interpretations is "quite apart" from outside reality and stimuli. It is my feeling that this cognitive-phenomenological model of practice is more appropriate for extended work on mid-life problems and crises. This is not a position unique to me, for the potential advantages of a combined cognitive and phenomenological approach to intervention in later adulthood were identified much earlier by other gerontologists (Baltes 1973; Thomae 1970).

It is important to note the full range of cognitive faculties. They include not only the intellectual and analytic functions but also sentience, imagery, vicarious experiencing, intuition, and so on. Furthermore, cognition and emotion are inextricably bound up with one another so that much of cognition is heavily emotion laden, and some cognitions would be meaningless without their emotional associations and energies. Therefore, cognitive therapy does not have to consist of a cold, intellectual "mind-trip." Indeed, most of the time it is not, often despite the orientation of the practitioner using it. On the other hand, the particular cognitive functions that the practitioner chooses to emphasize will definitely affect the nature and goals of treatment.

Let us take a look at the mediational and phenomenological models to see how the emphasis on different cognitive functions can affect the focus, techniques, and goals of practice. In the mediational model, the content focus is apt to be on symptoms of maladaptive patterns and clusters of personal rules or beliefs that contribute to certain categories of dysfunction, such as depression and anxiety. The techniques that tend to be favored are behavior modification, reality testing to authenticate or validate conclusions, and modeling approaches. The goals tend to be geared toward removing symptomatic patterns that block adaptive behavior.

The phenomenological model, on the other hand, will tend to focus on personal meanings of experiences and thought processes concerning those experiences, and will serve to clarify notions of the self in past, present, and future terms. The treatment process is seen as a mutual one, whereby person and practitioner engage in a kind of Socratic dialogue and problem solving. Techniques rely on empathic understanding and facilitation to help the person expand perceptions of self and reality. Goldstein identifies the goals of the phenomenological model to be "development of greater integrity and a more autonomous approach to the demands of living" (Goldstein 1982, 552). While I would not disagree with this self-actualization goal, I would add that this model is also appropriate for overcoming pervasive and often chronic problems in living such as several of those depicted in this book.

Clearly, the meditational and phenomenological models should not be seen as mutually exclusive in practice. The cognitive-behavioral approaches are apt to be highly effective in short-term cases with clearly delineated or targeted problems which are to be removed within a designated period of time. The cognitive-phenomenological is apt to be more appropriate for extensive work with long-standing or pervasive psychosocial problems of the dimensions of mid-life crises. It should also be noted that cognitive-behavioral techniques can be used effectively in long-term treatment to help the person cope, in the early stages when there are physiological as well as behavioral symptoms related to the stress which need to be relieved before more extensive cognitive work can begin.

Some therapists have been critical of cognitive therapy because of what they see as a split in the practitioner's thinking about cognition and affect. They believe that cognitive therapy does not give enough credence to the affective and emotional components of treatment. Jack L. Rubins (1980), a training and supervising analyst in the Karen Horney Institute, is one of those who has written quite effectively about this. He noted that in Horney's conception, the development of cognition in childhood clearly follows and is influenced by affect. That is, the child's affect or feelings of helplessness are pervasive and automatic, and they precede the cognition of the events with which they are associated. Therefore, the distorted affect is the precursor of the distorted cognition. This seems to run counter to the cognitive position that says that thinking shapes emotion and behavior. In fact, it might not run counter, but it is clear that Rubins is particularly critical of certain cognitive-behavioral approaches that tend to stress behavior modification and action in order to change dysfunctional emotions. In his view, this does not give credence to the prior and preemptive place of affect in emotional problems. He says:

> A sizable percentage of neurotic patients are action-oriented. They are constantly asking what they should do to find the magic cure. In effect, the mechanical manipulation only feeds into the neurotic compulsive emphasis on doing, which is a predetermined defense against awareness of the larger self (Rubins 1980, 198).

This is probably true of quite a few situations and of many coping efforts in the psychosocial crises of mid-life. It was especially true of Allan Kahn in Chapter Three, whose manic activity pattern did indeed act as a defense against awareness of the larger problem, and where the behavioral techniques just fed into his compulsiveness. So, one can accept the validity of some of Rubins' points but it is not necessary to accept his premise that affect is preemptive in treatment. The chicken-and-egg question of cognition and affect is not all that crucial in practice. Even if affect was there first, there is nothing to say that cognitive change cannot bring about emotional change. After all, much psychotherapy is based on the assumption that the informed application of the patient's adult cognition can serve to bring to light and overcome infantile ideas and emotions as they affect adult functioning. There is also nothing to say that evocative emotive techniques will work any more directly or effectively in dealing with emotional problems. They might, or they might not, as in the case of Ralph Kane who did not change despite the evocative techniques of Gestalt therapy.

Rubins is probably correct, though, about the relative ineffectiveness of attacking the more intransigent, pervasive, or characterological emotional problems through the use of direct, rational-cognitive disputational techniques. This can also be true concerning the difficult psychosocial problems involved in mid-life crises. It turned out to be true in at least two of the cases when rational-cognitive decision-making techniques were used in dealing with difficult life choices. Let us look at these two cases again because, as Levinson (1978) says, such choices are crucial factors in adult transitions and in negotiating the movement from one developmental stage and life structure to another.

The case of Doris Pierson in Chapter Three and Linda Craft in Chapter Four involved the use of Irving Janis's (1982) balance sheet procedure, which is essentially a cognitive decision-making technique. In retrospect, it can be said that it produced mixed results in the Pierson case and misleading results in the Craft case. It will be recalled that it was used to help Doris Pierson to decide whether to remain in her marriage or not. The balance sheet, on which she had to list reasons for and against remaining in the marriage, as well as for and against separating, produced a stalemate in which she generated an equal number of pro and con reasons for both options. However, when she used Janis's technique of projecting herself one year into the future under each option, and then to simulate an interview with her therapist following each option, she unequivocally chose to remain in the marriage. It was her emotional response to enacting the scenario of separation that led to her decision, because she became very anxious and concerned that she would probably go into a depression if she separated. This was a good example of how a cognitive approach can evoke a good deal of emotion. However, her final decision was to remain in a shaky and unsatisfactory marriage. Furthermore, her decision did not prevent her from going into a clinical depression, which had to be worked out in further therapy.

The balance sheet technique seemed initially to have worked extremely well for Linda Craft. Her decision to leave the Albany area for Tampa was unequivocal because of the overwhelming number of reasons she generated in favor of doing so, compared with the reasons for staying. She was very enthusiastic about the technique, probably because she was a well-organized "doer" who liked the structured, no-nonsense rationality of the procedure. At any rate, she later changed her mind when she found her sister and brother would be moving out of the Tampa area. This turned out to be fortunate, because she still had to work through her mid-life transition and the unsettled love relationship which she almost ran from.

Why did this straight-forward cognitive technique, which after all is only a variation of the basic problem-solving model being used so widely in business as well as the human services, fare so poorly in these cases? I suspect that it was too direct and simplistic in its rationality and in practically forcing decisions in complex and momentous life situations. Even the Direct Decision Therapy of Harold Greenwald (1973) does not take such a frontal approach, for he always finds out more about the people he works with and carefully studies the context of their current lives. He helps them generate alternative options, and for this, Janis's balance sheet procedure can be an excellent device, but he never pushes for a decision. Further, he never pushes people to act on their decisions, "because that would make it more difficult for them to change when they are ready" (Greenwald 1973, 16). He found in his practice that to be purposely "willful" in such momentous matters does not work in the long run.

The practitioner who probably did the most to provide insight into this difficult area of will, will power, and decision making was Leslie Farber of the William Allanson White Institute. In a number of essays later published in a book entitled *The Ways of the Will* (Farber 1966), he proposed two different realms of the will, which he based on his psychiatric practice and research. His first realm of the will is not experienced consciously by the person as an *act* of the will; it has to be inferred after an *event*. In effect, Farber suggests that the most important choices people make in life are not consciously experienced as choices. It is only after the fact that it can be determined that a choice has actually been made. This type of will has a *direction* in the life of a person but it does not have discrete *objectives or goals*. Although it provides movement and directionality to a person's life, it is not immediately and directly available to scrutiny.

The second realm of will is much more in line with the common sense notion of will power. This is the conscious component of will which is experienced during the act or event. Unlike the first realm, it presses toward some specific goal in a very conscious, intentional, and utilitarian way. The goal is known from the beginning, and it tends to consist of some objective end state, such as obtaining a graduate degree, learning to drive a car, a specific weight loss, and so on. In this realm the person can actually articulate the process by saying something like, "I will do this in order to achieve that."

Many people, and this includes psychotherapists, often mistakenly attempt to make the conscious will of the second realm do the work of the will of the first realm. The problem with attempting this is conveyed by the following statement:

> I can will knowledge, but not wisdom; going to bed, but not sleeping; eating, but not hunger; meekness, but not humility; scrupulosity, but not virtue; self-assertion or bravado, but not courage; lust, but not love; commiseration, but not sympathy; congratulations, but not admiration; religiosity, but not faith; reading, but not understanding. I would emphasize that the consequence of willing what cannot be willed is that we fall into a distress we call anxiety (Farber 1966, 15).

Thus, Farber sees anxiety as a function of the relationship between the two realms of the will. He has formulated this into what he calls a phenomenological definition of anxiety, as follows: "Anxiety is that range of distress which attends willing what cannot be willed" (Farber 1976, 27). This definition could very well fit the anxiety that led to Allan Kahn's panic attack, as described in Chapter Three. He wanted to "will" the nurturance, security, and protection provided in his marriage, as well as the integrity of his family, perhaps as a recognition of his own finiteness and mortality. His precipitous choice or decision to leave his job and become self-employed at home represented an instance of the second realm of the will attempting to do the work of the first.

This is an extremely valuable distinction Farber has made, and we will return to it again later in the chapter. For the moment, however, we are concerned with its clinical implications. These implications are that the two realms of will have to be approached differently in therapy. The second purposeful and conscious realm can be approached directly by techniques like Janis's balance sheet procedure, by encouragement and other forms of reward and reinforcement, or even by exhortation from the therapist. The first realm, however, has to be approached indirectly, insightfully, and emphatically by the therapist, because it literally has to be "lived" rather than "willed" by the client or patient. This calls for a careful and sensitive transactional process between practitioner and person and then between the person in his or her assumptive world and the realities of the outside world. It is actually a process many of us learn to carry out through life experience, in the course of aging and maturing. Sometimes, and for some people, it is necessary to seek help in carrying it out, particularly at those junctures and transitions in adult life when critical choices have to be made. Then, it is a question of "working through" rather than "working on" the problems of the first order of will.

One particular approach I have found helpful in doing this is Gendlin's (1981) technique of "experiential focusing." It is a technique based in large part on the phenomenological ideas of Merleau-Ponty, and it involves having the person experience and focus on a bodily, precognitive sense of the problem or problems with which he or she is currently coping (Gendlin 1973). The therapist then guides the person through the several steps in the procedure, which may or may not be sufficient to gain new insight or a new perspective on the problem or dilemma. The procedure can be repeated over time as the person gains more and more insight, and the procedure can be carried out with or without the guidance of the therapist. It is a way of gaining access to the kind of directionality implied in Farber's first (unconscious) realm of will. Space is too limited for its full presentation here, but Gendlin (1981) has given a full, book-length explanation of it. I have found it useful not only in this type of decision-making situation, but in clinical work with some other life transition problems.

The potential value of a dialectical perspective on the problems and processes of adult development has been mentioned several times up to this point. Now it is time to indicate its potentialities for intervention and clinical treatment. Kegan (1982) has proposed a dialectical approach within a phenomenological framework for counselors working with adults who are troubled by the conflicts, contradictions, dilemmas, and choices facing them in transitional states and crises:

> The counselor is trying to hold the door open to them [the conflicts, etc.] in his choice to resonate *to the experience* that having such a problem may entail, rather than to help solve the problem, or try to make the experience less painful. He chooses the phenomenological perspective because his loyalty is to *the person in her meaning-making,* rather than to her state or balance. He is seeking to join the *process* of meaning-evolution, rather than solve the problems which are reflective of that process (Kegan 1982, 274).

This is very consistent with the cognitive-phenomenological approach noted above. It also speaks to the limitations I have found with some of the cognitive-behavioral approaches which "attempt to solve the problems that are reflective" of a developmental, growth process. The need to *resonate* to the experience of conflict and contradictions is the dialectical aspect of the treatment approach.

How is this worked out in practice? It is essentially a dialogical process between the counselor and the person. It is what Friedman (1985) has referred to as "the healing dialogue in psychotherapy." As such, it begins with the nondirective empathic approach outlined in Chapter One. It is interesting to note that both Kegan (1982, 278-82) and Rychlak (1973, 504-06), a leading proponent of dialectical treatment methods, provide clinical examples of dialogical/dialectical methods that draw directly from the work of Carl Rogers.

The difference between them and Rogers, however, is that they consciously bring into the clinical dialogue the contradictions and polarities the person is experiencing. These are made explicit so that the person can make sense or meaning out of them and arrive at a personal synthesis of them in a growth process. It represents a form of conceptual encounter, as described in Chapter Two, in which the counselor highlights the implicit polarities, contradictions, and ambivalences so that the person can synthesize them in the process of change.

A great many techniques and methods of both assessment and treatment have been mentioned so far: cognitive, cognitive-behavioral, phenomenological, dialectical, and so on. The practitioner/reader is probably wondering at this point how, or if, all of these can be brought together in any cohesive or integrative sense for actual application in practice. As mentioned earlier, this is not intended to be a "how to" book for clinical practitioners, but rather one that might add to the understanding of mid-life transitions. However, I have attempted to integrate these cognitive and phenomenological methods for the purpose of clinical practice in another book (Sherman 1984). The chapters on treatment methods and the case illustrations of their application in differential problem situations might prove helpful to clinical practitioners who are interested in applying them in a systematic way.

IMPLICATIONS FOR LIVING THE MIDDLE YEARS

The phrase "*living* the middle years" was used in preference to "living *in*" the middle years" in the title of this section for a particular reason. The words "living *in*' tend to emphasize the temporal limitations of the middle years; of time left, of old age, and of death. It will be recalled from the discussion at the beginning of the book that many of the emotional problems and crises of the middle years are generated by reactions to the recognition of personal finiteness and mortality. Much of the manic activity and much of the willful decision making seen in a number of the cases presented here was generated by that recognition. If any one implication can be drawn from this, it is the need to consciously accept the reality of this finiteness without attempts to deny or ward it off and without frantic compensatory efforts to accomplish the goals of the idealized self within the time and energies left in the middle years. Those are indeed the way one becomes trapped in living *in* rather than *living* the middle years.

This acceptance is much easier said than done, but let us take a look again at some of the clinical, research, and theoretical material we have covered to see what can be done to facilitate this. As far as the clinical material is concerned, there is something that can be learned from the essentially cognitive approach which was used in most of the cases. It is noteworthy that Goldstein (1982) identified the primary thrust of the cognitive-phenomenological as one of helping the person develop "principles for living" which would provide "a more autonomous approach to the demands of living." Now, this sounds downright philosophical in orientation, and in many respects it is. What is needed in the middle and later years of life is a more "philosophical" outlook on life. When Peck (1968) says that it is necessary to learn to value wisdom over physical powers in the middle years, that is what he is talking about. But, even in the purely clinical sense, as distinct from the developmental one, it should be evident from much of the case material that there was a need for philosophical changes in the assumptive worlds of the persons in treatment. This holds true for much of psychotherapy in general. One behavioral therapist, for example, noted that follow-up studies of cases treated by behavior therapy showed that durable outcomes usually require philosophical as well as behavioral changes (Lazarus 1971).

It is important to note that the core idea in the cognitive approach goes back at least to around 100 A.D. when the Greek philosopher, Epictetus, noted that men are not disturbed by things but by their *perceptions* of things. This core idea is represented by the "B" in Ellis's (1962, 1974) ABC theory of emotions, which has been referred to a number of times in the book. This is a powerful idea which can be quite helpful even to people who do not go into psychotherapy. It is recognition, as well as intelligent and sensitive use, of this idea that seems to explain why some self-help books have been found to work for some people (Rychlak 1979). What it does is to help a person develop a corrective form of introspection, a purposive introspection, rather than to simply react behaviorally or emotionally without attempting to understand what is impelling the behavior or feelings.

Some of this introspective capacity should develop in the normal course of aging. It will be remembered that Neugarten (1968) identified this phenomenon in her empirical studies of the middle and later years, and she called it an increasing "interiority" of the personality. She felt the process served the function of enabling the person to narrow down and identify the core values in his or her life so that they could be lived by the person, similar to Erikson's concept of ego integrity. Gould (1978) identified the same kind of process in somewhat different terms when he said the mid-life is the time to "overcome remaining internal prohibitions and correct whatever distortion, misperceptions and misunderstandings that have prevented us from becoming authentic, whole people." He goes on to say that thereafter the "life of inner-directedness finally prevails" as does the credo, "I own myself."

Certainly, the core element in the cognitive approach can help one to identify many of these distortions, misperceptions, and misunderstandings. These distortions and misperceptions can then be disputed and changed on the basis of knowledge that has been obtained from study and research in adult development. This knowledge can help to explicate some of the "principles for living" which seem to fit with a more adaptive, "philosophical" approach to life in the middle years. These tend to be life-enhancing attitudes and beliefs which operate against certain myths and imperatives that people often feel they must live out in the middle years. For example, many middle-aged people question whether they are doing "meaningful things" in the time they have left in life. This question, though common and perhaps even socially normative for the middle years, is essentially a destructive one. It promotes the unhealthy and unnecessary idealized striving noted earlier. It is the "time left" element that is most destructive, so one principle would be not to accept the "time left" premise, and instead find one's core values and live currently in line with them. Just the search is worthwhile, so there should not be an added imperative to do something "meaningful," though that might come of its own volition, as in Farber's "first order of will."

Another point related to this is the insidious impact of social as well as personal timetables for whatever activities, attainments, and positions are appropriate or inappropriate for middle age. It might be added that this refers to the timetables of developmental theorists, as well as societal timetables. These can exert powerful influences on peoples' lives and they disregard individual differences, capacities, interests, and needs. They need to be made explicit in one's introspective cognitive review, especially when it comes to making important life decisions. These should not be made on the basis of societal or even "scientific" timetables.

Another principle which could be proposed is that there needs to be an acceptance of some limitations in one's self and one's life, which cannot be overcome in the middle or in the later years. In the current push for self-realization and self-satisfaction, we often lose sight of the fact that people are complex and cannot realize all aspects of themselves. Furthermore, by making certain choices in life, the person shuts off other options. By choosing to marry, one relinquishes certain aspects of personal freedom. If Warren Cates decides to choose the life of singlehood, he thereby relinquishes the possibility of the continuing type of intimacy available in couplehood. As Erich Fromm (1956) put it, "Man has choices . . ." but "whatever he chooses he builds a structure, in which certain orientations are dominant and others necessarily follow."

Elliott Jaques (1980) points to another potential principle in noting that in mid-life "one's work need no longer be experienced as perfect." There should be no need for "obsessional attempts at perfection" and the work process should be carried out far enough . . . so that the work is good enough." I would like to suggest that this concept of "good enough" be carried thoroughly into one's work life in the middle years. It overcomes the stultifying and stagnating effects of perfectionism and enhances the feelings and realities of creativity, productivity, and accomplishment.

Finally, it is important to be aware of the fact that we cannot will perfection, self-realization, and quite a number of other unrealistic imperatives that continue to drive us, usually without our awareness, during our middle years. Too often individuals, like Ralph Kane in Chapter Four, attempt to will themselves into love, intimacy, spontaneity, or any number of desired (imperative) states. The resulting frustration, despair, and sometimes depression is often immense.

Furthermore, we should be aware that we don't *have* to make the "right" and "correct" choices, or forever be damned. Most of this damning turns out to be self-damnation and it can be exceptionally demoralizing in the middle years. The freedom inferred in the choices and decisions we *can* make includes the freedom to fail. It must be recalled that we cannot will wisdom. We are finite creatures, limited by our circumstances and our perspectives, and this reality of the human condition has to be accepted in the middle years. The idea that there has to be an answer or a solution to everything represents an intolerance of ambiguity; a failure to recognize or come to terms with the complexities of human life.

If there was one troublesome issue that ran throughout the cases in his book, it was separation/individuation. This is an issue that exists throughout life from infancy on, not just during mid-life. However, the issue and theme was so prominent in the cases that it needs to be addressed further. It will be recalled that even the most individuated person of all the cases, Alice Decker in Chapter Six, held on to the illusion that she was not an effective, autonomous decision maker. One therapist, Hellmuth Kaiser (Fierman 1965), made particular note of this phenomenon and called it the "illusion of fusion." He noted that when his patients were faced with the necessity to make decisions, they would attempt to surrender their autonomy and would try to create an illusion of fusion through duplicitous communication with him. He found this to be so widespread that he considered it to be a "universal symptom," and he felt it was strongest when the individual has to confront his or her "basic aloneness," which tends to happen when he or she has to make a decision and take action.

This is an important observation to keep in mind because even the more individuated among us will revert to the illusion of fusion and fail to make choices, or will act out of fear. Whether the illusion of fusion is universal or not is open to question, but it does refer to the kind of childhood consciousness that Gould (1978) claims holds us back from making necessary changes in our adult development. He claimed it was the adult equivalent of childhood separation anxiety and sometimes, as Jaques would claim about the mid-life crises, it is abandonment anxiety. So one of the most regressive forces in midlife is this fear of separation, fear of aloneness. It represents the regressive pull of "embeddedness," as that concept was explicated by Schachtel (1959) and Kegan (1982) and as it was represented in several cases here. Warren Cates in Chapter Six, for example, had it to such an extent that he could barely contemplate a separation, even a trial one, in the troubled reattachment relationship he had established after his marital separation.

Quite a few people in their middle years have found out of necessity that they can indeed live without the other person, and some of them have found, paradoxically, that this experience enables them to live with another person in a different way because the old need/fear dilemma has been dissipated. Allan Watts (1940) has said, "Before you unite you must first divide." Being able to divide and separate can enable one to become more whole, and this will help to dissipate the fear of loss of boundaries and the illusion of fusion in a new relationship. Thus, true individuation allows for a mature relationship with another. Sometimes middle-aged people who do not have a basic problem with separation/individuation in any clinical diagnostic sense still have the distorted fear or belief that they could not survive without the other person. Women in particular, Gould would say, have this belief because they have been socialized into believing they need a "protector" (husband), by their parents, family, or society. Consequently, this is a belief which often has to be disputed, either in or out of therapy, in the middle years.

This formative process between individual and family and the underlying separation/individuation issue has been aptly described:

> A child growing up in a nuclear family learns that a human being is a creature who: is born into a family he did not choose, has needs and feelings and thoughts and ambitions—which are or are not, filled, expressed, shared, and encouraged—and eventually becomes an independent individual, ready to address the world—and the family that nurtured him—on his own terms.
>
> What endures for an individual is his own individuality—his experience of his individuality—and that occurs in the now, connected, of course, to many other nows of personal consequence. An individual, inspired with subjectivity, spurred by the urgencies of personality, armed with self, single-handedly takes on time in mortal combat. Time wins, of course, but the battle may be glorious. We are all, needless to say, individuals, and most of us are the better for it (Farber 1976, 231).

This kind of awareness of one's mortality, together with the choice to *live* one's middle years—with all their pitfalls, challenges, and opportunities for new, unfettered happenings and meanings—should be the fruit of the midlife experience. This life-stance or choice cannot be summed up any better than Alice Decker did in the last chapter: "I go forward with confidence to living, to 'becoming.'"

BIBLIOGRAPHY

Aguilera, D.C., and Messick, J.M. 1982. *Crisis intervention: Theory and methodology.* St. Louis: C.V. Mosby.

Ainsworth, M.D.S.; Blehar, M.C.; Waters, E. and Wall, S. 1978. *Patterns of attachment.* Hillsdale, N.J.: Erlbaum.

Allport, G.W. 1955. *Becoming: Basic considerations for a psychology of personality.* New Haven: Yale University Press.

Allport, G.W. 1961. *Pattern and growth in personality.* New York: Holt, Rinehart and Winston.

Arieti, S. 1978. "Psychotherapy of severe depression." In *Mild and severe depression,* edited by S. Arieti and J. Bemporad. New York: Basic Books.

Arnkoff, D.B. 1981. "Flexibility in practicing cognitive therapy." In *New directions in cognitive therapy,* edited by G. Emery, S.D. Holon, and R.C. Bedrosian. New York: Guilford Press.

Atwood, G.E., and Stolorow, R.D. 1984. *Structures of subjectivity: Explorations in psychoanalytic phenomenology.* Hillsdale, N.J.: The Analytic Press.

Aylwin, S. 1985. *Structure in thought and feeling.* London: Methuen.

Baker, K., 1972. *Philosophical dictionary.* Spokane, Wash.: Gonzaga University Press.

Baltes, P.B. 1973. Prototypical paradigms and questions in life-span research on development and aging. *The Gerontologist* 13: 458-67.

Baltes, P.B. 1979. "Life-span developmental psychology: Some converging observations on history and theory." In *Life-span development and behavior* Vol. 2, edited by P.B. Baltes and O.G. Brim. New York: Academic Press.

Bannister, D. 1965. The rationale and clinical relevance of repertory grid technique. *British Journal of Psychiatry* 3:977-82.

Bannister, D., and Fransella, F. 1971. *Inquiring man: The theory of personal constructs.* London: Penguin Books.

Bannister, D., and Mair, J.M.M. 1968. *The evaluation of personal constructs.* London: Academic Press.

Beck, A.T. 1976. *Cognitive therapy and the emotional disorders.* New York: International Universities Press.

Beck, A.T., and Emery, G. 1979. *Cognitive therapy of anxiety and phobic disorders.* Philadelphia: The Center for Cognitive Therapy.

Beck, A.T., and Greenberg, R.L. 1974. *Coping with depression.* New York: Institute for Rational Living.

Beck, A.T.; Rush, A.J.; Shaw, B.F.; and Emery, G. 1979. *Cognitive therapy of depression.* New York: The Guilford Press.

Bell, A., and Weinberg, M. 1978. *Homosexualities: A study in diversity among men and women.* New York: Simon and Schuster.

Berger, P.L., and Luckmann, T. 1966. *The social construction of reality.* Garden City, N.Y.: Doubleday.

Berlin, S.B. 1976. Better work with women clients. *Social Work* 21:492-97.

Bernard, J. 1972. *The future of marriage.* New York: Bantam Books.

Blasi, A. 1976. "Concept of development in personality theory." In *Ego Development: Conceptions and Theories,* by J. Loevinger. San Francisco: Jossey-Bass.

Bolgar, H. 1965. "The case study method." In *Handbook of clinical psychology,* edited by B. Wolman. New York: McGraw-Hill.

Bowlby, J. 1969. *Attachment and loss.* Vol. 1, *Attachment.* New York: Basic Books.

Brim, O.G. 1976. Theories of the male mid-life crisis. *The Counseling Psychologist* 6:2-9.

Broughton, J.M. 1981. Piaget's structural developmental psychology. *Human Development* 24:78-109.

Browning, D.S. 1973. *Generative man: Psychoanalytic perspectives.* Philadelphia: Westminster Press.

Bruner, J.S. 1966. *Toward a theory of instruction.* Cambridge, Mass.: Harvard University Press.

Buckley, W. 1967. *Sociology and modern systems theory.* Englewood Cliffs, N.J.: Prentice Hall.

Budner, S. 1962. Intolerance of ambiguity as a personality variable. *Journal of Personality* 30:29-50.

Buhler, C. 1962. *Values in psychotherapy.* New York: Free Press.

Buhler, C. 1968. The course of human life as a psychological problem. *Human Development* 2:184-200.

Butler, J.M., and Haigh, G.H. 1954. "Changes in the relation between self-concepts and ideal concepts consequent upon client-centered counseling." In *Psychotherapy and personality change,* edited by C.R. Rogers and R.F. Dymond. Chicago: University of Chicago Press.

Butler, R. 1963. The life review: An interpretation of reminiscence in the aged. *Psychiatry 26*, 65-76.

Cantril, H. 1957. Perception and interpersonal relations. *American Journal of Psychiatry* 114: 119-26.

Caplan, G. 1964. *Principles of preventive psychiatry.* New York: Basic Books.

Cath, S. 1980. "Suicide in the middle years: Some reflections on the annihilation of self." In *Mid-Life: Developmental and Clinical Issues,* edited by W.H. Norman and T.J. Scaramella. New York: Brunner/Mazel.

Chiriboga, D. 1981. "The developmental psychology of middle age." In *Modern perspectives in the psychiatry of middle age,* edited by J.G. Howells. New York: Brunner/Mazel.

Chiriboga, D. 1982. Adaptation to marital separation in later and earlier life. *Journal of Gerontology* 37:109-14.

Chiriboga, D., and Cutler, L. 1980. "Stress and adaptation: A life span study." In *Aging in the 1980's: Selected contemporary issues in the psychology of aging,* edited by L. Poon. Washington, D.C.: American Psychological Association.

Chomsky, N. 1968. *Language and mind.* New York: Harcourt, Brace, Jovanovich.

Combs, A.W. 1949. A phenomenological approach to adjustment theory. *Journal of Abnormal and Social Psychology* 44:29-35.

Combs, A.W.; Richards, A.C.; and Richards, F. 1976. *Perceptual psychology: A humanistic approach to the study of persons.* New York: Harper & Row.

Combs, A.W., and Snygg, D. 1959. *Individual behavior: A perceptual approach to behavior.* New York: Harper and Row.

Costa, R.T., and McCrae, R.R. 1976. Age differences in personality structure: A cluster analysis approach. *Journal of Gerontology* 31:564-70.

Costa, R.T., and McCrae, R.R. 1980. "Still stable after all these years: Personality as a key to some issues in aging." In *Life-span development and behavior,* Vol. 3, edited by P.B. Baltes and O.G. Brim. New York: Academic Press.

Costa, R.T.; McCrae, R.R.; and Norris, A.H. 1981. Personal adjustment to aging: Longitudinal prediction from neuroticism and extraversion. *Journal of Gerontology* 36:78-85.

Datan, N. 1976. "Male and female: The search for synthesis." In *Dialectic: A humanistic rationale for behavior and development,* edited by J.F. Rychlak. Basel, Switz.: S. Karger.

Datan, N. 1980. "Midas and other mid-life crises." In *Mid-life: Developmental and clinical issues,* by W.H. Norman and T.J. Scaramella. New York: Brunner/Mazel.

de Rivera, J. 1977. *A structural theory of the emotions.* New York: International Universities Press.

de Rivera, J., ed. 1981. *Conceptual encounter: A method for the exploration of human experience.* Washington, D.C.: University Press of America.

de Saussure, F. 1966. *Course in general linguistics.* London: McGraw-Hill.

Dilthey, W. 1976. "The development of hermeneutics." In *Selected Writings,* edited and translated by H.P. Rickman. Cambridge: Cambridge University Press (original work published 1947).

Eagleton, T. 1983. *Literary theory: An introduction.* Minneapolis: University of Minnesota Press.

Ellis, A. 1962. *Reason and emotion in psychotherapy.* Secaucus, N.J.: Citadel Press.

Ellis, A. 1974. *Humanistic psychotherapy: The rational-emotional approach.* New York: McGraw-Hill.

Ellis, A. 1977. *How to live with and without anger.* New York: Reader's Digest Press.

Elwell, F., and Maltbie-Crannell. 1981. The impact of role loss upon coping resources and life satisfaction of the elderly. *Journal of Gerontology* 36:223-32.

Erikson, E.H. 1959. *Identity and the life cycle: Selected papers.* New York: International Universities Press.

Erikson, E.H. 1963. *Childhood and society.* 2d ed. New York: Norton.

Erikson, E.H. 1968. *Identity: Youth and crisis.* New York: Norton.

Farber, L.H. 1966. *The ways of the will.* New York: Basic Books.

Farber, L.H. 1976. *Lying, despair, jealousy, envy, sex, suicide, drugs, and the good life.* New York: Basic Books.

Fierman, L.B., ed. 1968. *Effective psychotherapy: The contribution of Hellmuth Kaiser.* New York: Free Press.

Fiske, M. 1979. *Middle age: the prime of life?* New York: Harper and Row.

Fiske, M. 1980. Tasks and crises of the second half of life: The interrelationship of commitment, coping, and adaptation. In *Handbook of mental health and aging,* edited by J.E. Birren and R.B. Sloan. Englewood Cliffs, N.J.: Prentice-Hall.

Folkman, S., and Lazarus, R.S. 1980. An analysis of coping in a middle-aged community sample. *Journal of Health and Social Behavior* 21: 219-39.

Foreyt, J.P., and Rathjen, D.P., eds. 1978. *Cognitive behavior therapy: Research and application.* New York: Plenum Press.

Frank, J. 1974. *Persuasion and healing: A comparative study of psychotherapy.* New York: Schocken Books.

Freeman, A. 1981. Dreams and images in cognitive therapy. In *New directions in cognitive therapy,* edited by G. Emery, S.D. Hollon, and R.C. Bedrosian. New York: Guilford Press.

Frenkel-Brunswick, E. 1949. Intolerance of ambiguity as an emotional and perceptual personality variable. *Journal of Personality* 18:108-43.

Frenkel-Brunswick, E. 1950. Personality theory and perception. In *Perception: An approach to personality,* edited by R.R. Blake and G.V. Ramsey. New York: Ronald Press.

Friedman, I. 1955. Phenomenal, ideal, and projected conceptions of self. *Journal of Abnormal and Social Psychology* 51: 611-15.

Friedman, M. 1985. *The healing dialogue in psychotherapy.* New York: Jason Aronson.

Fromm, E. 1956. *The art of loving.* New York: Harper and Row.

Gadamer, H. 1976. *Philosophical hermeneutics.* Berkeley: University of California Press.

Gardner, H. 1972. *The quest for mind.* New York: Alfred A. Knopf.

Geertz, C. 1983. *Local knowledge: Further essays in interpretive anthropology.* New York: Basic Books.

Gendlin, E. 1962. *Experiencing and the creation of meaning.* New York: Free Press.

Gendlin, E. 1973. "Experiential phenomenology." In *Phenomenology and the social sciences,* edited by M. Natanson. Evanston: Northwestern University Press.

Gendlin, E. 1981. *Focusing.* 2d ed. New York: Bantam Books.

Gendlin, E., and Tomlinson, T.M. 1967. "The process conception and its measurement." In *The therapeutic relationship and its impact,* edited by C. Rogers. Madison: University of Wisconsin Press.

Giele, J.Z. 1980. Adulthood as transcendence of age and sex. In *Themes of work and love in adulthood,* edited by N.J. Smelser and E.H. Erikson. Cambridge: Harvard University Press.

Gilligan, C. 1982. *In a different voice: Psychological theory and women's development.* Cambridge: Harvard University Press.

Golan, N. 1981. *Passing through transitions: A guide for practitioners.* New York: Free Press.

Goldstein, H. 1982. Cognitive approaches to direct practice. *Social Service Review* 56:539-55.

Goodman, L.M. 1981. *Death and the creative life.* New York: Springer.

Gould, R.L. 1978. *Transformations: Growth and change in adult life.* New York: Simon Schuster.

Guidano, V.F., and Liotti, G. 1983. *Cognitive processes and emotional disorders.* New York: Guilford Press.

Gutmann, D. 1969. "The country of old men: Cross-cultural studies in the psychology of later life." In *Occasional papers in gerontology,* edited by W. Donahue. Ann Arbor: University of Michigan Press.

Haan, N.A. 1969. A tripartite model of ego functioning values and clinical research applications. *Journal of Nervous and Mental Disease* 148: 14-30.

Hampden-Turner, C. 1981. *Maps of the mind.* New York: Collier.

Heidegger, M. 1962. *Being and time.* New York: Harper and Row (original work published 1927).

Heider, F. 1958. *The psychology of interpersonal relations.* New York: Wiley.

Heider, F. 1959. *On perception and event structure and the psychological environment.* New York: International Universities Press.

Hill, R. 1963. "Generic features of families in crisis." In *Crisis intervention: Selected readings,* edited by H.J. Parad. New York: Family Service Association of America.

Holmes, T.H., and Rahe, R.H. 1967. The social readjustment rating scale. *Journal of Psychosomatic Research* 2:213.

Horney, K. 1945. *Our inner conflicts: A constructive theory of neurosis.* New York: Norton.

House, J.S. 1974. Occupational stress and coronary heart disease: A review and theoretical integration. *Journal of Health and Social Behavior* 15:12-27.

Howard. R.J. 1982. *Three faces of hermeneutics: An introduction to current theories of understanding.* Berkeley: University of California Press.

Howells, J.G., ed. 1981. *Modern perspectives in the psychiatry of middle age.* New York: Brunner/Mazel.

Husserl, E. 1970. *Logical investigations I & II.* New York: Humanities Press (original work published 1900).

Husserl, E. 1970. *The crisis of the European sciences and transcendental phenomenology.* Evanston: Northwestern University Press (original work published 1936).

Husserl, E. 1973. "Phenomenology." In *Phenomenology and existentialism,* edited by R.M. Zaner and D. Ihde. New York: G.P. Putnam's Sons.

Husserl, E. 1977. *Phenomenological psychology.* The Hague: Nijhoff (original work published 1962).

Ihde, D. 1986. *Experimental phenomenology: An introduction.* Albany: SUNY Press.

Jacobsen, E. 1938. *Progressive relaxation.* Chicago: University of Chicago Press.

Janis, I.L., ed. 1982. *Counseling on personal decisions.* New Haven: Yale University Press.

Janis, I.L., and Mann, L. 1977. *Decision making: A psychological analysis of conflict, choice, and commitment.* New York: Free Press.

Jaques, E. 1965. Death and the mid-life crisis. *International Journal of Psychoanalysis* 46: 502-14.

Jaques, E. 1980. "The midlife crisis." In *The course of life: Psychoanalytic contributions toward understanding personality development.* Vol. 3, edited by S.I. Greenspan and G.H. Pollock. Bethesda: National Institute of Mental Health.

Jung, C.G. 1964. *Man and his symbols.* Garden City, N.Y.: Doubleday.

Jung, C.G. 1971. "The stages of life." In *The portable Jung,* edited by J. Campbell. New York: Viking.

Kane, R. 1976. "Two studies on the experience of depression." Master's thesis, Clark University, Worcester, MA.

Keen, E.A. 1975. *A primer in phenomenological psychology.* New York: Holt, Rinehart & Winston.

Kegan, R. 1982. *The evolving self: Problem and process in human development.* Cambridge: Harvard University Press.

Kelly, G.A. 1955. *The theory of personal constructs: A theory of personality.* Vols. 1 and 2. New York: Norton.

Kerlinger, F.N. 1973. *Foundations of behavioral research.* New York: Holt, Rinehart and Winston.

Kerlinger, F.N. 1979. *Behavioral research: A conceptual approach.* New York: Holt, Rinehart and Winston.

Kimmell, D.C. 1978. Adult development and aging: A gay perspective. *Journal of Social Issues* 34:113-30.

Klein, G.S. 1970. *Perception, motives and personality.* New York: Alfred A. Knopf.

Klein, M. 1948. *Contributions to psychoanalysis.* London: Hogarth Press.

Klein, M.H.; Mathieu, P.L.; Gendlin, E.T.; and Kiesler, D.J. 1970. *The experiencing scale: A research and training manual.* Vol. 1. Madison: University of Wisconsin.

Kruger, D. 1981. *Phenomenological psychology.* Pittsburgh: Duquesne University Press.

Kuypers, J.A. 1972. Internal-external locus of control, ego functioning, and personality characteristics in old age. *The Gerontologist* 12:168-73.

Lazarus, A.A. 1971. *Behavior therapy and beyond.* New York: McGraw-Hill.

Lazarus, R.S. 1966. *Psychological stress and the coping process.* New York: McGraw-Hill.

Lazarus, R.S.; Kanner, A.; and Folkman, S. 1980. "Emotions: A cognitive-phenomenological analysis." In *Theories of emotion,* edited by R. Plutchik and H. Kellerman. New York: Academic Press.

Levinson, D.J.; Darrow, C.N.; Klein, E.B.; Levinson, M.H.; and McKee, B. 1978. *The seasons of a man's life.* New York: Alfred A. Knopf.

Levi-Strauss, C. 1963. *Structural anthropology.* New York: Basic Books.

Levy, N.J. 1981. "The middle-aged male and female homosexual." In *Modern perspectives in the psychiatry of middle age*, edited by J.G. Howells. New York: Brunner/Mazel.

Lewin, K. 1935. *A dynamic theory of personality.* New York: McGraw-Hill.

Lewin, K. 1951. *Field theory in social science: Selected theoretical papers.* New York: Harper.

Lieberman, M.A., and Tobin, S.S. 1983. *The experience of old age.* New York: Basic Books.

Lifton, R.J. 1968. Protean man. *Partisan Review* 35:13-27.

Lifton, R.J. 1976. *The life of the self: Toward a new psychology.* New York: Simon and Schuster.

Lindemann, E. 1944. Symptomatology and management of acute grief. *American Journal of Psychiatry* 101:141-48.

Loevinger, J. 1976. *Ego-development: Conceptions and theories.* San Francisco: Jossey-Bass.

Lowenthal, M.F. 1980. "Intentionality: Toward a framework for the study of adaptation in adulthood." In *Being and becoming old,* edited by J. Hendricks. Farmingdale, N.Y.: Baywood Publishing.

Lowenthal, M. Fiske; Thurner, M.; and Chiriboga, D.A. & Associates. 1975. *Four stages of life: A comparative study of women and men facing transitions.* San Francisco: Jossey-Bass.

Lynd, H.M. 1958. *On shame and the search for identity.* New York: Science Editions.

Mahler, M. 1979. *Separation-individuation.* New York: Jason Aronson.

Mahoney, M.H. 1974. *Cognition and behavior modification.* Cambridge, Mass.: Ballinger.

Marrow, A.J. 1969. *The practical theorist: The life and work of Kurt Lewin.* New York: Basic Books.

Meichenbaum, D. 1977. *Cognitive-behavior modification: An integrative approach.* New York: Plenum Press.

Merleau-Ponty, M. 1962. *Phenomenology of perception.* New York: Humanities Press (original work published 1945).

Merleau-Ponty, M. 1964. *Signs.* Evanston: Northwestern University Press (original work published 1960).

Merleau-Ponty, M. 1964. *The primacy of perception.* Evanston: Northwestern University Press.

Merluzzi, T.V.; Glass, C.R.; and Genest, M., eds. 1981. *Cognitive assessment.* New York: Guilford Press.

Moss, C.S. 1970. *Dreams, images, and fantasy: A semantic differential casebook.* Urbana, Illinois: University of Illinois Press.

Mucchielli, R. 1970. *Introduction to structural psychology.* New York: Avon.

Neugarten, B.L. 1968. "The awareness of middle age." In *Middle age and aging,* edited by B.L. Neugarten. Chicago: University of Chicago Press.

Neugarten, B.L., ed. 1968. *Middle age and aging: A reader in social psychology.* Chicago: University of Chicago Press.

Neugarten, B.L. & Associates. 1964. *Personality in middle and late life.* Chicago: University of Chicago Press.

Neugarten, B.L.; Havighurst, R.J.; and Tobin, S.S. 1961. The measurement of life satisfaction. *Journal of Gerontology* 1:134-43.

Newman, B.M., and Newman, P.R. 1979. "Later adulthood: A developmental stage." In *Dimensions of aging: Readings,* edited by J. Hendricks and C.D. Hendricks. Cambridge, Mass.: Winthrop.

Norman, W.H., and Scaramella, T.J. 1980. *Mid-Life: Developmental and clinical issues.* New York: Brunner/Mazel.

Notman, M.T. 1980. "Changing roles for women in mid-life." In *Mid-life: Developmental and clinical issues,* edited by W.H. Norman and T.J. Scaramella. New York: Brunner/Mazel.

Novaco, R.W. 1975. *Anger control: The development and evaluation of an experimental treatment.* Lexington, Mass.: D.C. Heath, Lexington Books.

Novaco, R.W. 1978. "Anger and coping with stress." In *Cognitive behavior therapy: Research and application,* edited by J.P. Foreyt and D.P. Rathjen. New York: Plenum Press.

Osgood, C.E.; Succi, G.J.; and Tannenbaum, P.H. 1957. *The measurement of meaning.* Urbana: University of Illinois Press.

Parad, H.J., ed. 1965. *Crisis intervention: Selected readings.* New York: Family Service Association of America.

Parkes, C.M. 1971. Psycho-social transitions. *Social Science and Medicine* 5:101-115.

Peck, R.C. 1968. "Psychosocial developments in the second half of life." In *Middle age and aging,* edited by B. Neugarten. Chicago: University of Chicago Press.

Pettit, P. 1975. *The concept of structuralism: A critical analysis.* Berkeley: University of California Press.

Piaget, J. 1954. *The construction of reality in the child.* New York: Basic Books.

Piaget, J. 1970. *Structuralism.* New York: Basic Books.

Polyani, M. 1966. *The tacit dimension.* Garden City, N.Y.: Doubleday.

Rabkin, R. 1977. *Strategic psychotherapy: Brief and symptomatic treatment.* New York: Basic Books.

Raimy, V. 1975. *Misunderstandings of the self.* San Francisco: Jossey-Bass.

Rakos, R.J., and Schroeder, H.E. 1980. *Self-directed assertiveness training.* New York: Guilford Press.

Rapoport, L. 1965. "The state of crisis: Some theoretical considerations." In *Crisis intervention: Selected readings,* edited by H.J. Parad. New York: Family Service Association of America.

Ricoeur, P. 1981. *Hermeneutics and the human sciences.* Cambridge: Cambridge University Press.

Riegel, K. 1976. The dialectics of human development. *American Psychologist* 31:689-99.

Rogers, C.R. 1965. *Client-centered therapy.* Boston: Houghton Mifflin.

Rogers, C.R. 1980. *A way of being.* Boston: Houghton-Mifflin.

Rokeach, M. 1973. *The nature of human values.* New York: Free Press.

Rosenberg, M. 1979. *Conceiving the self.* New York: Basic Books.

Rosow, I. 1973. *Socialization to old age.* Berkeley: University of California Press.

Rotter, J.B. 1966. Generalized expectancies for internal versus external control of reinforcement. *Psychological Monographs, 80,* issue #609.

Rubin, L. 1979. *Women of a certain age: The mid-life search for self.* New York: Harper & Row.

Rubin, L. 1983. *Intimate strangers: Men and women together.* New York: Harper & Row.

Rubin, T.I. 1975. *Compassion and self-hate.* New York: McKay.

Rubins, J.L. 1980. On cognition, affects, and Horney theory. *The American Journal of Psychoanalysis* 40:195-212.

Runyan, W.M. 1982. In defense of the case study method. *American Journal of Orthopsychiatry* 52:440-46.

Rychlak, J.F. 1973. *Introduction to personality and psychotherapy: A theory-construction approach.* Boston: Houghton Mifflin.

Rychlak, J.F. 1979. *Discovering free will and personal responsibility.* New York: Oxford University Press.

Ryff, C.D. 1982. Successful aging: A developmental approach. *The Gerontologist* 22:209-14.

Ryff, C.D. 1985. "The subjective experience of life-span transitions." In *Gender and the life course,* edited by A.S. Rossi. New York: Aldine.

Ryff, C.D., and Dunn, D.D. (1983, November). "Life stresses and personality development: A life-span developmental inquiry." Paper presented at the American Gerontological Society Meeting, San Francisco, CA.

Ryle, A. 1975. *Frames and cages: The repertory grid approach to human understanding.* London: Sussex University Press.

Sartre, J.P. 1966. *Being and nothingness: An essay on phenomenological ontology.* New York: Washington Square Press.

Schachtel, E.G. 1959. *Metamorphosis.* New York: Basic Books.

Sheehy, G. 1981. *Pathfinders.* New York: Morrow.

Sherman, E. 1981. *Counseling the aging: An integrative approach.* New York: Free Press.

Sherman, E. (1982, April). "Comparative adjustment and coping strategies of men and women to mid-life family crises." Paper presented at the annual meeting of the American Orthopsychiatric Association, San Francisco, CA.

Sherman, E. 1984. *Working with older persons: Cognitive and phenomenological methods.* Boston: Kluwer-Nijhoff.

Slater, P. 1965. *The principal components of a repertory grid.* London: Vincent Andrews & Co.

Smelser, N.J., and Erikson, E., eds. 1981. *Themes of work and love in adulthood.* Cambridge: Harvard University Press.

Snygg, D. 1941. The need for a phenomenological system of psychology. *Psychological Review* 48:404-24.

Spiegelberg, H. 1965. *The phenomenological movement: A historical introduction.* The Hague: Martinus Nijhoff.

Spiegelberg, H. 1972. *Phenomenology in psychology and psychiatry.* Evanston: Northwestern University Press.

Spielberger, C.D.; Gorsuch, R.L.; and Lushene, R.E. 1970. *STAI manual for the state-trait anxiety inventory.* Palo Alto, Cal.: Consulting Psychologists Press.

Strauss, E. 1966. *Phenomenological psychology: Selected papers.* New York: Basic Books.

Tamir, L.M. 1982. "Men at middle age: Developmental transitions." In *Middle and late life transitions,* edited by F.M. Berardo. Beverly Hills, Cal.: Sage.

Thomae, H. 1970. Theory of aging and cognitive theory of personality. *Human Development* 13:1-16.

Troll, L.E. 1975. *Early and middle adulthood.* Belmont, Cal.: Wadsworth Publishing.

Turner, N.W. 1980. Divorce in mid-life: Clinical implications and applications. In *Mid-life developmental and clinical issues,* edited by W.H. Norman and T.J. Scaramella. New York: Brunner/Mazel.

Vaillant, G.E. 1977. *Adaptation to life.* Boston: Little, Brown.

von Bertalanffy, L. 1951. *Problems of life.* New York: Harper and Row.

von Bertalanffy, L. 1968. *General systems theory: Foundations, development, application.* New York: George Braziller.

Wallerstein, J.S., and Kelly, J.B. 1980. *Surviving the breakup: How children and parents cope with divorce.* New York: Basic Books.

Watts, A.W. 1940. *The meaning of happiness.* New York: Harper and Row.

Wegner, D.M., and Vallacher, R.R. 1977. *Implicit psychology: An introduction to social cognition.* New York: Oxford University Press.

Weis, R.S. 1973. *Loneliness: The experience of emotional and social isolation.* Cambridge: M.I.T. Press.

Weiss, R.S. 1975. *Marital separation.* New York: Basic Books.

Wheelis, A. 1969. How people change. *Commentary* 47:56-66.

Whitehead, A.N. 1969. *Science and the modern world.* New York: Free Press.

Witkin, H.A. 1962. *Psychological differentiation.* New York: John Wiley.

Witkin, H.A. 1965. Psychological differentiation and forms of pathology. *Journal of Abnormal Psychology* 70:317-36.

Witkin, H.A., and Goodenough, D.R. 1981. *Cognitive styles: Essence and origins.* New York: International Universities Press.

Witkin, H.A.; Oltman, P.K.; Raskin, E.; and Karp, S.A. 1971. *A manual for the embedded figures test.* Palo Alto, Cal.: Consulting Psychologists Press.

Wolpe, J. 1973. *The practice of behavior therapy.* New York: Pergamon Press.

Wrong, D. 1961. The oversocialized conception of man in modern sociology. *American Sociological Review* 6:183-93.

Yalom, I.D. 1980. *Existential psychotherapy.* New York: Basic Books.

Zung, W.W.K. 1965. A self-rating depression scale. *Archives of General Psychiatry* 12:63-70.

INDEX